Beyond Religion and the Secular

Also Available from Bloomsbury:

Free Zone Scientology
Aled Thomas

Gnosticism and the History of Religions
David G. Robertson

Rethinking Religion and Politics in a Plural World
Julia Berger

Beyond Religion and the Secular

Creative Spiritual Movements and their Relevance to Political, Social and Cultural Reform

Wayne Hudson

BLOOMSBURY ACADEMIC
LONDON · NEW YORK · OXFORD · NEW DELHI · SYDNEY

BLOOMSBURY ACADEMIC
Bloomsbury Publishing Plc
50 Bedford Square, London, WC1B 3DP, UK
1385 Broadway, New York, NY 10018, USA
29 Earlsfort Terrace, Dublin 2, Ireland

BLOOMSBURY, BLOOMSBURY ACADEMIC and the Diana logo are trademarks of
Bloomsbury Publishing Plc

First published in Great Britain 2023
This paperback edition published 2024

Copyright © Wayne Hudson, 2023

Wayne Hudson has asserted his right under the Copyright,
Designs and Patents Act, 1988, to be identified as Author of this work.

For legal purposes the Acknowledgements on pp. vi–vii constitute
an extension of this copyright page.

All rights reserved. No part of this publication may be reproduced or transmitted
in any form or by any means, electronic or mechanical, including photocopying,
recording, or any information storage or retrieval system, without prior
permission in writing from the publishers.

Bloomsbury Publishing Plc does not have any control over, or responsibility for,
any third-party websites referred to or in this book. All internet addresses given
in this book were correct at the time of going to press. The author and publisher
regret any inconvenience caused if addresses have changed or sites have ceased
to exist, but can accept no responsibility for any such changes.

A catalogue record for this book is available from the British Library.

Library of Congress Control Number: 2022940111

ISBN: HB: 978-1-3503-3171-6
        PB: 978-1-3503-3175-4
        ePDF: 978-1-3503-3172-3
        eBook: 978-1-3503-3173-0

Typeset by Integra Software Services Pvt. Ltd.

To find out more about our authors and books visit www.bloomsbury.com
and sign up for our newsletters

Contents

Acknowledgements   vi

1   Rethinking the Terrain   1
2   The Baháʼís: Prosociality and Global Civilization   21
3   Soka Gakkai and Cosmic Humanism   38
4   Ananda Marga and Utopian Futurism   52
5   Brahma Kumaris: Modernism on the Way to Apocalypse   67
6   The Church Universal and Triumphant: The Democratization of Counterfactuality   80
7   The Charismatic Latter-day Saints   95
8   Conclusion   111
Appendix: Latter-day Saint Doctrinal Innovations   124

Glossary of Technical Terms   132
Notes   134
Bibliography   169
Index   192

Acknowledgements

In writing this book, I have benefited from the help of many people. First, I would like to thank my colleagues in Canberra who have commented on text especially Jonathan Cole, Scott Cowdell and Michael Gladwin. A special thanks to Bernard Doherty, a leading scholar of New Religious Movements, who helped me to orient myself in this growing field.

Individual chapters have benefited from input and corrections from scholars associated with the movements I discuss. My discussion of the Bahá'ís is indebted to critical commentary from the distinguished Bahá'í scholar Moojan Momen and from suggestions from Natalie Mobine of the Canberra Bahá'í community. My discussion of Soka Gakkai is heavily indebted to my friend Greg Johns and to detailed corrections provided by Joan Anderson and other Soka members. I also wish to acknowledge the inspiration of Richard Causton and the late Yong Fu who originally aroused my interest in this movement.

My discussion of the Brahma Kumaris is indebted to the inspiration and scholarship of my friend and colleague Julia Howell who first introduced me to the movement and to the leading Brahma Kumaris scholar Tamasin Ramsay who commented in detail on the text. I was also privileged to meet the late Dadi Janke as well as members of the Brahma Kumaris in Brisbane.

My work on Ananda Marga is indebted to two Ananda Marga scholars Sohail Inayatullah and Marcus Bussey, both of whom commented on the manuscript and provided help with bibliographical literature.

My chapter on the Church Universal and Triumphant is indebted to my friend Virginia Herbert and to the staff of the Church who provided much-needed help with bibliographical details. I also wish to thank Marie Huttley-Jackson of the Canberra branch of the Church for her comments and criticisms.

My knowledge of the Latter-day Saints has developed over many years. It has benefited from my long friendship with the leading Mormon scholar Richard Bushman. The Latter-day Saint scholar Terryl Givens also commented on the manuscript, as did David Schak and the Australian Latter-day Saint scholar Keith Thompson. I also benefited from being hosted by the Church in Washington and Provo, where I met eminent Latter-day Saint scholars.

I must also thank my two research assistants, Lauren Barclay and Thyme Hansson for their outstanding work in correcting and preparing the manuscript. Both were unsparing in devoting their time to what were often technical tasks. I also wish to thank my editor at Bloomsbury, Stuart Hay, and Bloomsbury's reviewers who suggested improvements to the text.

My largest debt by far, as always, is to Catherine Hudson who commented on all the drafts. I wish also to thank my sons Charles and Raphael who encouraged and supported me while writing this study and kept me at the project during a period of ill health. Thank you also to family and friends who have encouraged and supported me throughout the book's writing.

This book ranges over a vast terrain and engages with many different geographic and linguistic contexts. It has not been easy to do them all justice and some readers may find the level of detail overwhelming. However, my wider aim is to modify in certain respects how we think about religion and the secular.

My work in this area would not be possible without the continuing support and assistance of Charles Sturt University's Australian Centre for Christianity and Culture, in Canberra, where I enjoy excellent facilities, have learned and generous colleagues and benefit from the expertise of first-class administrative staff, Hazel Francis and Sarah Stitt. I would also like to acknowledge the consistent support of two Directors of the Centre, James Haire and Stephen Pickard, and of Ross Chambers. I have also benefited from affiliations and scholarly contacts with the University of Tasmania and the Australian National University.

1

Rethinking the Terrain

Has 'religion' anything to offer humanity as it attempts to come to terms with a world shaped by advanced science and technology? A widely held view is that it has not. Those who hold this view tend to maintain that religion is outmoded and harmful, that its beliefs are false, and its practices superstitious and repressive. A more complex assessment is possible, however, one that takes account of the heterogeneous contents and activities falling under the 'religion' label. Positive and negative evaluations of 'religion' may both be too generalized to be really helpful, especially if 'religion' is one-sidedly associated with false beliefs. Traditional organizations deemed religious may sacralize unjust arrangements and also oppose a wide variety of progressive reforms. Those who recognize this are sometimes less inclined to attend to more controversial spiritual movements. This study suggests this may be a mistake. Indeed, I suggest, to the contrary, that some movements of this type have creative features that may be relevant to political, social and cultural reform.[1] My argument here assumes that generic conceptions of religion need to be problematized and that more rigorously contextual approaches are needed to materials traditionally deemed religious by Europeans. This much is not too controversial. Indeed, a large literature now shows that European generic conceptions of religion work can work badly for actual empirical cases.[2]

Once we do not assume *a priori* that religion has to involve some determinate type of world view (for example, belief in supernatural beings or forces), or that religion hinges on some determinate type of experience (for example, an experience of the sacred or the numinous), or that religions require social marking of a certain type (for example, a distinction between the 'sacred' and the 'profane'), materials traditionally associated with 'religion' can be read in more searching ways.

Spiritual movements

In this volume, I consider six contemporary spiritual movements that are more creative than is generally supposed. I uncover rich terrain in movements that are sometimes written off as irrational or even dangerous. In the process, I take some first steps towards a different way of thinking about the cultural productivity of movements with controversial doctrines and indeed, religion more generally. At a time when the future of what was once called religion is open to doubt, and there is a widespread search in advanced countries for forms of spirituality which can take historical religion's place, we need to recognize that creative developments can be realized in older organizational forms. Attending to these spiritual movements can help us perceive how such admixtures operate, and this, in turn, makes possible an advance beyond modern stereotypes. My aim in the longer term is to rethink the relationship between Enlightenment, modernity and religion. The studies in this volume advance this project in modest ways. The spiritual movements I discuss all attempt to reassert spiritual traditions in response to the challenges of modernization. In the outcome, they are all more modern in some respects than one might expect.

My approach to these issues is indebted to the work of the German Jewish Marxist philosopher Ernst Bloch (1885–1993) and to his project of attending to the utopian surplus found throughout human experience and across both natural and cultural worlds.[3] Bloch held that utopian contents appeared in a vast range of materials, which signalled more maximal reality contents than those currently realized in the world at hand. This led him to associate utopian contents in both nature and culture with developing real possibilities. My approach in this volume is also influenced by my work on the Enlightenment and modernity, specifically my studies of the English Deists, in which I sought to rehabilitate the thought and activities of these underestimated figures, and to show how some reforms central to modernity derived in part from them.[4]

This volume displays the same commitment towards rehabilitating those who have been caricatured or overlooked, and towards finding possible sources of reform where others have chosen not to look.[5] Drawing both on my work on Bloch and my work on the Enlightenment, I emphasize the importance of *utopian perspectives, model ideas* and *utopian intentionality.* That is, I attend not only to what has become actual in these movements, but also to what they may indicate about what is lacking in the contemporary world and what may become possible in the future. In this context, instances of *concrete utopianism* are particularly important because they draw attention to arrangements and reforms that are already realistic or will become so. My approach here is a version of *utopian realism* for which the utopian does not refer to a perfect society to come, but to the way in which cultural and historical materials provide anticipatory drafts of better contents, arrangements and practices that can be found in a realized and effective form in the world at hand. Utopian realists are not utopians in a political or social sense and do not expect that the contradictions and tensions that pervade human life will ever be resolved. However, they are ameliorists who think that improvements are possible in many different areas.

In this chapter, I set out my general approach to the terrain, define key terms and explain how my approach differs from that found in the existing literature. I place particular emphasis on obstacles to understanding which have made it harder to appreciate the creativity of these movements, and then introduce my own disaggregative approach, which I suggest brings this creativity into clearer view. I begin with matters that are primarily terminological. The term 'spiritual movement' identifies a movement with significant spiritual concerns. It does not imply that various movements are instances of a more general type. The spiritual movements I discuss are all, to some degree, controversial. They are all, to a degree, non-mainstream, but of different types and significance. Some have been studied more closely than others. Each of them, however, has a seer or prophet at its apex, and each of them generates or brings forward spiritual practices and cognitive materials, which are arguably of greater value than popular treatments of them suggest.

In discussing these spiritual movements, I do not disregard the substantive research already undertaken by historians and sociologists, amongst others.[6] Historians have long written about spiritual movements with counterfactual doctrines, especially those involved in major political or social or cultural change. Contemporary spiritual movements have also received considerable attention, from sociologists interested in social and cultural change, from social anthropologists and from scholars in the field of religious studies. A formidable literature has developed, replete with many insights.[7] As might be expected, much of the sociological literature on these movements studies their emergence and growth under conditions of rapid social change. As a result, the social character of these movements is well understood, including their tendency to have recurrent features, including new scriptures, mythological narratives, revealed cosmology and unfamiliar doctrines along with worship practices and extensive formational training.[8]

Although this literature often displays considerable sophistication, it tends to treat these movements as expressions of *something else*. For example, social forces, or conflicts between social groups, or else these movements are seen as examples of cultural difference, so that the crucial question becomes how one movement differs from another without consideration of cognitive or evolutionary constraints. Again, many of those who study spiritual movements accept forms of social relativism and/or non-essentialist accounts of social properties. The activities of these movements are listed and described, but there is little emphasis on their potential significance, let alone on the possibility that they may have features which are anticipatory in certain respects. If, however, these movements are read with reference to utopianism, which is now understood in less Eurocentric ways and as including spiritual or religious movements,[9] then their realistic features are less surprising since, as is well-known, religious utopian communities often succeed.[10]

Obstacles to understanding

Why has the creativity of these movements not received more attention? I suggest that a number of conceptual obstacles have made it hard to recognize the creativity of these spiritual movements.

The prejudice against positivity

The creativity of these movements has been occluded by a tendency to accept, consciously or unconsciously, *the prejudice of some sections of the European Enlightenment against positivity* or doctrines and practices accepted on the authority of spiritual traditions, a prejudice which often leads to underestimating the significance of doctrines and practices deemed to derive from authority rather than reason.

Positivity was a term deployed by some strands of the European Enlightenment critical of religious beliefs and practices to designate *beliefs and practices based on supernatural claims or religious authority*. For Enlightenment thinkers of this type, beliefs and practices based on supernatural claims or religious authority had negative associations because positive religion tended to be particularistic and characterized by concepts and information that could not be arrived at by reason, in contrast to the precepts of natural religion and morality that could in principle be known by all and by reason alone. The German philosopher Kant (1724–1804) provided the most famous exposition of such a view in his celebrated text *Religion within the Limits of Reason Alone* (1793). Kant identified religion in the strict sense with 'pure moral faith', as opposed to historical faiths, which could only have particular validity for those who had access to the records on which it rested. Granted his attempt to characterize religion within the limits of reason alone, the actual doctrines and practices of a spiritual tradition were only valuable if they instilled the moral principles which were the real substance of true religion.[11]

It was the philosopher Hegel (1770–1831) who famously theorized *positivity* as a condition into which Christianity had fallen, as doctrines and practices grounded on the authority of tradition or revelation prevailed over the dictates of reason and morality.[12] The young Hegel implied a negative evaluation of reliance on such doctrines and practices. Indeed, he hinted that reliance of this kind was a falling away from true religion based on reason and nature. This Enlightenment prejudice against positivity, which was not shared by all strands of the Enlightenment, influenced the outlook of many German Jewish intellectuals and can be found, for example, in the work of the great Jewish Enlightenment thinker Moses Mendelssohn (1729–86), in the works of the religious socialist Moses Hess (1812–75), and also in the work of the outstanding Jewish economic historian and sociologist Max Weber (1864–1920). It also influenced large parts of German Protestant theology up to and even beyond Karl Barth (1886–1968).

Subsequently, this prejudice against positivity influenced the development of the sociology of religion in German, French and English. Social and cultural anthropologists, to be fair, approached spiritual movements somewhat differently, and were more inclined to take the spiritually based doctrines, practices and institutions of the peoples they studied seriously, partly because they were often well-versed in the relevant languages and contexts. Social and cultural anthropologists, however, often studied spiritual cultures in functionalist terms, asking what functions they fulfilled in the societies in which they were found, and also in particularistic comparative ethnographic terms, emphasizing how the beliefs and the rituals of one people differed from those of another people not that far away. For the most part, analysing spiritual movements with an eye to alternative ways of organizing socio-cultural reality in the future was not seen as part of their discipline.

In this volume, I qualify the prejudice against positivity by showing that in some cases *positivity can have creative features*. I do not reject outright the criticisms of positivity advanced by Kant and Hegel among others, and

I recognize that uncritical acceptance of positivity can impose limitations, including cognitive, ethical and organizational blocks.

The prejudice against counterfactual doctrines

Some strands of the Enlightenment also propagated a more general prejudice against counterfactual doctrines, whether derived from supernatural authority or not. It did so because such doctrines were deemed to be false, and to be likely to underwrite popular superstition and arbitrary power. There was also a conviction that the progress of the sciences depended upon exposing and overthrowing such doctrines. Those who held such views failed to confront the possibility that such doctrines played a positive as well as a negative role in individual lives and human history. They also failed to grasp that many of their own doctrines were counterfactual, while inclining to a good/bad dualism, which aligned with their own conceptions of true and false. This prejudice was attacked at the time by Christian thinkers, such as the German philosopher J. G. Hamann (1730–88), and subjected to major assault by the German Romantics. Nonetheless, the focus on counterfactual doctrines continued into the nineteenth century, when it influenced applied intellectuals, whether scientists, lawyers, doctors or academics.

Today this prejudice can be challenged both by empirical examples and by research in the natural sciences, including cognitive science.[13] The term 'counterfactual' is currently used in multiple and often confusing senses.[14] Here by 'counterfactual doctrines' I mean doctrines that involve states of affairs not found in ordinary life. The term 'counterfactual' characterizes the type of doctrine and does not prejudge the question of its truth. This is the contemporary cognitive science sense as opposed to how the term is used by historians and many Humanities scholars to mean expressing what has not happened or is not the case.

Generic conceptions of 'religion'

Apart from the prejudice against positivity and the prejudice against counterfactual doctrines, the creativity of these spiritual movements has also been obscured by *generic conceptions of religion*. Although generic conceptions of 'religion' have been problematized in the scholarly literature for some time, there has been resistance to the implications of such problematization, largely on the pragmatic ground that talk of 'religion' is too established to be dispensed with. Be that as it may, there are grounds for treating generic conceptions of religion with caution, in so far as generic conceptions of religion may tend to misdirect our inquiries in certain respects. Generic accounts of 'religion' encourage us to find what we expect, and to identify what we find as 'religious', which may or not be the case. They may also lead us to assume that the sacred and the secular are separate in these movements, when this may not be the case.

After Durkheim, the distinction between the sacred and the profane or secular became fundamental to a great deal of anthropology and sociology of religion, and central to general theories of secularization. More recent research, however, problematizes the sacred as often associated with cruelty and violence, and also tends to deny that modern secular societies in the West are free of religious or even theological elements.[15] Islamic and Jewish scholars now complain that the Western secular society is really Protestant Christian, and not some sort of neutral state to which all cultures can aspire.[16] This does not mean that the distinction between the sacred and the secular is without value, but it does warn us not to assume it too quickly without careful consideration of particular contexts. Questioning generic conceptions of religion, in contrast, removes an obstacle to understanding these movements. Generic accounts of 'religion' encourage immaterialist and ethereal constructions of 'the spiritual'. Spiritual movements may provide formations of the self, enhance capacities, set up political parties, promote social reform and run major educational networks. They may also run businesses and accumulate wealth and power. In controversial cases, they may sell sex and drugs, launder money, hide criminals, and pile up weapons, to give only straightforward examples.

The term 'New Religious Movements' may also be sometimes misleading for the same reasons if it is taken to imply that movements of very different kinds are 'religious', and that the elements of these movements are unified by their religious features. This term can also go with an emphasis on the strange or controversial doctrines that the movement is alleged to teach, and a related tendency to imply that what the movement does follows from its doctrines. As we will see, this can be misleading, not because doctrines are unimportant, but because these movements are often heterogeneous amalgams and not primarily religious confessions. If we study spiritual movements without assuming that they are examples of generic religion, we will often be surprised by what we find.

Once the traditional religious-secular dualism is questioned, a different way of thinking about the cultural productivity of spirituality becomes possible.

It becomes clear, for example, that these spiritual movements are engaged in various so-called secular activities, often with considerable success. Once the traditional focus on doctrines and on their truth or falsehood is qualified, it is also possible to find value both in many of the cognitive materials these movements provide and in some of their spiritual practices. Once a less prejudiced attitude is taken towards the positivity of these movements, possible contributions to alternative arrangements can be noted in an astonishing range of areas, including philosophy, science, politics, ethics, social reform, economics, medicine, psychology, education, medicine, law, agriculture, international relations and cultural organization.

The claim that spiritual movements may produce ideas and practices that can help to reshape political, social and economic life is hardly new. It was central to the work of Max Weber and to the role he gave the Protestant ethic in the emergence of capitalism. More recently, the Italian philosopher Giorgio Agamben (b.1942) has studied the Franciscan monasticism of the twelfth century as a form of life not under the rule of law, and suggested that the Franciscans' detailed rules of life based on common use and not ownership may provide a model for a form of life still to come.[17] Nevertheless, it is perhaps more unusual to relate this claim to controversial movements with counterfactual doctrines.

Conceptions of the secular

Dualistic conceptions of the secular have also impeded the study and evaluation of these movements. In recent decades, the Western term 'secular' has become controversial both because historians have become unhappy with the older accounts of the term and because Muslim scholars have complained that the term is covertly Christian and assumes a privatized conception of religion which will not work for Islam.[18] In the context of spiritual movements the term is problematic if it is used to imply that the societies in which these movements operate are secular when they are not explicitly religious, and if it is taken to imply that movements alleged to be religious may not have secular features. And for contextual reasons the whole attempt to separate the secular from the spiritual can often be misleading. Many of these movements arose in societies in which spiritual traditions played both a political and a legal role and several of them retain theopolitical tendencies. None of these movements assume that the most important truths about the universe can be stated without regard to spiritual considerations, while many of them are engaged in what we might call worldly enterprises. This, however, is easier to see once we do not assume conceptions of the secular which occlude such admixtures and/or impose separations which only make sense in societies with particular types of governmental and legal regimes. Treating the 'secular' as heterogeneous and various by country, century and domain on the other hand allows us to characterize what we find more precisely and opens up new horizons for research.

Creativity

The creativity of these movements has also been neglected because of the tendency in much of the literature to associate creativity with absolute innovation and high cultural achievements. This perspective is outdated, but it lingers on in the assumption that movements with counterfactual beliefs will have mediocre cultures, and will attract people who are needy rather than people with initiative and capacity. My approach to these movements challenges this conception of creativity. I do not miss the fact that many contributions made by these movements are in part adaptations of earlier developments. I do not, however, reduce creativity to unprecedented innovation understood in Romantic terms. Rather, I take creativity to occur at various levels of social and cultural organization under specific conditions.

In my view, creativity is to be expected in a range of areas under modern social, economic and cultural conditions, and it is its *absence* which needs to be accounted for by reference, for example, to unequal distributions of wealth and power, by reference to ineffective institutions, and by reference to systems of hegemonic cultural power, which prevent or punish challenges to old ideas. Consistent with this, spiritual movements often arise in less developed contexts, and take off with marginalized social strata. Predictably, the creativity found in these spiritual movements often takes the form of *cultural productivity* or innovative further development of existing cultural resources. This creativity can occur in unexpected places. The results do not necessarily belong in the art gallery or in the culture museum, although they may do so, but they do provide new cultural and social possibilities for those in the movements, who often encounter them for the first time. Here there is a parallel with sixteenth and early seventeenth century Protestantism in Europe which produced little that was absolutely new, but revolutionized the social and cultural experience of those who became involved in it by initiating them into both cultural materials and social and economic arrangements which transformed their lives.[19]

I do not, of course, suggest that the creativity of these movements is ignored in the existing literature. However, there is little sense in the existing literature of how positivity and creativity are connected in these movements. Instead, there is a tendency to construe the creativity of these movements as a matter of a series of add-ons, with no structural link to the cognitive materials and practices which also characterize these movements. Here, in contrast, I take the creativity of these movements to be linked to the utopian intentionality they display in various manifestations, as well as to contextual factors. This creativity includes the exemplification of alternative possibilities that might inform our choices as well as the generation of thought experiments and practices that may be models for later developments.[20]

A disaggregative approach

In seeking to problematize the bias against positivity, the prejudice against counterfactual doctrines, and the role of generic conceptions of religion in understanding these movements, I deploy *a disaggregative approach* which proposes that many elements found in these movements can be studied in their own right. Adopting a disaggregated approach implies a rejection of social holism in the sense of the claim that the nature of a social form determines the character and operation of its elements. It does not deny that the elements disaggregated exist together and sometimes interact. Disaggregation is a methodological device, not a social ontological thesis. A disaggregative approach makes it possible to revisit many materials labelled 'religious' without stereotyping spiritual performances in terms of allegedly irrational doctrines and without assuming that the creativity of religious organizations stands or falls with the doctrines allegedly associated with them. Indeed, religion is often now characterized in terms that do not involve truth claims. The French philosopher Bruno Latour, for example, claims that religion and science are not in competition because religion is not propositional, but transformational. Religion, it seems, aims at veridiction, not information or truths about extensional realities.[21]

Disaggregating 'religion' in this way means, however, that different elements historically associated as 'religion' may have different futures. Social and personal uses of projectivism and counterfactuality may increase in advanced techno-scientific cultures moving out of the social processes in which the repression of the non-mundane was crucial to the success of early industrialism. Again, various thought experiments, practices, spiritual technologies and organizational forms found in spiritual movements may be redeveloped or redeployed in new constellations which may or may not lack the characteristics associated with them in the historical past. In the case of the spiritual movements I discuss, it is fair to ask whether they have negative characteristics that limit or distort their creative features. I do not address this issue in this volume, although it will be clear that I think that some of the negative characterizations of these movements are caricatural or overstated. The value of the approach I adopt, however, does not depend on how the balance between negative characterizations and creative features is weighted. Rather it depends on the potential value of the creativity I find, just as the potential value of the Mongol stirrup does not depend on our judgement of Mongol violence or our evaluation of the authoritarian tendencies of Genghis Khan.

My disaggregative approach goes to a larger attempt to change how we think about developments that have been labelled 'religious' in the context of future organization of political, social and cultural life. Here my approach has a background in a moderate naturalism which identifies tendencies, thought experiments, portable features and repertoires. On my account, spiritual movements can be culturally productive and generate narratives, symbols, rituals and practices, even forms of life.

Specifically, *the cognitive materials* made available by spiritual movements need to be construed in terms that capture their purchase without reducing them to true or false doctrines; *the spiritual practices* associated with these spiritual movements need to be studied as such; the *political, social, economic and cultural contributions* made by these movements need to be considered without importing a generic conception of religion. Equally, although these movements all have traditionalist elements going back before the modern period, they all have some postreligious features. The *organizational forms and arrangements* found in these movements need to be studied without reducing them to the aims or intentions of the actors involved in such movements.

Nothing I have said here should be construed as implying that there is only one correct way to work with materials labelled 'religious'. Nor do I deny that work is needed to expose the cognitive blocks religions encourage, the ethical retardation that they may promote, and the organizational problems that they may render difficult to solve. Nothing in my approach denies that materials associated with 'religion' may have been sources of mystification and repression at both individual and collective levels. Nor does it miss the fact that allegedly 'religious' organizations and practices have sometimes inspired hatred and violence. My discussion, however, does open the way for new approaches to cognitive materials, practices, political, social and cultural activisms and organizational forms that appear in movements labelled 'religious'.

I do not, of course, deny that phenomena can be located which can be construed as religions. My point is that we should not assume too quickly that these phenomena are instances of generic religion or that this religion is religion as European scholars have understood it. Instead, alleged instances of 'religion' need to be historicized and contextualized, and close attention then needs to be paid to what kinds of activities are under discussion since the activities falling under generic terms may differ quite dramatically over space and time.[22] Many scholars would now accept this. However, I take the argument one stage further and suggest that it may be a mistake to assume that we know what kind of phenomena these phenomena are, or how they should be understood. Instead, we *need to look*, without reading in European conceptions of generic religion. It is then possible to study these phenomena in a way which allow us to see aspects of them we either did not see before or did not see so clearly.

My disaggregative approach is influenced by theoretical developments in philosophy and the natural sciences which allow for dispositional features that are likely to be present other things being equal. It does not imply extreme nominalism or any claim that the various elements found in these movements are completely discontinuous. Obviously, they tend to impact on each other. Nor is the selection of some movements rather than others intended to be prejudicial. Obviously other movements might have been chosen instead. Many of them, however, have been much studied or are not especially controversial. One case, the Anthroposophical movement, deserves extended treatment elsewhere. Again, my attention to disaggregated elements recognizes that one element may be more important in one movement and less important in another. To explain why this is the case, I give the context in which each movement emerged, and underline aspects of this context which shape the movement thereafter.

I now discuss each of the elements on which I focus in turn.

Cognitive materials

The *cognitive materials* associated with these movements are arguably undervalued in the existing literature, even though they are extensively noted and described, largely because it is assumed that these materials contain pre-modern residues that do not involve cognitive, social or cultural advances. In attending to these cognitive materials and to doctrines based on them, I rescind from the tendency to construe counterfactual doctrines as such residues, even as evidence of intellectual error or superstition.

Here it is crucial to distinguish between the doctrines found in these movements' cognitive materials or thematized from them and the actual beliefs of members of these movements. My approach attends to the former. Obviously, such doctrines may impact on the actual beliefs of members. However, they need not do so, and there often is a significant difference between the multiple ways actual members understand the doctrines of a movements and the way they are understood and explained by its intellectual elites. Thus no one suggests that ordinary Western Christians understand what theologians mean by *hypostasis* or *theosis*, although both doctrines are arguably of outstanding intellectual importance. In the same way, I argue for the potential importance of the doctrines found in these movements rather than the considerably simpler beliefs most members may have.

My approach here gains support from the contemporary re-evaluation of counterfactuality in a range of disciplines, suggesting that counterfactuality may play a part in sentience, as it obviously does in memory, that some forms of counterfactuality, including forms nineteenth-century people dubbed 'religion', may be forms of evolutionary adaptation, and may in some contexts have helped to form the human bodies and minds. In this volume I do not enter into the technical problems raised by the term 'counterfactual', which many writers deploy in confused and different senses. I do, however, raise the possibility that people in advanced technological societies may choose in a range of contexts in the longer term to privilege fictionality over literal truth. My approach here allows me to treat many cognitive materials more sympathetically than they have been treated in the past in a way that allows for the role of *fantastic* and of *projective imagination*. The term 'fantastic' is used for narratives in the realist mode, which escape the standard dualism between truth and fiction. Here I extend this usage to cover narratives and reports that possess a luminosity which does not collapse into ordinary facts. The concept of projective imagination takes account of cases in which human beings throw non-mundane contents into the surrounding world. It covers cases which probably should not be construed as instances of claims to propositional truth.

Again, in discussing cognitive materials found in these spiritual movements I suggest that these materials may sometimes contain *model ideas or thought experiments* in both rational discursive and para-rational forms. The term 'thought experiment' signals that cognitive materials deployed by spiritual movements can be construed in terms of the cognitive operations they involve, conventional assumptions they challenge and the counter-empirical moves they make. The implication is that such materials are often of more interest from a cognitive point of view than a traditional true/false analysis of their claims would suggest.[23] These model ideas, where model ideas are thought experiments capable of later development, possibly in substantially different contexts, may be more valuable than is often realized.[24]

Here again my approach may seem radical in so far as it implies a less judgemental view of such fictionality as may be involved. Once again there are theoretical reasons for this. There are now developments in philosophy,[25] literary studies and religious studies[26] that imply that fictionality may be basic rather than derivative in some contexts. There is also now an extensive literature exploring the relationship between fictionality[27] and possible worlds theory,[28] and also a more restricted literature on the relationship between fictionality and religion. Less attention, however, has been paid to how fictionality relates to human spirituality, both individual and collective. There are studies of historical fiction, religious fiction and fiction-based religions,[29] as well as publications on invented religions[30] and hyper-real religions based on popular cultures.[31] These studies suggest formal continuities across traditional divides between fact and fiction. They also raise issues about how possibilities which appear in fiction, including fantasy texts, embody conceptual and/or metaphysical possibilities. Given these shifts of perspective, the fact that many spiritual movements have counterfactual doctrines may not be entirely negative. I do not suggest, however, that the effects of embracing or deploying counterfactual doctrines can be adequately established at this point, despite well-known research on brain plasticity and health, although scholars are now attempting to show their formative effects on the body more generally.

This is not to deny that a case may be able to be made that these movements are not unproblematic, that their controversial reputations may have a basis in evidence, that many of them involve authoritarianism or practise various forms of indoctrination. Obviously relying on positivity has its negative side, as Hegel argued. Again, adopting counterfactual doctrines may have serious negative consequences both for the individual and for the group, although I think this needs to be studied in detail, rather than simply inferred from an assumption that truth is all that human beings need.

I do not, however, explore how far the adoption of counterfactual doctrines relates to sociological considerations, including the structure and trajectories of particular social strata. My approach to cognitive materials accepts that subjective beliefs may be crucial to specific contexts, as Evans Pritchard famously argued.[32] However, I do not concentrate on how these cognitive materials are internalized using specific habits of reading. I do, however, suggest that these cognitive materials can sometimes be studied for possibilities that might be realized more fully or differently in later contexts. Cognitive materials in the form of cosmosophy or an enchanted interpretation of the universe as opposed to a cosmology adopted on theoretical grounds, revealed philosophy of history, and revealed science can all be read, I suggest, in this way. For obvious reasons I concentrate on cognitional materials that are publicly available, even though at least one movement, Ananda Marga, has secret teachings as a resource.

Spiritual practices

I also attend to the *spiritual practices* these movements provide for their members. In most cases, these practices are seen as enlivening the personal life and life praxis of members. In the case of movements influenced by Indian theosophy, the claim is stronger, and members believe that their practices can change their minds and bodies as well as their present and future karmas. Here there are significant differences between Ananda Marga, the Brahma Kumaris and the Church Universal and Triumphant, all of whom provide practices with a background in Indian theosophy and Tantra, and the Bahá'ís and the Latter-day Saints, whose practices tend to be more exoteric, although some practices may have esoteric aspects. For example, the reading of mystical texts in the case of the Bahá'ís and secret temple doctrines and ordinances in the case of the Latter-day Saints.

Spiritual practices may contribute to both the formation of the self as well as to community and identity formation, and also to the moral qualities associated or not associated with particular social bonds. Here my approach can be related to the work of the French scholar of late antiquity Pierre Hadot (1922–2010), and to the work of the French philosopher Michel Foucault (1926–84). I distinguish *esoteric practices* which aim to significantly modify bodies and minds from *exoteric practices*, which do not aim at measurable physical and spiritual changes but operate more on the personality, self or psyche. I do not imply, however, that exoteric practices are inferior to esoteric practices. I also accept that some exoteric practices may help ordinary people live extraordinary lives. And I assume that some such practices may sometimes migrate from the contexts in which they originally occurred, just as practices developed for spiritual purposes in monasteries provided organizational models for the later organization of factories. I also associate esoteric practices not only with transformed perceptual experience, but with the acceptance of forms of cosmosophy, where a cosmosophy is an enchanted interpretation of the universe. All of these movements provide a form of cosmosophy for their members.

Political, social economic, educational and cultural contributions

Spiritual movements may also make political, social, economic, educational, agricultural, medical and cultural contributions to their contexts and beyond them. In some cases, they do so because their central concerns require the whole organization of life to change. If so, this may be a significant consequence of their more counterfactual doctrines, and also an example of how such doctrines may have more impact than their credibility or lack of it might suggest. Obviously, the assumption that one's movement possesses unique information about the future and/or about the best social, economic and cultural order may motivate efforts to transform the world. Equally, the assumption that the world is about to end may make some actions more urgent than others

All these considerations feature in the spiritual movements I discuss. However, it is more difficult to determine whether a particular contribution follows from central doctrines of the movement, a significant intellectual advance associated with the movement, from contextual considerations or from the need to expand or consolidate the movement. In practice, different spiritual movements come up with many different examples of activism, with the exact nature of each intervention and its relationship to others and to the movement differing from case to case.

Emerging postreligion

Finally, all the spiritual movements I discuss have elements of emerging postreligion, in the sense of organizations of spirituality that do not insist on adherence to traditional beliefs, practices or moral codes. All the spiritual movements discussed in this volume demonstrate a degree of social creativity in loosening the bonds of tradition in some respects, even though in other respects they are all committed to some pre-modern doctrines and practices. How far, and why they do so, differs from case to case, but in all these movements there are features which a generic conception of religion might not lead one to expect, and in many of them there are elements of *futuristic ecumenism*, pointing beyond traditional spirituality altogether.

Organizational forms

I also attend to the organizational forms found in these movements. In doing so, I take a more realist approach to organizational forms than is found in much of the literature, one that implies that organizational forms have recurrent tendential features. Specifically, I entertain a version of organizational materialism found in some forms of comparative historical sociology, specifically, in the work of the German sociologist Georg Simmel,[33] who drew attention to cultural developments that changed subjective but not objective cultural and social forms, and in the works of the historical sociologists Michael Mann[34] and Toby Huff, with their emphasis on the long-term consequences of the presence or absence of specific organizational forms.[35] This work emphasizes that the choice of some organizational forms rather than others has long-term consequences, independent of the intentions and beliefs of the social actors,[36] and in some cases may restrict the history of a movement and its impact. Specific organizational forms may have particular organizational limits.[37] My approach to organizational forms is not crudely deterministic, but it does imply probabilities that bear on how the presence and absence of organizational forms relates to their ability to work for personal, social, economic and cultural change. It also recognizes that organizational forms may work for insiders in ways outsiders are insensitive to. These movements provide enclaves within which members experience community and meaning.

Emphasizing the need to study the organizational forms these movements adopt implies that what the actors think they are doing is not always decisive. It also suggests that some and not other personalities may be supported by some and not other organizational forms. However, I do not deny that some organizational forms require particular beliefs, just as they may support some rather than other personality types. Similarly, I do not deny that organizational forms may promote certain types of cognition, and restrain others. On the contrary, I think this aspect of the development of spiritual movements deserves more attention than it has received. Further, such organizational forms can sometimes be important for reasons that do not depend on the aims and purposes of its adherents.[38]

Organizational forms may also be studied for their impact on specific social strata or parts of the population. Clearly the provision of spiritual enclaves is important for oppressed minorities and for spiritual seekers. Likewise, different organizational forms may be appropriate to agricultural populations needing to maintain linkages and community for both economic cooperation and security and for urbanized wage workers wanting to advance their careers and educational attainments. As this implies, spiritual movements may develop as vehicles for the purposes of some social strata and then turn into vehicles for others. Thus Soka Gakkai began as a vehicle for Japanese mainly from lower socio-economic strata needing education and community, and then became a vehicle for the advancement of more secure social strata. Almost all these movements have proven attractive to spiritual seekers in Western countries, while two of them – the Bahá'ís and the Latter-day Saints – have had outstanding success with underprivileged populations in South America and Africa.

Once again, however, I resist attempts to read organizational form off activities that outsiders find offensive such as recruitment practices or arrangements designed to separate members from the society outside. None of these movements should be assumed to be cults or sects unless such characterizations can be shown to be appropriate and more revealing than others that might be suggested.

Summary of chapters

The chapters that follow discuss six spiritual movements and take account of both the cultural and linguistic contexts in which they arose and of their subsequent movements beyond them.

I begin Chapter 2 with the Bahá'ís, a spiritual movement originating in Persia that draws on positivity in working to bring about a global ecological civilization. I show that a movement with Adventist features is more creative than might be expected, and provides its members not only with rich cognitive materials and spiritual practices, but also with political, legal, economic and administrative proposals about how a better global order might be organized. Specifically, I claim that the Bahá'ís can be construed as an outstanding contemporary utopian movement having both positive and negative intentional features, even as a movement that in some respects may be ahead of the world at hand.

In Chapter 3, I consider the case of Soka Gakkai, a Japanese spiritual movement that has developed from an aggressive sect into a form of Buddhist humanism.

Despite its controversial reputation in Japan, I show that Soka Gakkai redeploys earlier Nichiren Buddhist utopianism to promote many innovations including rich cognitive materials, an ethical thought based on value creation, its own forms of education and a wide range of political, economic social and cultural contributions.

In Chapters 4 and 5, I consider two controversial Indian Hindu movements, Ananda Marga and the Brahma Kumaris. These movements come from very different backgrounds, but both are deeply connected with Hindu cosmic historicism based on revealed positivity. Ananda Marga is an Indian spiritual movement that combines Indian philosophy and esotericism with Bengali futurism. Despite its controversial reputation, I show that Ananda Marga is not only radically modern but futurist, and promotes a universalist philosophy, revealed cosmosophy and science, new economic and social thought, and a holistic approach to education. It also engages in multiple social and cultural initiatives and has postreligious features. The Brahma Kumaris, in contrast, have relatively few philosophical ideas and are much more Hindu Adventist than they first seem. Nonetheless, they too have an unexpected creative side. Although they operate within an Indian cyclical theory of history that predicts world destruction and apocalypse, the Brahma Kumaris reinterpret this to justify an unprecedented emphasis on the leadership of women as well as a vast range of social, economic and cultural activism. They also have a range of post-religious features.

In Chapter 6, I turn to a contemporary Christian theosophical spiritual movement that originated in the United States. The Church Universal and Triumphant has been seen at times as a dangerous doomsday cult. This, I suggest, does not capture the original features of the movement which, despite its partial immanence in what Partridge calls 'occulture', that is, popular cultural occultist trends, has radical pluralist and possibly post-truth features.[39] Once again, there is an unsuspected creativity at work in this movement, a creativity which I thematize as the democratization of counterfactuality to the point where the legitimation of claims and the sources of spiritual symbols and practices may be relatively irrelevant. Indeed, what critics see as extreme syncretism can better be construed, I suggest, as a form of postmodern spirituality which has escaped the censorship of tertiary cultures.

Finally, in Chapter 7 I consider the case of the Latter-day Saints. Unlike Latter-day Saint accounts which claim exclusive originality for the Church and hostile accounts which assume that Mormonism is a religion with incredible beliefs, I construe the Latter-day Saints as *a charismatic spiritual movement* that changes structurally over time. I sidestep debates about whether or not the Latter-day Saints are Christian. Instead, I attend to the remarkable creativity that characterizes the movement, including the revealed positivity that the Saints have received. I also take reports of experiences of ingression and vivid spiritual experience to be central to the Latter-day Saints and their achievements, however these experiences are to be explained. Moreover, I find creativity in the cognitive materials the Saints possess, in the positivity they deploy in developing strong families and spiritual bonding, and in the organizational efficiency they display in many different areas. The Conclusion explores the wider implications of these case studies and the need to think beyond inherited conceptions of religion and the secular.

Obviously, the question of what religion has to offer humanity in advanced technological societies remains open. The studies in this volume clear the way, however, for a more informed discussion of this question. Once prejudices from sections of the Enlightenment are put aside and generic conceptions of 'religion' are problematized, the focus then falls on what is creative about these spiritual movements and whether it matters. Raising the issue of whether spiritual movements can be culturally productive shifts the ground.[40] Once we think of movements labelled 'religious' as emancipatory in some respects, it becomes possible to grasp these movements' involvement with counterfactuality as a feature, and to begin to think about whether this feature allows their members to distance themselves from the social world in which they find themselves. Indeed, it may be necessary to rethink the ways in which Enlightenment relates to modernity if it turns out that some of what has been labelled 'religious' can be construed as anticipatory or futuristic. I do not, of course, attempt to predict the future. However, I do suggest that disaggregating 'religion' and questioning dualistic conceptions of 'religion' and 'the secular' makes possible a modest advance.

2

The Bahá'ís

Prosociality and Global Civilization

Let your vision be world embracing ...

Bahá'u'lláh

Now the new age is here and creation is reborn.
Humanity hath taken on new life. The autumn hath
gone by, and the reviving spring is here.
All things are now made new ...

'Abdu'l –Bahá

In this chapter, I consider the case of the Bahá'ís, a spiritual movement that directly challenges the European prejudice against positivity, that is, the prejudice and practices accepted on the authority of spiritual traditions. The case of the Bahá'ís also provides a powerful postsecular challenge to the growth-obsessed capitalist world by insisting on the need for a meaningful telos, then providing it. No Enlightenment thinker hostile to religion imagined that positivity could be *ahead of the world at hand.* That something like this could be possible is also a direct challenge to Western secularism and opens up the possibility of a form of Messianism based on actual arrangements rather than future events. It also suggests that under certain circumstances developments dubbed 'religious' can contribute to human social progress. Unlike most other spiritual movements, the Bahá'ís advance a prosocial positivity which can make a claim of this kind in some respects. This positivity encourages behaviour that benefits others and takes account of their needs, behaviour that reforms existing social and cultural relations and brings about a greater level of ethical awareness and action in society as a whole. As a result, their positivity can be seen as concrete utopian and relevant to future forms of life.

This is the perspective I will bring to their spiritual practices, their social and cultural activism and their administrative and organizational innovations. In making an argument of this kind I do more than report diverse matters of fact. I suggest that significant cultural productivity occurs where contemporary scholarship often does not expect it, and that inherited generic conceptions of religion have led us to misunderstand how counterfactual doctrines, advanced values and innovative arrangements arise and relate. I also imply that socio-economic factors influence and over-determine spiritual movements and their fate, but do not satisfactorily explain the content of the utopian surplus found in such movements.

The Bahá'ís are known internationally for their multi-faith ecumenism, their promotion of global government and peace, and their emphasis on the education and the rights of women. With rare enthusiasm, they attempt to bring all races, religions, peoples and cultures together, and endeavour to promote economic justice and human development. Indeed, they are arguably the most progressive spiritual movement in the world. Like Quakers, the Bahá'ís are an ethical minority critical of Western materialism and militarism, who attempt to promote a more harmonious world. Like Quakers, they reject pessimistic views of human nature and social order. Unlike Quakers, however, who have little positivity and can even be free of definite doctrines, the Bahá'ís base their radicalism on revealed positivity over a wide area. Their creativity is also of a distinctive kind. The Bahá'ís do not advance unprecedented ideas or practices, although there are exceptions. Rather they mobilize already extant indications, extend their application and/or intensity, and bring them together in a constellation of efforts directed at a new global civilization.

The context

The Bahá'í movement developed out of a millenarian Islamic background in nineteenth-century Persia.[1] Bahá'í prehistory is complex and controversial, and mainly important because it signals a sophisticated cultural context in which a remarkable religious teacher could appear. In 1844, in a world pervaded by Adventist expectations, a young Persian merchant proclaimed himself to be 'the Báb' or the Gate. A follower of Shaykh Ahmad Ahsá'í of Bahrain (1756–1825), who taught that the Imams pre-existed and were the causes of creation, the Báb adopted Shaykhite esoteric teachings and Neoplatonist metaphysics, numerology and magic,[2] and "advanced an explosive apocalyptical outlook". He wrote a revealed book, the *Bayán*, to replace the Quran in both Arabic and Persian, and revealed a new dispensation which abolished Sharia law and concubinage. The Báb also seems to have envisaged the establishment of a theocracy. He was uncompromising towards those who failed to recognize his high office, and claimed at various times to be the occulted Sh'ia twelfth Imam and a new prophet abrogating Islam.[3] The Báb was executed by firing squad in 1850.[4] In 1863 one of his followers, Mirza Husayn-Ali Nuri, the son of a wealthy government minister, known as Bahá'u'lláh, declared himself to be the Manifestation of God for this age,[5] and wrote tablets to the Pope and the world's rulers commanding them to obey him. His claim to exalted status was evidenced by his chanting wonderful texts in classical Persian and Arabic at great speed. When, however, Bahá'u'lláh's brother, who was the leader of the movement appointed by the Báb, refused to recognize Bahá'u'lláh's claim to be a new Manifestation, this led to violence between their followers and Bahá'u'lláh was imprisoned for his claims and activities for some forty years.[6]

The tangled early history of the movement partly explains its subsequent fate, its persecution in Muslim countries and the importance to the Bahá'ís of organizational authority. The early Bahá'ís were a millenarian movement responding to modernity.[7] It was not unknown in nineteenth-century Persia for individuals to chant verses in order to indicate that they were inspired by God. What was new was the challenge that gradually emerged of a movement attempting to supersede Islam, and the development of the first mass-based globalist ideology in world history, a movement that was arguably more advanced ethically than much of the world around it. The Bahá'ís explain this development in terms of divine revelation, although there may have been German influences on the thought of Bahá'u'lláh, including the work of the German writer and philosopher Lessing (1729–81) who, like Bahá'u'lláh, saw the various world religions as contributing to the education of the human race.

To provide organizational authority Bahá'u'lláh appointed his eldest son, 'Abdu'l-Bahá (1844–1921), as the leader of the Bahá'í community and designated him as the 'Centre of the Covenant'. 'Abdu'l-Bahá journeyed to the West, attended Jewish, Christian and Muslim services, and gave the Bahá'í movement a strong interfaith dimension.[8] He had an ambitious conception of the new covenant and envisaged a worldwide political commonwealth as the goal for which the movement should be working. His successor, his grandson Shoghi Effendi (1897–1957), changed the movement again by creating an administrative framework, expanding and regularizing the electoral basis for the Universal House of Justice, the democratically elected Bahá'ís institution of governance, and directing the expansion of the movement by issuing a series of plans.[9] After Shoghi Effendi's death a new phase began in 1983 when Bahá'ís were urged to seek out ways in which they could become involved in the social and economic development of the communities in which they lived. Henceforth, Bahá'ís opened their study circles, children's classes, youth groups and devotional meetings to surrounding populations. Subsequently, they experienced exceptional growth and currently have more than seven million members in 210 countries from over 2,000 different ethnic backgrounds. In effect, an Adventist movement from a sectarian background became a worldwide spiritual movement intent on prosocial anticipation. In doing so, it reinterpreted some of the Bab's teachings in modernist or pragmatist terms.

Cognitive materials

The Bahá'ís have vast cognitive materials that provide them with religious, philosophical and ethical ideas,[10] which summon them to strive for universal enlightenment and to work for the establishment of 'divine civilization'.[11] These materials can be read for personal exaltation without addressing the literal truth or falsity of their contents. Indeed, for some members of the movement this reading can become a spiritual exercise leading to ascent.

The Bahá'í cognitive materials take the form of high-quality literature in Persian and Arabic.[12] Bahá'u'lláh's most important writings include the *Kitáb-i-Aqdas*, literally the *Most Holy Book*, which is his book of laws, the *Kitáb-i-Íqán*, the *Book of Certitude* and the Gems of Divine Mysteries.[13] There are also a number of mystical texts. *The Seven Valleys* sets forth the stages of the path to higher consciousness and eventually towards God, while *The Hidden Words* summarizes truths.[14] These cognitive materials show that positivity can be culturally productive in ways that do not depend on a dualism between true and false, and that model ideas of some portability can be found in materials traversed by counterfactual beliefs. They contain ontological innovations, a philosophy of history, a revealed cosmosophy and practical ethics.

The ontological innovations found in the writings of 'Baha'u'llah are gradually gaining attention from professional philosophers and theologians, especially in the remarkable writings of the Bahá'í process theologian Roland Faber, who finds a radical pluralism in them, a non-dual unity of the unmanifest Divinity and its Primal Manifestation, as well as parallels to many Buddhist doctrines.[15] On this interpretation the Manifestation brings advanced ideas and introduces a radical pluralism which renovates older philosophical materials for new evolutionary purposes. The Bahá'ís also have a philosophy of history based on Manifestations, a philosophy that gives them a hermeneutics to apply to specific historical developments. According to the Baháʼís, God is unknowable and inconceivable, but his attributes appear in the Manifestations translated into human terms.[16] Manifestations are human beings who function as divine physicians, whose task is to contribute to the collective learning process of humanity. They bring new spiritual capacities that awaken human populations to new forms of action, and these changes, in turn, reflect changes in the spiritual world because the physical and the spiritual worlds correspond and there is interpenetration between the worlds. The Manifestations receive their revelation without an intermediary. They constitute a single, ongoing divine educational process for humanity.[17] On a maximalist account, the Manifestations pre-exist and are omnipotent, omniscient and infallible, another kind of being altogether, immaculate in their personal lives, beings through whom God establishes covenants with humanity. On a modernist account, the Manifestations are high beings with special cognitive capacities who use the same techniques as artists, and we need to become artists in order to understand them.[18] The theory of Manifestations implies that religious traditions are organic and lose their efficacy over time, so that when they then become obstacles to social progress a new Manifestation appears.[19]

Baháʼi theology implies that linear evolution occurs in both religion and social organization.[20] The Baháʼís construe all religions as *vehicles for the education of humanity*, a perspective which changes the crucial question from 'Are the beliefs of this movement true?' to 'Does this movement make contributions to the education of the human race?' According to the Baháʼís all religious founders are equal, and witness to the same truth in historically different forms and all religions are the outer expression of the divine reality.[21] When God sends a Manifestation, there are changes in the outward form of religion and in spiritual capacity, and each Manifestation reveals more than the one before it. However, they are also relative, in that the present teaching will later be revised. No other spiritual movement has transcended the Enlightenment's understanding of religion in this way, although related developments can be found in some forms of Hindu reformism which accept multiple revelators and spiritual paths and see no problem in syncretism provided the emotion of evolution towards spirituality is maintained.

The Baháʼís, however, are less dependent on current science than this suggests, partly because they have a *revealed cosmosophy* or an enchanted interpretation of the universe, deriving from Middle Eastern sources, and including hermetic and alchemical elements. This cosmosophy allows members to imagine a spiritual universe which is not the physical universe that immediately appears and to feel at home in a structure that is both meaningful and wondrous without abandoning the scientific cosmology of the natural sciences. The Baháʼís also hold that there are no essential differences between revelation and science, and that all human beings have been created to carry forward an ever-advancing civilization.[22] Accordingly, Baháʼís teach that science and religion must be in harmony. Consistent with this, some recent Baháʼí writers argue that the Baháʼí scriptures contain ecological teachings about humanity's relationship to nature.

According to Baháʼí cosmosophy, reality has several metaphysical levels, and everything is interrelated. The highest of these levels is the divine realm of unicity (*aḥadīya*), wherein only God's essence and his essential attributes exist. According to the Baháʼís the universe is eternal, and creation out of nothing is impossible. Again, the soul is immaterial and eternal, not in space or time, and does not enter the body. On some interpretations this means that it is to be understood in non-dualist terms. Moreover, the human being can consciously acquire 'the consciousness of reality', live in conscious at-one-ment with the eternal world, and experience eternal life.[23] After death the soul journeys through many worlds beyond space and time, in which its spiritual development in the physical world becomes the basis for judgment and advancement. Heaven and Hell are spiritual states of nearness or distance from God. On this view, life in the physical world is important for the spiritual development of human beings and the metaphorical nature of the physical world[24] reflects the spiritual world.[25] Hence, in a sense, the physical creation is perfect.[26] Salvation, however, involves *motion towards perfection* in both the physical and the spiritual worlds.[27] In practice, many Baháʼís do not over-attend to the occult cosmology their scriptures assume.[28] Some, however, find parallels between the esotericism of Baháʼuʼlláh's writings and contemporary physics, including a non-sensible ether, the emergence of space and time from quantum entanglement, and a non-physical continuum behind matter and electromagnetism.[29]

Finally, the Baháʼí cognitive materials include *a practical ethics*, based on demonstrating the perfections of God in one's life and on a specific view of justice as directed towards recognizing and consolidating the unity of humanity.[30] The Baháʼís do not believe in original sin or the Devil. Evil only arises as a result of human failure to turn to the good. On other issues, however, they are more traditional. The Baháʼís reject polygamy,[31] divorce is discouraged and young people must gain the permission of all parents before marriage. Homosexuality is not permitted. The Baháʼí teachings on marriage call it a fortress for well-being and salvation, and they locate the family as the foundation of the structure of human society. At the same time, the Bahá'ís are committed to a strong egalitarian family life. On the whole, their ethics have an open or future-oriented dimension. Interracial marriage is highly praised in the Bahá'í scriptures, and there are indications that in the longer term they will be able to accept a broader conception of family life. The Bahá'ís are also exceptionally ethical in ordinary life. In practice they seem to mainly universalize ethical ideals already found in Buddhism, Christianity and Islam. They have no controversial ethical ideals to propose, although they arguably have more success in living up to existing ethical ideals than many other groups.

To sum up, the Bahá'í cognitive materials stimulate new thinking in many different areas, while encouraging Bahá'í s to think in terms of further developments still to come.

Spiritual practices

Guided by their cognitive materials, the Bahá'ís follow a range of spiritual practices designed to promote a *non-sectarian spirituality practices*. Here the utopian intentionality towards a possible future spiritual development is striking, even though the details are more nondescript. The Bahá'ís have no body of infallible doctrines, no rituals, sacraments or clergy, and they allow free forms of worship in which, in addition to certain fixed prayers, individuals can choose their own words and music. Their house of worship services include readings from many traditions and are open to everyone. This pattern of worship is to some extent new, and points to a possible confluence of spiritual traditions. Nonetheless, some of their spiritual practices are fairly traditional, although based on revelation. There is a religious tax, a duty to go on pilgrimage, the reading of tablets at shrines, prayers for the dead, a nineteen-day sunrise-to-sunset fast each year, eleven Holy Days, a festival every nineteen days and an obligatory prayer each day using fixed words, forms and bodily movements.[32] At the level of personal spirituality, however, the Bahá'ís have an intense devotion to the person and teachings of Bahá'u'lláh, a sense of his personal charisma, which they attempt to realize in many different contexts, and a sense of a covenant that binds them to the current Manifestation. In practice, historical and cosmic perspectives merge and the Bahá'í calendar associates the names of the days and the weeks with the perfections associated with the divine names. They have no esoteric practices and the esoteric residues in their tradition are not emphasized, although clearly they were present in the Báb.[33]

Positivity as a guide to achieving a global civilization

Unlike most other spiritual movements, the Bahá'í movement is shaped by positivity that provides concrete guidance about how to achieve a global civilization. In doing so, they exemplify a profound turn to the prosocial or voluntary behaviour intended to benefit others, especially behaviour that is helpful and characterized by acts of kindness and compassion. As the Manifestation for this age, the Bahá'ís believe that Bahá'u'lláh brings the revelation of a new world order and a global civilization based on the unification of humanity. This global civilization will require a new global consciousness, new values and a new vision of humanity's future. Moreover, Bahá'u'lláh revealed *political institutions, legal arrangements and organizational forms.* These include the Universal House of Justice in Haifa, The Institutions of the Learned, originally the Hands of the Cause of God and now the Continental Board of the Counsellors, all of which operate on markedly prosocial principles.

The Bahá'í difference lies in the prosocial character of their arrangements, including government by elected councils, and processes of consultation and collective action. These arrangements assume the unity of God, the unity of religion and the unity of humanity, but their coherence is practical rather than ideological. The Bahá'ís do not seek to impose their preferences on others or imagine that their own activities by themselves will bring the global civilization about. On the other hand, they do regard their consultation process as a superior way of proceeding in human political and social affairs and also envisage the establishment of houses of justice throughout the world providing a qualitatively new type of non-hegemonic governance and administration. The Bahá'ís are unqualifiably optimistic, and believe that a complete restructuring of the political, social, economic and cultural life of humanity is now becoming possible. Hitherto, all areas of life have been organized in hierarchical structures. However, humanity has now reached the threshold of maturity, which makes it possible for human organization to be restructured in terms of the absolute equality of free and autonomous individuals. The Bahá'í social programme involves a just system of world government, a universal language, a world-collective security arrangement and an international court of arbitration. Guided by the central leadership of the Bahá'í community, the Bahá'ís promote a radical programme of prosocial practices and attempt to free human structures from conflict, competition and violence. Moreover, they apply this perspective to industry, the family and to international affairs,[34] and envisage a more egalitarian and participative society in which all class, racial and gender hierarchies have been abolished.

Bahá'u'lláh's *Kitáb-i-Aqdas* and *The Will and Testament of 'Abdu'l Bahá* are the foundational documents of the Bahá'í administrative order. In these arrangements there is no separation of powers, although there is a separation of function between the House of Worship and the House of Justice. Each organizational layer elects the next above it by secret plurality of voting. They also have many other institutions such as the Centre for the Study of Sacred Texts, and the Ruhi Institute at Puerta Tejadia Columbia whose programmes have been successful over much of the world.[35] There are detailed arrangements, such as government by elected councils, and processes of consultation and collective action. These arrangements are important because they embody cooperation and fraternity as real-world alternatives to arrangements based on competition and the survival of the fittest. Unlike the dominant arrangements in Western societies, they are radically prosocial in that they attempt to discourage competition and conflict. Moreover, consistent with these concrete practical orientations, Bahá'ís conceive of the administration of their movement as a spiritual practice, in effect, sacralizing ordinary life to an unexpected degree.

The Bahá'ís also have *revealed political arrangements*, including a specific understanding of the state and government derived from Bahá'u'lláh's writings. The Bahá'ís pursue the goal of a political system free from partisanship, parties and campaigning, indeed all mimetic rivalry. They practise a non-political type of decision making in which those who serve are chosen from the rank and file by secret ballots without nominations. At local, regional and national levels the Bahá'ís elect members to nine-person spiritual assemblies. There are also appointed individuals working at various levels, including locally and internationally, to propagate the teachings and protect the community. The Universal House of Justice, first elected in 1963, remains the supreme governing body, and its nine members are elected every five years by the members of all national spiritual assemblies. Much is made of the practice of consultation (*mashvirat*), the role of councillors appointed for five years and the tasks of the World Centre. Nonetheless, the Bahá'ís do not seek to impose their preferences on others or imagine that their own activities by themselves will bring the global civilization about.

Consistent with their marked prosocial bias, the Bahá'ís also maintain that many problems can be resolved by cooperation and consultation.[36] These arrangements are sometimes seen as a Bahá'í alternative to Western liberal democracy. The Bahá'ís are divided, however, about whether their political and social thought implies theocracy.[37] Some recent approaches align Bahá'í political thought with pluralism and even postmodernism.[38]

At a global level the Bahá'ís envisage the establishment of a world commonwealth in which nations, races, classes and creeds are closely and permanently united. The unification of humanity will take the form of a world federal system, ruling the whole earth with unchallengeable authority.[39] There will be a world legislature, a Supreme Tribunal, controlling the resources of all nations and legislating for them. Each nation will elect two or three representatives proportionate to their population. There will also be a world metropolis as the centre of the new world civilization, a world language, a world script and literature and a world currency. A world executive will be backed by an international force. Economic barriers and restrictions will be abolished along with class distinctions and unjustifiable distributions of wealth. Over time, state sovereignty and rivalry will decline and be replaced by mutualism and cooperation.[40] Problems that cross national borders will be adequately addressed including prostitution, terrorism and refugees. A world constitution will reconcile aristocracy and democracy.[41] The actual steps towards this goal are modest. They include proposals that nations make binding covenants fixing national frontiers, limiting armaments and removing governments in breach, as well as support for an international judiciary and international law. It remains to be seen whether their proposals can help to actually achieve these goals or whether their contribution is more to agitate for changes which may be realized in a different form later. Here there may be parallels with the Quakers who opposed slavery very early and then later proposed radical prison reform, both developments brought about in part by the work of others.

All these instances of revealed positivity can be construed, I suggest, as instances of concrete utopianism. In so far as a utopian intention appears, it is possible to detect a challenge to the world as it is currently. Nonetheless, because the concrete utopian indications are found in historical particulars they may turn out to be inadequate or misleading. Those who keep faith with the vision have to keep their eyes on the horizon as much as on what currently has managed to appear.

Socio-cultural activism for a global civilization

In all their activities, the Bahá'ís have a well-defined teleological goal: the achievement of a global civilization, which is understood as the next stage of ever-advancing human development. The Bahá'ís are socio-cultural activists and make valuable contributions in many different areas. They work not only for the advancement for women throughout the world, but also the overcoming of national, religious, racial and economic divisions, and the protection of religious, political and ethnic minorities. They promote respect for all races and cultures, accept the equality of peoples and oppose all forms of despotism and oppression. They also promote the case for international law and advocate disarmament. Despite their traditional family ethics, the Bahá'ís also attempt to pioneer a new family life based on the equality of men and women, and a just system of government. They promote a socio-political utopia in which government by force is replaced by administration, and a new society is developed in which every space is seen as an organizational centre for learning. The Bahá'ís are particularly concerned to promote education for development, including spiritual education for children and the education of girls, and place special emphasis on the spiritual capacities of youth. Currently there are some 600 schools run on Bahá'í principles. They have also pioneered a new type of spiritual education in the form of study circles designed to inculcate both knowledge of the faith and the skills needed to spread it to others. These study circles are supervised by some 300 training institutes. The generalized progressivism of the Bahá'ís is exceptional (not least in its radical revaluation of the rights of women), especially within the context of the Global South, where the most active and advanced Bahá'í communities now live. It is based on concrete organizational innovations such as youth empowerment programmes, followed by cluster reflection meetings. The Bahá'í difference is to prepare for a future perfect social order by making micro-social innovations now.

To bring the unification of humanity closer, the Bahá'ís insist that economic problems are connected with spiritual problems.[42] They work for the elimination of extremes of wealth and poverty, and for greater equality of income distribution. They are also committed to socio-economic progress, including many socio-economic development projects throughout the world. Envisaging cooperative economics concerned to achieve spiritual and not only economic goals, the Bahá'ís promote organicist conceptions of economics and made specific proposals for the reform of agriculture.[43]

Over the longer term, the Bahá'ís envisage humanity emerging from its preliminary phase into a phase in which all religions work together in a spirit of fellowship, and all peoples are united in a new global society. In this context, they are active promoters of global human rights. Nonetheless, although Bahá'ís welcome all religions as forms of the truth in historically conditioned forms and read texts from all traditions during their services, Bahá'í ecumenism has not led often to in-depth engagement, partly because Bahá'ís have often tended to follow a progressivist scheme in which other religions lead up to their own.[44] Recently, however, ecumenical engagement of a higher order can be found in the books of the distinguished scholar Roland Faber who avocates that religions in the future become transreligions.[45] Currently the Bahá'ís are working to revive and treasure Indigenous religions worldwide.[46] Here again they are arguably ahead of the world at hand, and quick to advance utopian ideals with the capacity to become mainstream in stages over time.

The Bahá'ís understand that their utopian goals will not be achieved overnight, and also that early organizational drafts will require revision. However, they are convinced that each individual can engage in forms of social transformation which will cumulatively make a difference. Moreover, they believe that vast numbers of small initiatives in over 15000 communities around the world can have an effect. They see their micro-activism as providing a social laboratory in which a new model of social organization is gradually emerging. In so far as Bahá'ís try to integrate spirituality and universal education with gender equality and vibrant community, there may be some basis for their hopes. They have certainly had some success with rejuvenating local communities, just as they have proposed media reforms.[47]

Bahá'í activism also includes cultural activities of many kinds. The Bahá'í emphasizes beauty in all aspects of life, but the most conspicuous manifestation of their cultural creativity is their outstandingly beautiful temples which are designed to represent paradise on earth. These temples are often very modern. They also maximize the use of sacred space and gardens. As an art form, they are concrete utopias in Ernst Bloch's sense, utopias that embody the universalist humanism the Bahá'ís are working to achieve.[48] The movement has also inspired many artists, including the potter Bernard Leach, the jazz trumpeter Dizzie Gillespie and the artist Mark Tobey.[49] Overall, Bahá'í cultural activism is impressive, but not yet perhaps entirely adequate to the scale of their claims for a new Manifestation.

Postreligious features in the context of a covenant

The basis of unity for the Bahá'ís is the Covenant between the Manifestation and his followers. When combined with other elements, this means that the movement has postreligious features. Despite their residual involvement in Middle Eastern religious practices, the Bahá'ís emphasize that each person must judge for themselves in religious matters and associate the Faith with advancement in all the branches of knowledge. As Bahá'u'lláh's grandson Shoghi Effendi wrote:

> The independent search after truth, unfettered by superstition or tradition; the oneness of the entire human race, the pivotal principle and fundamental doctrine of the Faith; the basic unity of all religions; the condemnation of all forms of prejudice, whether religious, racial, class or national; the harmony which must exist between religion and science; the equality of men and women, the two wings on which the bird of humankind is able to soar; the introduction of compulsory education; the adoption of a universal auxiliary language; the abolition of the extremes of wealth and poverty; the institution of a world tribunal for the adjudication of disputes between nations; the exaltation of work, performed in the spirit of service, to the rank of worship; the glorification of justice as the ruling principle in human society, and of religion as a bulwark for the protection of all peoples and nations; and the establishment of a permanent and universal peace as the supreme goal of all mankind – these stand out as the essential elements [of the teachings of Bahá'u'lláh].[50]

As in other spiritual movements, there is an emphasis on spiritual transformation, including ascent through different levels of consciousness, a path Bahá'u'lláh mapped out in mystical writings addressed to Sufi audiences. Moreover, salvation applies to societies as well as individuals and there is no dualism between personal and social salvation. However, neither Bahá'ís cosmology nor doctrine nor Bahá'í spiritual psychology should be understood as fixed.[51]

More generally, the Bahá'ís *reframe religion,* and associate it with new ideals and the social education of humanity. Indeed, they understand their own religion as a new stage in the religious evolution of humanity, one that brings together all that was learnt in the past and raises it to another level. Although they refer to themselves as a 'faith', Bahá'ís define 'faith' as first conscious knowledge and then the practice of good deeds.[52] For them the purpose of religion is to inspire moral change and to promote the social and economic development of humanity. Religion is the educator of humanity and its ambit is very wide. Bahá'ís emphasize the salvation of society, and not only individuals, and understand religion as dealing with all aspects of life.[53] This means that the Bahá'í faith has a larger goal than the religions of the past. It aims to shape a new global social reality, to change the current organizations of nations and global institutions, and ultimately to produce a new race. Accordingly, Bahá'ís see themselves as going beyond the Christian ethic of love for individual human beings, and as advancing to a new ethic of love for the world and a conception of the religious group as a unified community. They receive a new global religious identity from the movement, and see themselves as global citizens helping to educate others.

The Bahá'ís have no absolute interpretation of their faith, and allow a degree of *interpretative pluralism*.[54] Currently within the unity of the Bahai community there are Bahá'í traditionalists and Bahá'í modernists who recognize that interpretation of the faith and its institutions will change as it expands. Some Bahá'í modernists exploit relativistic sounding statements by Bahá'ís to imply that Bahá'ís can provide a radically new understanding of philosophy and religion. Some Bahá'ís insist that their religion allows for the independent investigation of truth and that science and religion correct each other. In addition, they take a critical view of the early more dogmatic phases of the movement and concede that the science in the scriptures is antique. Bahá'í intellectuals recognize that the community so far is transitional and full of residues, and that at any one time it is a mixture of what should be and what is inherited from the past.[55] Modernists gloss esoteric Shaykhite teachings as global pragmatism. They qualify the traditional claim to infallibility, stress the literary character of their scriptures, and the gulf between theory and practice. In the long run, it seems likely that Bahá'í ideology will change, especially since most members are now found outside the Persian world in Africa, India and South America.

According to the leading Bahá'í scholar Moojan Momen, the standard construction of the Bahá'ís as another world religion in competition with the others is a distortion of its real nature. This construction reflects the present stage in its historical development when its leaders and intellectuals have largely interpreted the Bahá'í teachings in accordance with their own Middle Eastern/or broadly Abrahamic cultural perspectives.[56] On Momen's view the Bahá'í faith is *a metareligion*, not another religion that has come to take the place of the existing religions. It is *a way of looking at the religious experience of the whole of humanity*. Moreover, in the future, people from other cultures, Hindus, Theravada and Mahayana Buddhists, Chinese religionists and native peoples, will produce their own interpretations and developments of the Bahá'í Faith from their own cultural and religious viewpoints which maybe scarcely recognizable to us who know only the Bahá'í Faith today. For Momen, the Bahá'í faith is in its early birth phases and still evolving, and he envisages that Bahá'ís in the future will be very different from now when they are still immersed in practices and beliefs that predate the Manifestation. Whereas the older teachings subordinated the individual to the will of society, modernist interpretations emphasize the need to allow the faith to unfold and that the movement is still at a very early phase of its development.[57]

Consistent with this, Baháʼís increasingly define their religion in terms of *education for lifelong learning* and establish centres of teaching and learning. This shift towards lifelong learning is a significant renegotiation of traditional religion and a radical transcendence of traditional ideas which assume that one spiritual tradition has exclusive access to the truth.[58] In the same way, because the revelation is about transformation rather than doctrines the movement can allow a good deal of freedom of belief.

Organizational forms

As we have seen, the Baháʼís have organizational revelations. They have not, however, been free from organizational conflicts. There have been expulsions of Covenant breakers who reject the decisions of the Universal House of Justice and also difficulties with individuals who claim to be later Manifestations than Baháʼuʼlláh. The Baháʼí emphasis on unity does not mean that it is always achieved. The movement is also more authoritarian than its public profile suggests, and strong claims are made for the infallibility of the Manifestation and the Writings. On the other hand, no test or control of this infallibility is provided. There is also internal censorship (all writings about the faith are to be submitted to a prepublication review committee), and those who disobey the divinely established leadership were denounced at one time as 'covenant breakers'. There are also structural tensions between Baháʼí proto-globalism and an exclusivist organizational form and ideology. Baháʼí feminism also has its limits, and no women serve on the Universal House of Justice, although they are vocal in local and national spiritual assemblies. It is also fair to note that the movement has many traditional features, which more modernist Baháʼís would regard as residual. For example, the Baháʼí community is united by law, and is a legally constituted organism, but is more collectivist than it first appears. Divine law has been revealed, and must be obeyed. In contrast to Islamic legalism, however, this law is non-static, and can be continually revised and extended by the administrative authorities. Nonetheless, Baháʼí law is not Western, and is based on justice rather than love. For Baháʼís law hinges on the fulfilment of obligations and on the community's right to self-defence. It includes specific requirements such as the payment of a dowry and specific punishments, including death penalties and proposals for an inheritance tax.[59] At this stage it is difficult to detect anything like a new philosophy of law, although modernist writers increasingly adopt flexible stances and attempt to move beyond the revealed law paradigm with which they began. This suggests that they are in transition from a Middle Eastern movement to organizational arrangements more consistent with their goal of a global civilization.

Conclusion

In this chapter, I have only dealt with some aspects of the Bahá'í movement. I have omitted the severe persecution they have suffered in Iran, and have also not dwelt on the considerable contributions they are making to development in many parts of the world. I have also made less than I might of their philosophy of history, based on Manifestations. This is because I think that their philosophy of history may not illumine empirical cases in detail, as their very limited studies of Christianity illustrate. The Bahá'ís are ultra-ecumenical and even accept that Christ's death on the cross purified the world. However, the belief that Bahá'u'lláh fulfills and in a sense brings back all the teachings of the previous great prophets inevitably confers on the movement a sense of superiority which needs to be established rather than assumed. In practice, whole civilizations are denied a Manifestation. Thus, according to Shoghi Effendi, Confucius and Lao-Tzu were not Manifestations, and Guru Nanak and Mani are probably discounted as well. Bahá'ís are also inclined to declare themselves to be the only modern global religion and to interpret other religions in terms of their own soteriological scheme.[60] Again, their philosophy of history can sometimes give the Bahá'ís a superior attitude towards earlier spiritual traditions, just as it embroils them in perpetual and irresolvable conflicts with Islam. These problems are reduced, it is true, if the central content of the revelation is interpreted as unlimited pluralism and relativism. But then the resulting syncretism may not lead to superior explanations. What really matters about the Bahá'ís is their attempt to introduce and build a global civilization, a goal which has effects in itself, and one that gains relevance as they increasingly pioneer new prosocial forms of life designed to be compatible with it. To a striking degree, the Bahá'ís are introducing ideas, practices and organizational arrangements which point beyond a civilization constructed around hierarchies and discrimination. The Bahá'í movement is also modelling postreligious forms of spirituality in which generalized learning may come over time to replace doctrine and cult. The fact that *a movement beyond positivity is based on revealed positivity* is a paradox of the first importance. Clearly the Bahá'ís provide creative models for alternative forms of life in many areas.

The Baháʼís may be the first spiritual movement to map a path to a global ecological civilization. Their efforts to do so can be construed as concrete utopianism, limited by historical conditions. The Baháʼís's are unusual among spiritual movements because they attempt to be the future now in a way that will help bring it into being. They do so without the benefit of Tantric practices, unlike Ananda Marga, and without positive knowledge of future events, unlike the Brahma Kumaris. In their multiple activities the Baháʼís signal the inadequacy of Enlightenment prejudices against positivity and counterfactual doctrines. They also signal, and, in part, exemplify the need to go beyond traditional dualistic conceptions of religion and the secular.

3

Soka Gakkai and Cosmic Humanism

Introduction

In this and the following two chapters, I discuss Soka Gakkai, Ananda Marga and the Brahma Kumaris, movements originating respectively in Japan, Bengal and Pakistan. Each of these movements has been strongly criticized at times. My concern here, however, is to draw attention to the cultural creativity of these movements which has not always been acknowledged. In each case there is a complex linguistic and cultural background, of which some members are only partially familiar, and in each case pre-modern cultural survivals are associated with attempts to be ultra-contemporaneous as rich traditional materials in Sanskrit, Bengali, Chinese and Japanese are re-morphed for contemporary purposes.

In what follows, I read Soka Gakkai, Japan's largest religious organization, as a modernist movement promoting a completely laicized Buddhism as well as progressive social developments both in Japan and internationally, while addressing issues not yet solved in Western cultures, including how to provide structured organization for autonomous lay spiritual life, how to promote advanced socio-cultural practices among the public more generally, how to connect personal spiritual practice and concern for the environment and how to articulate a humanism grounded in a cosmosophical account of the universe. Unlike most commentators, I construe Soka Gakkai as promoting a concrete utopianism combining discipline and excellent organization with socio-cultural vision. Soka Gakkai's utopianism here has some relation to earlier forms of utopianism based on the teachings of Nichiren in Japan which combined an emphasis on the harmony of religion and science, the end of gender inequality, the celebration of the unity of all and the goal of the unity of all races.[1] In Soka Gakkai, however, this utopianism takes a pacifist and progressive form. Unlike Ananda Marga and the Brahma Kumaris, Soka Gakkai is not crucially dependent on positivity because it understands traditional Buddhist teachings in allegorical terms. Moreover, the movement is modernist, like the Brahma Kumaris, and not futurist like Ananda Marga. That is, it modernizes older traditions but does not specify what changes will occur in the future as a basis for action now.

Although Soka Gakkai shares some of the eclecticism found also in other forms of engaged Buddhism in Asia, and also the same tendency to valorize developments in East Asian Buddhism as the key events in cosmic history, no Buddhist movement has done more to transcend traditional Buddhism in order to focus upon a cosmic humanism, where humanism implies reverential participation in nature. No other Buddhist movement has been so successful in translating traditional Buddhist teachings into a universal ecology with global appeal. And no other Japanese movement has successfully traversed so many languages and cultures. Soka Gakkai also provides experimental models of shifts which all spiritual traditions may need eventually to make: from particularistic exclusivism to universal cosmic humanism, from ritualism and priesthood to spiritual republicanism and from sectarian self-maintenance to other directed social, economic and cultural contributions.

The context

Soka Gakkai, the Society for the Creation of Value, is a Japanese Buddhist lay organization with some twelve million members in 192 countries, including between 5 to 10 per cent of all Japanese. Emerging out of the economic and social turmoil of the 1920s, Soka Gakkai has grown exponentially, both in numbers and in resources, since 1945. It has major membership around the world,[2] although in Japan itself, with a change of social conditions, its growth has now peaked.[3] The movement is famous for its emphasis on chanting as a way to reach objectives in practical life. It is also known for its peace witness and its militant environmentalism. In the discussion which follows I find more evidence of creativity than any previous treatment of the movement in English. I also suggest that the enthusiastic activism that characterizes the movement, as well as its openness to new social and cultural developments, can be related to the reinterpretations of Buddhist positivity which the movement promotes.

Founded by the Japanese educational reformer Tsunesaburo Makiguchi (1871–1944) in 1930, Soka Gakkai has changed over time from the Soka Kyoiku Gakkai (Value-Creation Education Society), propagating Nichiren Buddhism among educators, to the Soka Gakkai, promoting Buddhism among all Japanese, to Soka Gakkai International, promoting Nichiren Buddhism throughout the world. It has retained, however, a strong emphasis on forms of internal discipline and on the conversion of outsiders.[4] Beginning with mainly working-class members, it now attracts more educated and prosperous strata, many of whom are women. Indeed, an openness to women's emancipation is one of Soka Gakkai's many progressive features.

Members of Soka Gakkai follow a modified version of the Buddhism of the thirteenth-century Japanese reformer, Nichiren (1222–82), sometimes dubbed the Japanese Luther. Nichiren criticized traditional Buddhism for encouraging passivity and resignation, and attacked the élitism, asceticism and world renunciation of Buddhist monasticism in Japan according to which ordinary people could not become Buddhas in their present lifetime without becoming monks. Instead, he promoted a lay Buddhism for ordinary people. Nichiren's Buddhism subsequently became associated with ethnocentric nationalism and an exclusivist attitude to other forms of Buddhism. Soka Gakkai's mutation of Nichiren's Buddhism, however, transcends this history, including the more obscure aspects of its beginnings,[5] and places the emphasis instead on social and cultural transformation. In its short history, the movement has mutated from an aggressive sect denouncing all other religions as evil into a modernist movement seeking ecumenical dialogue with other religions and humanity generally.[6]

This transformation is largely the achievement of Soka Gakkai's post-war leader, Daisaku Ikeda (b.1928), a self-educated layman turned spiritual teacher, a prolific writer and an intellectual interested in art, photography, philosophy, poetry and music. Although not a seer or a prophet, Ikeda has a status in Soka Gakkai which puts him beyond ordinary mortals. He has produced countless books and engaged in dialogues with a wide range of eminent figures.[7] Ikeda has given Soka Gakkai a comprehensive vision,[8] based on both a passionate commitment to Japanese civilization and a vast knowledge of Western writers and intellectuals, although his career has not been free of controversy in Japan.[9] Without separating himself from the movement's founding heroes,[10] Ikeda has changed the movement from an evangelical sect, holding huge rallies and using aggressive methods, to a mainstream movement encompassing a wide diversity of views and concerned to promote peace, a sustainable environment and global citizenship.[11] He is a committed humanist reformer and a dedicated globalist, and these characteristics have given Soka Gakkai a radical edge. Ikeda has also maintained to some extent the strong religion or rigid bonding character of Soka Gakkai, while modernizing it from within. It is this combination of radical humanist modernism and rigid bonding which accounts for much of the movement's success internationally, while in Japan itself the rigid bonding makes sense for lower social strata seeking to rise. For such strata, Soka Gakkai provides an ideology, a national family and effective social and cultural disciplines as well as a wide range of opportunities to expand their knowledge and social skills. However, this combination of hierarchy and democratization may morph over time.

Cognitive materials

Soka Gakkai provides its members with a wide range of cognitive materials at different levels of difficulty. The major texts are the *Lotus Sutra*, the works of Nichiren, and, most important, President Ikeda's writings. In addition, a deeper grounding in Buddhist philosophy and cultural history is now available through the publications of its Institute of Oriental Philosophy in Tokyo, with the result that intellectually minded members have access to a wide range of Buddhist philosophical texts. In practice, the most important cognitive materials may be found in Ikeda's re-interpretations of the thought of Nichiren and of the work of the two first presidents of the organization, Tsunesaburo Makiguchi and Josei Toda (1900–58). These materials provide members with a completely laicized and largely modernist version of Buddhism. In this remake, the Mahayana theory of the 3,000 realms (*ichinen sanzen*) and many other doctrines are given allegorical meanings,[12] and Soka Gakkai miracle stories including Toda's first epiphany (his realization that the Buddha of the *Lotus Sutra* is 'life itself') and his second epiphany (his experience of being present at 'the Assembly on Eagle Peak' referred to in the *Lotus Sutra*), become allegories of Enlightenment.

None of the cognitive materials deployed by Soka Gakkai are explicitly esoteric, although some of them may well have had esoteric dimensions in earlier centuries. For current purposes, Ikeda transposes Nichiren Buddhism into a new humanism for the twenty-first century, based on a 'human revolution' in the life of each person, enabling followers to develop their capacities and express their individualities.[13] Here he makes an advance that may be relevant to social reform worldwide.[14] According to Ikeda, the 'human revolution' is what idealistic social movements of various kinds sorely lack. Indeed, Ikeda goes so far as to write that:

> Under the sway of the nineteenth century cult of progress, we have fervently devoted ourselves in this century to enhancing the structure of society and the state, labouring under the delusion that this alone is the path to human

happiness. But to the extent that we have skirted the fundamental issue of how to reform and revitalise individual human beings, our most conscientious efforts for peace and happiness have produced just the opposite result.[15]

This revolution is set out in two serialized novels by Ikeda, *The Human Revolution* and *The New Human Revolution*. For Soka Gakkai, a Buddha is one who dedicates their life to *kosen-rufu* or 'widely declaring the *dharma*', the realization of the ideals envisaged in the *Lotus Sutra*. There is no strong distinction between the physical and the spiritual. Through struggling against and overcoming obstacles members can transform their destiny and attain Buddhahood in their lifetime. In this way, Buddhism becomes a practice of self-help based on 'doing our human revolution'. Buddhahood is revealed through challenging every aspect of our life; it exists nowhere else. In the same way, a relationship of non-duality between the individual and its surroundings becomes more important than magical practices, and the traditional Buddhist doctrine of dependent origination or the claim that everything that exists is dependent on something else is reinterpreted as a sophisticated theory which privileges internal over external causes.

In contrast to the world denial and passivity of traditional Buddhism, Soka Gakkai members attempt to become successful and wealthy. There is no need to become free of desires: desires can be realized. However, a strong commitment to social-ethical life is required. Like the founder of Opus Dei, Escrivá de Balaguer, Ikeda teaches that spirituality has to do with performing one's work exceptionally well. So far from promoting an otherworldly spirituality, Ikeda holds, with Nichiren, that 'The true path lies in the affairs of this world'.[16] For Ikeda, Buddhist practice takes place in the real world and in society. It does not guarantee a life free of problems, but motivates the individual to overcome life's challenges. Indeed, according to Ikeda, Buddhism enables us to succeed in every aspect of our lives. Accordingly, prayer becomes a struggle to overcome our weakness and lack of confidence in ourselves and to elevate our life conditions. The Buddha is the true entity of life, Life is eternal, eternal life is the true self and the true self is co-extensive with the universe and exists for all eternity.[17] What is involved here is nothing less than a concept of human sovereignty in the universe.[18]

In effect, Soka Gakkai translates Nichiren's Buddhism into *a cosmic humanism* that implies that the human being is to be identified with the whole universe, and can affect the environment around them, consistent with the Buddhist principle of *esho funi*, the oneness of the person and the environment. The connection between humanism, the universe and the environment amounts to a model ideal of potential relevance to human beings everywhere in the age of the Anthropocene. It provides a personal horizon for the movement's militant environmentalism, a horizon often lacking in the lives of many environmentalists in the West, who struggle to integrate a secular self-conception with personal experience of the unity of nature.

Soka Gakkai members are also introduced to *a revealed cosmosophy* which brings out the significance of traditional Buddhist doctrines for human beings with a modern scientific world view. For this cosmosophy, the whole universe is a single life entity, governed by a single mystic law, and there is no unchanging or nondependent entity. There is no distinction in principle between mind and matter, physical and spiritual; inner and outer are related, and all of life has both physical and spiritual aspects. These ideas are fused with a reassertion of the traditional Buddhist doctrine of nine levels of consciousness and of the claim that the pellucid structure of pure consciousness experienced in Enlightenment is the cosmic ultimate with elements of the contemporary sciences.[19] Indeed, the Buddhist view of the simultaneity of cause and effect and privileging of internal over external mechanical causation can be used to challenge Western notions of linear causality.[20]

This modernist transformation of traditional Buddhism allows karma to be reinterpreted as 'what returns', without going into the traditional doctrine of transmigration. Likewise, Nichiren's 'mystic law' becomes universal life, of which we are all embodiments; death and life are parts of the same eternal life of the universe. There is no separate self (the self really refers to the universe), and no soul to survive death, but this does not preclude the rebirth of the individuality out of intermediate existence (*ku*) when conditions are ripe. The intermediate state of existence is used to explain how Buddhism, while correlating with the discoveries of the contemporary sciences, nonetheless allows for long-term internal causality across lives, such that the circumstances of a child's birth reflect both its karma and the physical conditions studied by the natural sciences.[21] And in a further countermove against Western historicism or the doctrine that where you are in history is what matters, each individual is to learn to live the present moment in such a way that contact is made with the cosmic Buddha nature, which is a very demanding ideal by any standards. They are to engage with the moment as a moment of time without beginning.

Finally, Soka Gakkai also gives members access to a sophisticated modern ethics based on *value creation*, an ethics that is radically open because new values can be created in the future. This ethics emerged as part of a Japanese reception of the ethical thought of the German philosophers Friedrich Nietzsche (1844–1900) and Max Stirner (1806–56), a reception which impacted on Makiguchi. In the

German context value creation implied that traditional values were expressions of decadence and/or heteronomy and that individuals could and should create new values more in keeping with their real instinctual and other needs. However, in Nietzsche the implication was that traditional Western values were those of slaves rather than of the *Übermensch*, while Stirner emphasized the need for ethical individualism rather than ethics imposed by others. Soka Gakkai retains neither of these themes. Instead it adopts and reasserts Makiguchi's approach to ethics based on the creation of value as a real-life concern, not the study of values or the rational justification of values:

> When we speak of creation, we refer to the process of bringing to light whatever has bearing on human life from among elements already existing in nature, evaluating these discoveries, and through the addition of human effort further enhancing that relevancy. In other words, creation reworks the 'found order' of nature into an order with special benefits for humanity. Strictly speaking, then, *creation* applies only to value and not to truth, for truth stops at the point of discovery.
>
> Of course, there are times when we may just discover value. To highlight things that were simply never noticed before and make them apparent is an act of discovery, not creation. But when someone brings together previously unrelated things to the manifest benefit of humankind or builds upon earlier works to increase their relevance that is called invention, origination, or creation.[22]

Makiguchi insisted that value was a matter of benefit, not truth: something intrinsically connected with human beings, their orientations and life practices, and realized and judged within life activities.[23] Unlike American pragmatists such as William James (1842–1910), by whom he was influenced, he held that truth does not change, but value does. This interpretation gives Soka Gakkai the ability to avoid canonizing older moral judgements, while endorsing new developments in both general ethics and sexuality.

Taken together, these cognitive materials re-orient the lives of members towards ethically based action in the world at hand, while providing countermoves against both the meaningless Western universe and against the traditional ethics imposed by religious authorities. It is not clear that these cognitive materials, with the exception of the *Lotus Sutra*, are read in a particularly contemplative way. However, they provide members with the resources to ally personal spiritual transformation with work for reform in many different areas, not only a modernist transformation of Buddhism with implications for social and cultural reform but major model ideas such as cosmic humanism, allegorical cosmosophy and value creation.

Spiritual practices

Soka Gakkai provides members with what it sees as uniquely powerful spiritual practices which effectively democratize traditional Nichiren Buddhism. Soka Gakkai members chant a single Japanese sentence (*Nam-myoho-renge-kyo*), along with the first part of the second chapter, and the verse section of the sixteenth chapter, of the *Lotus Sutra* morning and evening before a printed scroll called the *Gohonzon*, a piece of paper which is a transcript of a calligraphy by Nichiren preserved at the Nichiren Shôshû temple near Mt. Fuji. Chanting to the *Gohonzon* summons forth one's Buddhahood and has cosmological as well as existential effects. When believers chant, they believe that the Buddha's life state is realized from within their being. Chanting allows members to integrate their subjective state with objective reality, while at the same time polishing their lives by struggling to correct their faults. This is thought to activate the creative force inherent in all life and enables people to express their enlightened nature. Long-term family benefits are also expected from chanting. In the same way, Soka Gakkai members view prayer as fusing one's own being with the fundamental law of the universe and activating the depths of the human spirit.

The original Dai-Gohonzon, or ultimate worship object, was inscribed by Nichiren as a new kind of mandala, on which the phrase 'Devotion to the *Lotus Sutra*' (*Nam-myoho-renge-kyo*) was written vertically and surrounded by the names of Shinto and Buddhist deities to symbolize the absolute superiority of the *Lotus Sutra* over other religions and sects. It was then copied by successive high priests of the Nichiren Shoshu sect, and Soka Gakkai reproduces a copy made by Nichikan Shonin, Nichiren Shoshu's twenty-sixth high priest. *Nam-myoho-renge-kyo* is interpreted by Soka Gakkai to mean the activity of practising Buddhism (*nam*, devotion), the essential law of the universe and its phenomenal manifestation (*myoho*), simultaneity of cause and effect (*renge*, the lotus) and continuity in life (*kyo*, sutra or, more broadly, Nichiren's teaching).

In Soka Gakkai's practice the *Lotus Sutra*, as interpreted by the Chinese Buddhist philosopher Chih-i (538–597), becomes a meditation on the possibility of a de-hierarchized and post-ideological Buddhism, while Nichiren's writings become Scriptures, in which an ecological ethics can be found. Chanting to the *Gohonzon* is claimed to produce direct material rewards and to be the most effective way to become rich, healthy and happy in this life, just as it helps to overcome specific difficulties and to achieve specific objectives. More educated members emphasize that the goal is to become a Buddha in the sense of a human being full of courage, wisdom and compassion who creates something positive for oneself and others.

Apart from having faith in the *Gohonzon*, members perform 'assiduous practice' (*gongyo*) in the form of chanting twice daily, studying the works of Nichiren and Ikeda, attending weekly meetings and undertaking hierarchically ordered education courses. An enormous amount of graded and examinable study material is available. Members are encouraged to learn the technicata of Nichiren Buddhism, including the concept of the 3,000 realms in a single moment (*ichinen sanzen*) and the ten 'factors of life' (*jū-nyoze*), and to become involved in a range of cultural and social activities. Membership gives individuals *a structured spiritually oriented active life*. While spiritual practices are rigidly prescribed, there is remarkable freedom in other respects and memberships of other organizations are possible. There is no detailed prescriptive moral code, so that many of the burdens of more traditional religious practice are avoided. On the other hand, there is personal connection and community, reinforced by mentorship, friendship circles, small group memberships and common subscription to periodicals.

Political, Social, Economic, Educational and Cultural Contributions

According to Soka Gakkai, Ikeda's human revolution requires members to make multiple contributions to contemporary political, social and cultural life. Each person is responsible for creating world peace, social justice and the happiness of humanity and these outcomes require this-sided work by each individual for change. An emphasis on nature or the environment provides a crucial link between the Romanticization of nature and the capacity of the individual who engages with nature in appropriate ways to transform it. Members of Soka Gakkai are to be activist individuals and each human being is to transform his or her environment, and not simply to conform to it.

Among its many forms of activism, Soka Gakkai's peace witness is outstanding. In this area, Soka Gakkai has a remarkable record of opposing nuclear weapons worldwide and rearmament in Japan. Ikeda has worked for decades for the reform of the United Nations and for world peace, submitting peace proposals to the United Nations every year since 1983.[24] He has also maintained close links with China, and attempted to mitigate the hostility between China and Japan. He has established influential research organizations of influence, including the Toda Institute for Global Peace and Policy Research, which publishes an annual journal entitled *Peace and Policy*; the Institute for Oriental Philosophy, which republishes Buddhist classics, has a journal of Buddhist thought, and engages in ecumenical dialogue with other religions; and the Ikeda Center for Peace, Learning and Dialogue in Boston, which addresses a range of contemporary issues from bioethics, global education and the reform of capitalism to the promotion of peace. Overall, Soka Gakkai works effectively at many different levels for peace, including Ikeda's own practice of citizen diplomacy and emphasis on peacebuilding through dialogue.

Soka Gakkai also has a global socio-cultural vision. It calls for coordinated action in the world on behalf of others and the environment. Moreover, members are encouraged, in a finesse of a sermon by Buddha on Eagle Peak, to regard themselves as 'bodhisattvas of the earth', and to work for a global ecological civilization.[25] The contrast here with many forms of prosperity gospel Pentecostalism is striking. In effect, Ikeda's transformation of Nichiren Buddhism provides members with a positivity which gives them advanced cosmopolitan moral and social ideals. Given the exclusive particularism of traditional Nichiren Buddhism, this is remarkable achievement.

To achieve its goals of reforming both Japan and the international order, Soka Gakkai has established new institutions, including the *Komeito*, Japan's third largest political party, raising issues about the proper relation between what Westerners would call church and state.[26] Like Ananda Marga, Soka Gakkai embraces actual political struggle, even though Ikeda has worked to separate the Komeito and Soka Gakkai over time. As a political player, it has been a major opponent of Japanese rearmament and a strong advocate for friendship between Japan and China.

As part of its attempt to further value creation, Soka Gakkai has also been successful in assiduously providing education based on value creation, especially for less privileged strata. It has worked hard to realize its own interpretation of Makiguchi's educational ideas in various educational organizations. Makiguchi taught that the production of value needed to be central to ethical education, rather than the study of ethical systems and ethical reasoning. Here he inherited the practical concerns of American pragmatism, but gave them an even more this-sided and real-world definition by attempting to locate value in practical activities.[27] Where pragmatists such as Dewey attempted to relate truth to 'what works' or pragmatic consequences, Soka Gakkai has been successful in integrating Makiguchi's approach to education with a vision of global values and planetary citizenship.[28]

According to Makiguchi, education can be assessed by whether or not students acquire an ability to create value:

[Education] is not the piecemeal merchandising of information; it is the provision of keys that will allow people to unlock the vault of knowledge on their own. It does not consist in pilfering the intellectual property amassed by others through no additional effort of one's own; it would rather place people on their own path of discovery and invention.[29]

The concept of increasing the value creativity of students was revolutionary in the Japan of the 1930s, and still has radical implications for contemporary education.[30] Soka education emphasizes the need to integrate education with practical life. It implements Makiguchi's vision of education shared between the home, the school (conceived of as a mini-society where ideal social relations can be implemented) and the community. It is not based on theories of education or the works of philosophers, but on an orientation to real life, reverence for the environment and a strong sense of how geography and place condition human life. The ideal of Soka education is to produce well-rounded human beings who promote transformative change in the context of their local communities with both global and local vision. The unique creative potential of every individual is to be fostered, and they are to be imbued with an ethic of peace, social contribution and global consciousness. Makiguchi's radicalism is now exemplified in Soka University in Tokyo and at Soka USA at Laguna Hills, Orange County, where a remarkable campus in the fifteenth-century Renaissance style has been built. There are also Soka high schools, kindergartens and a women's college in Japan as well as many research institutes and university affiliations.

In the same way, to realize its cultural mission Soka Gakkai makes extensive use of contemporary magazines and media, and publishes a quality daily newspaper, the *Seikyo Shimbun,* as well as a weekly paper in English, the *World Tribune*. It has also established an art gallery for working people, the Tokyo Fuji Art Museum and the Min-On Concert Association which brings international cultural events to Japan and also set up community cultural centres in many countries. Here, Soka Gakkai identifies what it perceives as missing in the lives of its members and provides specific cultural innovations in response. These many activities involve several model developments:

- the provision of high cultural materials (art, music and current affairs) for a mass audience
- a mass movement promoting pacifism and concern for the environment
- a major political party with reformist goals
- value-based education integrating instruction with social practices and real life

Post-religious features

Despite its Buddhist character, Soka Gakkai's version of Buddhism has post-religious features. In Soka Gakkai's version of Buddhism, the meaning of 'religion' is reinterpreted to mean serving the real needs of people and finding solutions to the problems facing humanity. Consistent with this, Ikeda's humanistic Buddhism is a demanding religion based on strenuous practice. It involves the practice of both natural and social ecology, and Buddhism is said to teach oneness of self and the environment. Likewise, the earlier pattern of attempting to prove that all other forms of Buddhism were false has now been abandoned, with the result that there is little or no emphasis on exclusively correct doctrines. Further, Ikeda himself now concedes that Buddhism will never be the world's sole religion, and therefore urges members to engage in multifaith dialogue and concrete cooperation with other religions. In Ikeda's later teaching a movement towards *postreligion* becomes explicit, although he does not use this term. There are no images of Buddha, no monks in saffron robes, no temples or monasteries, no system of meditation, but only faith in a particular form of chanting. Traditional Buddhist doctrines are finessed. The traditional Bodhisattva ideal is widened to mean that each individual should seek to serve others, and the traditional Buddhist emphasis on withdrawal from the world is replaced by an activist philosophy of historical transformation. In place of the over-spiritualized concept of compassion often found in Mahayana Buddhism, there is a stress on the need to work hard, to struggle, to be courageous and to act to change circumstances.

According to Ikeda, it is now necessary to humanize religion in order to take full advantage of its transformative potential. Religions exist for the sake of people, not vice versa. In humanist mode, Ikeda can be seen as fusing Nichiren Buddhism with European personalism, as found in writers he admires such as Montaigne, Berdyaev and Maritain, and so gives it a decidedly non-Buddhist dimension, but one that appeals to young people undergoing Western individualization. Ikeda is especially impressed with Montaigne's delineation of personality as a distinct ontological level. In Ikeda's revision of Buddhism, the self-motivated changing of individual lives becomes central. Moreover, the *Gohonzon* exists only in the mortal flesh of those who chant and is not to be sought outside the self.[31] The true Buddha is *nam-myoho-renge-kyo*, and is inherent in ordinary people. None of the Buddhas or the bodhisattvas are outside the human being. These are radical ideas to propagate among lay audiences.

Organizational form

Soka Gakkai is more ethnic Japanese than its propaganda suggests, and possibly more rigid and authority-oriented in Japan itself than overseas. Like many other spiritual movements, Soka Gakkai struggles to find an organizational form appropriate to its goals. In effect, it has mutated from an authoritarian sect into an international movement working in multiple socio-cultural contexts. It retains, however, especially in Japan, a combination of top-down hierarchical leadership, with emergent individualism, albeit one structured around the ideals of group membership and following a mentor. Currently, Soka Gakkai lacks a clear successor to Daisaku Ikeda as a spiritual teacher, even though Minoru Harada has now replaced him as President. The movement has no authoritative model for how to respond to scientific and technological changes in the longer-term. It is not clear how the movement proposes to critique Japanese ethnocentrism in spiritual as well as other matters. Soka Gakkai currently has no general theory of social evolution, and no scientifically grounded response to the pluralism of spiritual traditions, including Indigenous traditions. Indeed, it is not impossible that the movement will drift back to ethnocentric Japanese models in any area not governed by specific teachings from Ikeda. To this extent, the gift of a charismatic leader may have led the movement to underestimate the need to develop new alternative institutional arrangements in several areas.

Conclusion

Despite these possible limitations, Soka Gakkai has a remarkable record as a movement that has developed from particularism to universal cosmic humanism, from ritualism and priesthood to spiritual republicanism, and from sectarian self-maintenance to other directed social, economic and cultural contributions. Given the war-time Japanese context which has shaped its development, its record of militant passivism stands out internationally as an example of how a spiritual movement can morally challenge defining features of the social and cultural world in which it emerges, and become a champion of advanced social causes and new education relevant to the whole world.

Soka Gakkai provides a model for how a spiritual movement which was originally narrow and ethnocentric can become universalistic and postreligious. The creativity of its cognitive materials, spiritual practices, ethics, social activism and education is clear, and needs to be explained by both the initiatives of an outstanding leader and by social changes within Japan that made it possible for humanistic reformism and rigid confessional bonding to coalesce. It is perhaps surprising that a movement that was initially more ethnocentric than many other forms of Buddhism now offers a model for a transition out of historical 'religion' altogether.

Soka Gakkai also demonstrates that personal transformation can be combined with work for political, social, cultural and educational reform. Soka Gakkai is distinctive, however, in its movement away from communal spiritual order and in its promotion of education based on value creation. However, as we shall see, unlike Ananda Marga, Soka Gakkai lacks plans for a vastly different and possibly transhumanist future. It also has no specific social utopia to propose and, unlike Ananda Marga, tends to work with existing political orders. On the other hand, Soka Gakkai involves a radical democratization and laicization of Buddhism in contrast to the remnants of Hindu hierarchy found in both Ananda Marga and the Brahma Kumaris. Indeed, all its many attempts at social creativity imply that lay people generally can operate as autonomous agents and achieve Buddhahood without the need for priests or other traditional spiritual authorities. Here it exemplifies a possibility with which Christians and Muslims have sometimes still to come to terms. The combination of a human revolution, cosmic humanism and an entirely laicized approach to political, social and cultural transformation is of international significance.

4

Ananda Marga and Utopian Futurism

Introduction

In this and the following chapter, I discuss two Indian Hindu spiritual movements – Ananda Marga and the Brahma Kumaris – which combine social, economic and cultural activism with Hindu cosmic historicism or the view that history is not linear but always passes through the same phases.[1] Ananda Marga, literally 'the Organization to propagate the Path of Bliss', is a socio-spiritual movement with a range of objectives not usually associated with a 'religion'. Aiming at both spiritual transformation and service to humanity, it is a reformed Hinduism with Bengali features, and arguably one of the most radical spiritual movements in the world.

Ananda Marga combines practices designed to bring about spiritual transformation, plans for political, social, economic and cultural revolution, and utopian futurism, a combination which directly addresses the failures of Communist movements in the twentieth century in the West. Its optimistic futurism makes it open to all manner of progressive ideas, including a global maximum and minimum wage, wealth for all rather than the few, universal basic assets, the social equality of women, gender and racial inclusivity, as well as sensitive to the contemporary relevance of Indigenous spiritualities. Ananda Marga's futurism, however, is not a Western futurism, but one concerned to end the Western domination of the world. Moreover, despite its militant progressivism, Amanda Marga is shaped by a classical Indian conception of macrohistory which allows members of the movement to know what the next phase of the historical cycle is likely to be.

Ananda Marga has been studied for its membership patterns and involvements in local communities,[2] but its utopian dimensions have not received the integrated treatment they deserve. As a reformed Hinduism, Ananda Marga rejects many older interpretations of Hinduism, and breaks with caste, religious intolerance, as well as traditional marriage and dowry practices, while committing itself to holistic reformism, pan-species ethical universalism, racial and gender equality, and world government. Here it inherits many elements of the Bengali Renaissance[3] pursued by Ram Mohan Roy (1772–1833) and Rabindranath Tagore (1861–1941), as well as the social reformism of Swami Vivekananda (1863–1902), the founder of the Ramakrishna Math and the Ramakrishna Mission. Whereas the Bengal Renaissance, however, was largely about Hinduism catching up with the West, Ananda Marga uses elements of Hindu tradition to develop solutions to problems the West has failed to solve.

A movement with allegedly one million adherents in 100 countries, Ananda Marga currently presents itself as a spiritual and social service organization offering free meditation training all over the world rather than as a religion. Much of its literature is about courses or trainings designed to promote mental, emotional and physical well-being. Its motto of self-realization and service to all gives little idea of its Hindu background.

The context

Ananda Marga was founded in 1955 in Jamalpur Bihar by the Bengali philosopher, linguist and polymath Prabhat Ranjan Sarkar (1921–90). The son of a railway official, Sarkar never completed his college degree at Vidyasagar College in Kolkata, but came to be regarded in India, under the name Shrï Anandamurti, as a realized master or the embodiment of supreme consciousness. His followers called him 'Baba' or Father in the Indian manner, and attributed to him occult powers and clairvoyant knowledge. Sarkar himself presented as a polymath and a spiritual teacher who held that external science needed to be supplemented by intuitive knowledge.

In its original Indian context Ananda Marga was associated with violent revolutionary objectives and accordingly its members are sometimes characterized as Hindu Anabaptists, a reference to the revolutionary Radical Protestants of the early sixteenth century.[4] The movement became popular in India in the 1960s but came into conflict with Indira Gandhi's government. In 1971, Sarkar was imprisoned on charges of conspiracy to murder members of Ananda Marga trying to leave the movement. He was jailed for seven years, but subsequently released with all charges dropped. Many international organizations took up his case, arguing that he was innocent. Between 1975 and 1977, Ananda Marga was banned in India, and some 400 schools were closed. Subsequently the Indian Supreme Court exonerated Sarkar, but his health was seriously affected by ill-treatment and allegedly poisoning in prison.

It is not clear how central violence was to Ananda Marga in its early phase. Ananda Marga accepts the need for extensive use of force in certain circumstances, and some wings of the movement were associated with violence, both in India and overseas. Sarkar himself was not opposed in principle to the use of force if injustice against the downtrodden could not be changed through social service and electoral changes, even though he denounced terrorism. When members engaged in violence to have him released from prison, Sarkar chastised them, telling them he would not gain his release through these means but through the judicial system. He may, however, have considered force to be justifiable when establishing a new utopian order, especially since he taught that it was possible to change the order of dominance in a social order or to reduce the degree of a negative cycle. On the other hand, Sarkar argued that violence in between epistemic eras was not necessary. If education and literacy were high, then a peaceful transition was more than likely. However, if they were not, then workers and peasants were likely to revolt against the powerful.

There are suggestions that some members of the movement in India in the 1970s and 1980s were open to seizing power through violence. One wing of the movement, The Universal Revolutionary Proutist Federation, claimed responsibility for terrorist attacks on Indian interests.[5] Whatever the truth of Ananda Marga's military activities, Sarkar saw violence, or at least the need to fight, as basic to human life, and did not retreat from an acceptance of warfare at both the local and the cosmic levels. However, Sarkar also saw war as the darkest spot in human history. He also taught that establishing and maintaining the Great Universe of co-operating living entities requires struggle between good and evil forces in the universe.[6] It is not clear whether Ananda Marga now entirely precludes violence if conditions change. The violence associated with the early days of the movement may also reflect specific features of the Indian context. Sarkar knew both the Bengali philosopher and political theorist Manabendra Nath Roy (1887–1954) and the political theorist and activist Subhas Chandra Bose (1897–1945), both of whom advocated new humanism and radical democracy, while supporting violent action in support of political and social reform.

Sarkar himself was astonishingly productive. The author of 5,018 Bengali songs (The Songs of the New Dawn), Sarkar was a polymath who wrote over

264 'books', many in Bengali, encompassing mysticism, cosmology, philosophy, sociology, history, education, medicine, ethics, bio-psychology, linguistics, economics, ecology, farming and music, as well as children's stories, poetry, fiction, comedy and drama.[7] He was also an accomplished linguist and left an unfinished twenty-six volume encyclopaedia on the Bengali language. He also developed a philosophy of language based on traditional Indian acoustic vowels. Sarkar saw himself as the harbinger of a new civilization, and he made contributions to education, medicine, science and economics, although his plan to build a utopian city has still to be realized. The range and quality of his achievements have not received the recognition they deserve.

The fact that Sarkar emerged in South East Asia is both striking and important. It means that he was able to address many different areas of life without feeling that he was pontificating outside his field. Consistent with this, Sarkar's approach to a huge number of questions was holistic rather than single discipline-based. His cultural and geographic location also allowed him to combine classical rural attitudes, including strong localism and a celebration of place, with urbanite futurism. The question remains as to why so much creativity is to be found in someone with a limited background and from a less privileged part of the world. Part of the answer has to do with the cultural wealth of Hindu civilization and the particular cultural strengths of intellectual elites in Bengal.

Cognitive materials

Although negative stereotypes of Ananda Marga give the impression that the movement is narrow and fanatical, Ananda Marga actually provides members with a wealth of cognitive materials, including some that combine traditional Indian and modern scientific concepts. Indeed, contrary to the movement's popular image, Ananda Marga arguably has more creative cognitive materials, including a range of model ideas, than any other Asian movement emerging in the twentieth century.

To appreciate how this can be the case, it is necessary to bracket the Enlightenment bias and allow that new developments may emerge from attempts to modernize tradition. Consistent with this, in formulating his spiritual philosophy Sarkar drew upon several traditional Indian systems, including classical Sāmkhya philosophy, Śaiva and Śakta Tantra, Bengali Vaishnavism and Vedanta.[8] He often defined traditional terms in non-traditional ways, gave traditional terms an expanded sense, or used the terminology of one tradition in the sense of another.[9] Mostly, he said new things in old languages.

At the heart of Sarkar's spiritual philosophy was *revealed cosmosophy* or an account of the eternal cycle of creation through which the universe passes. This cosmosophy is Sarkar's adaption of classical Sāmkhya dualist philosophy.[10] In Sarkar's philosophy, however, allowance is made for both immanence and transcendence (both *Nirguṇa* and *Saguna Brahman*), or a form of metaphysical monism that resembles Kashmiri Śaivism in some respects.[11] In contrast to the dualism of Sāmkhya philosophy, *puruṣa* and *prakṛti* become two aspects of one reality.[12] The physical universe is a metamorphosis of primordial psychic factors and cognition is inherent in matter. Consciousness is not the result of mental activity, and matter is not separate from consciousness.[13] Rather consciousness is cosmological and causal. The universe is created by the 'Supreme Consciousness', and exists in the 'Supreme Entity'. Its evolution follows a universal pattern. Pure consciousness is transformed into mind and then into the five elements that constitute matter.

Sarkar's spiritual philosophy was syncretic, but technically demanding. In 1986, however, Sarkar developed a theory of *microvita* with no precedent in Indian philosophy. According to Sarkar, microvita are extremely small subtle entities with both physical and psychic dimensions and real but invisible causal powers. These are units of consciousness and may be positive, negative or neutral.[14] There are fourteen types. Microvita are alive, and can transfer both ideas and viruses. They enter into atoms and change the structure of genes. They can also be used to change physical structure as well as the structure of the mind.[15] Ananda Marga writers construe Sarkar's microvita as revealed science correcting contemporary physics and astrophysics. They see his theory of microvita as implying a new view of mind, matter and consciousness and as anticipating a future unification of the mental and the physical sciences by implying that all solid objects are imbued with energy or life. Some claim that they make possible a new cosmology of a creative universe which has consciousness in all of its structures.[16]

This opens up the problem of whether (1) microvita stand alone as one of Sarkar's many contributions; or whether (2) they amount to a new scientific cosmology displacing in some respects Sarkar's early monist cosmosophy (*brahma cakra*) which was mainly philosophical, or whether (3) a synthesis of the two perspectives is possible. Different students of Sarkar's thought adopt different standpoints. What matters is that Sarkar's creativity here gives Ananda Marga members not only an intellectual investment in contemporary physics, astrophysics and mathematics, but also expectations that the future will be very different from the world that exists now.

Consistent with this, Sarkar himself left many indications about what the transhumanist future would involve, including predictions of a coming ice age, projections of major biological changes to human beings, plants and animals, and optimistic expectations of hyper-technologies. Children would be born without sexual reproduction and human beings would make their homes in the stars. For Sarkar, such forecasts were probabilities based on what he called time, place and person. For many members of Ananda Marga they seem to have become more or less certain.

In addition to microvita, but not entirely separate from them, Ananda Marga also has *a biopsychology* which expands the Tantric chakras and relates them to physiology, glands and the hormonal secretions of human physical and psychic states. This biopsychology once again combines traditional and scientific concepts.[17] In addition, Ananda Marga also has *a philosophy of mind*, according to which there are eight levels of consciousness (*kosas*) in interaction with the world.[18] The last three layers are identified with the causal mind in contact with the causal consciousness, from which the mind derives, and the third layer of the mind makes possible clairvoyance, dreams and intuitive telepathy. Ananda Marga attempts to integrate this philosophy of mind with contemporary physiology.

Ananda Marga also has *a revealed conception of history*, one which makes its members actively interested in the future and not disinclined to political action.[19] This revealed conception of history is based on the standard Hindu teaching which envisages an eternal repetition of the same cycles and so a rejection of Western linear conceptions of history. According to this conception, there are four successive ages, each dominated by a specific class in turn, to which particular arrangements are appropriate: the age of the workers, the age of the warriors, the age of intellectuals and the age of the capitalists, with correlative mentalities and social systems.[20] The conception further predicts that when a class of people struggle and rise to power, they cause a revolution in the physical and mental world, but then become corrupt and are overthrown. Revolution, however, is not the only possible future. There can also be evolution, and the cycle can also go backwards returning to the previous era. However, it may be possible for strong leaders to prevent a dominant class from clinging to power and exploiting other social strata.[21]

Here Sarkar reinterprets Hindu cosmohistoricism as an historical sociology, including predictions that the next world era will be a martial one. This historical sociology includes a political sociology which captures how dominant social strata exploit people and hang onto power, a historical sociology reminiscent at times of Marx. The cycles are fixed, but stages can be accelerated and exploitive phases can be shortened, just as periods of rapid change can follow periods of relative pause. In effect, Sarkar takes the classical Hindu view that the world or universe continually passes through the same five phases in a modernist direction. It is not clear whether Sarkar retained more of the cosmic version than his Western followers suggest, and also whether he left teachings reserved for higher levels of membership about such matters. Members of Ananda Marga believe that they know more about what will happen in the future than secular knowledges alone provide. What is striking is how easily Ananda Marga adopts a radical futurist outlook, one that embraces extensive technological and scientific change, even though its futurism is shaped by a Hindu cyclical macrohistory. Moreover, its view of the near future is optimistic, and does not include an expectation of an apocalypse. It has inspired the internationally important work of Sohail Inayatullah on future studies and the metafuture.org think tanks,[22] and a range of future studies publications. The peace scholar Johan Galtung was also inspired by Sarkar's work, arguing it is amongst the most important of the century,[23] and the economist Ravi Batra used Sarkar to develop his forecasts on the demise of capitalism.

Ananda Marga also has a *philosophy* in the Western sense. This philosophy is known as *Neohumanism*. It is a revision of humanism designed to modify or replace it by extending humanism to all living beings, including plants and animals, and rejects the humanist emphasis on self-bounded individuals.[24] Sarkar's Neohumanism builds on the radical humanism that the great Indian social reformer R. M. Roy set out in his classic text *New Humanism: A Manifesto* (1947). On this universalist view, all living beings belong to a universal family and deserve equal care and respect. Neohumanism explicitly excludes racism, caste and religious discrimination. It also involves a new conception of how human beings relate to nature,[25] just as the Ananda Marga emphasis on a vegan diet has ecological implications. Its wider implications are only now becoming evident. They include crucial elements for a future ecological civilization in which care for animals and plants goes with a just international distribution of wealth.

Ananda Marga also has a *universalist ethics* that rejects all discrimination on the basis of race, nationality, religion culture, class, gender or species. This ethics is radically environmentalist, and calls for an end to animal suffering. It includes a wider theory of rights to include non-human rights for animals and plants,[26] and a sixteen-point guide to ethical conduct in daily life.[27]

Taken together, these cognitive materials provide members of Ananda Marga with ways of understanding the world that set them apart as having access to privileged knowledge not easily obtainable outside the movement. This leads them to see themselves as ahead of the world at hand, and they do in fact have cognitively advanced teachings over a vast area. This raises the crucial question of whether these teachings are to be taken on faith, whether they are able to be confirmed by occult perception achieved by the movement's Tantric practices and/or whether they are compatible with or confirmed by current science. In practice, the movement tends to claim all three.

Spiritual practices

Ananda Marga encourages its members to achieve personal transformation and provides spiritual practices for the systematic training of both the body and the mind, as well as ceremonies which enhance bonding and create enclave effects. To achieve the spiritualization or self-realization needed to bring about and sustain change Ananda Marga prescribes demanding spiritual practices which are held to deliver great benefits to mind and body. These practices, summarized by Sarkar in sixteen points, amount to a system of non-dualistic *Tantra*, loosely based on Patañjali's Astānga yoga. They include a lacto-vegetarian diet and fasting as well as forty-two body practices to be performed once a day. Members of Ananda Marga use their yogic practices to raise the kundalini or the spiritual serpent at the base of the spine, which then makes a form of clairvoyance possible.[28] The aspirant learns meditation from a qualified teacher or *āchārya*, most commonly a monk or nun, but then is obliged to keep the lessons secret. This is the sense in which Ananda Marga provides members with a 'path of bliss', leading to an experience of pure consciousness or initiation.[29] These practices help fill the epistemological gap opened up by many of the movement's claims. They also introduce an element of elitism and secrecy since only those with occult powers are able to confirm many of the teachings and also to receive others that are not made public. The secrecy is justified on the grounds that each individual has an individual sound which only a guru can interpret correctly.

Ananda Marga's use of Tantra, which it takes to be a science, means that it has doctrines and practices which it only partly reveals, including esoteric training that leads highly committed followers to report significant spiritual experiences.[30] There is also an adaption of Buddha's eight-fold path[31] as well as devotional practices (*bhakti*) for final realization (*sadhana*).[32] The movement also has spiritual practices which are communal and esoteric at the same time. Ananda Marga recommends that its members practice collective meditation at least once a week. These meetings called *Dharma Chakras* are preceded by the singing of 'Songs of the New Dawn' composed by Sarkar, followed by a spiritual dance (*Lalita Marmika*), along with the chanting of a universal mantra (*kiirtan*). Before meditation, the Samgacchadhvam *mantra* is chanted. At the end of meditation, the Nityam Shuddham and the Guru Puja *mantras* are recited. Two other sacred dances, kaoshikii, the dance for mental expansion, and tandava, a vigorous dance to enhance the body, are also employed. Ananda Marga's use of Tantra means that spiritual transformation is achieved through body-based practices and the feelings rather than rationality alone. That is, a form of body enlightenment is the basis for spiritual enlightenment.[33]

Ananda Marga's approach to spiritual practices is now sometimes presented in less Indian forms as about mind-body integration or even embodied practices that invite grace in.[34] Nonetheless, despite extensive modernization, hierarchy and secrecy seem to some extent to prevail. In the same way, there is an Indian understanding of how *atma* relates to *paramatma* or the Supreme Consciousness which is more technical than popular presentations of the benefits of meditation suggest. Indeed, the Tantric training available in Ananda Marga is advanced and designed to produce real body and brain changes. Members convinced of the claims of the movement often report substantial changes of this kind as a result of their spiritual practice. It is also possible that these spiritual practices enhance the creativity of more gifted members, a phenomenon also found in some other spiritual movements relying on esoteric spiritual practices such as Anthroposophy.

Political, social, economic, educational and cultural contributions

Ananda Marga is exceptional among contemporary spiritual movements in promoting a specific and technically worked out alternative to the poverty and oppression found in much of the world at hand. This in itself confirms that, contrary to Enlightenment prejudice, positivity can be the source of radical creativity. Specifically, the movement has a new economic and social theory known as Prout (Progressive Utilization Theory), which Sarkar set out over some 1,500 pages.[35] Prout is as an alternative to both capitalism and communism, one that is fully environmental and one that aims at more than material and technological development. It is one of the most comprehensive utopias advanced in the twentieth century. It is fair to argue that this utopia is not itself directly revealed and comes from Sarkar. However, it is a utopia inspired by revealed positivity and this is the background which allows Sarkar to know which political, social and economic forms will be appropriate in the world emerging.

Prout attempts to achieve a new cooperative economic system, based on equity and sustainability long term, a system in which spirituality will be central rather than competition, collective welfare will prevail over profit, and transcendental ideals will prevail over self-interest. Under Prout, everyone has the right to equal opportunities of life and development, and there will be no discrimination on the basis of race, nationality or religion. The minimum requirements of food, clothing, housing, education and medical treatment will be guaranteed to all, along with continually increasing purchasing capacity. There will be no accumulation of wealth without the permission of society. Material goods will be common property and distributed to maximize the physical mental and spiritual development of all.

Prout will take effect in distinct stages. In phase one, there is inclusive incentive-based capitalism, but also a shift towards cooperatives, the use of artificial intelligence to enhance productivity and renewable green energy to power the world. These technological shifts lead to power shifts as well – a greater standard of living for local areas. In the next stage, work practically disappears as does ownership as a world of abundance is created. New technologies are regulated by a global government system. In Sarkar's system, the measure of economic advance will be people's purchasing power, and to increase this continually basic goods and services will be guaranteed, prices will be stable, wages will be periodically and progressively increased and collective wealth and productivity will be continually enhanced. There will be no absolute ownership of property, no privately owned corporations, no unemployment and all taxation will be at the point of production.

With Prout, Sarkar delivered a South Asian critique of Western urbanism, while attempting to outline strategies applicable to largely rural populations. In contrast to orthodox economics, he advocated a needs-based economics organized around agriculture, decentred local industries, the ideal of self-sufficient cooperative communities, the role of local people in decision making and the use of local materials.[36] Sakar's social vision combined a strong bias to communalism and localism with modernist reforms. Later writers have sought to build on these ideas to provide interpretations of late capitalism and also updated accounts of possible ways ahead.[37]

Prout does not seem to take much account of conflicts between liberty and equality, and there is a tension between Sarkar's advocacy of economic democracy, economic decentralization, based on cooperatives and local planning, and his support for political centralization. The majority of economic transactions will be through producers' and consumers' cooperatives. Most enterprises are to take the form of cooperatives run by workers who are local people. Economic decisions are to be made by local people, local goods are to remain in the local area and local materials are to be used for the development of the region. These emphases are meant to correct the ills of urbanism as they manifest in South East Asian countries. However, they do not exclude larger concerns. As part of Prout there are also plans for eventual world government, a world constitution, a bill of rights for animals and plants as well as humans, an ombudsman and a global militia.

Prout also has some problematic aspects. The role of law in Prout, for example, is less developed. Sarkar insists that Western law should not simply be imposed and that account must be taken of the consciousness and culture of Indigenous peoples. There will also be cooperation between the genders, ending patriarchy. The overall ethic will be Neohumanistic, with planetary identity and weaker religious, national and ethnic associations. Further, Prout also has a less democratic side. Age-based suffrage is to be abolished, and only the politically conscious will be allowed to vote. Supreme power is to be placed in the hands of an elite of spiritually based revolutionaries (*sadvipras*) organized into executive, legislative and judicial boards governed by a Supreme Board. Sarkar envisaged these moralists as being able to change the order of dominance within the social order to prevent it from exploiting other classes. He also envisaged them establishing their own parallel structure with monitoring functions.[38] Transcending familiar dualisms, Prout allies small-scale private enterprises with state-run public utilities, a federalist world system and more proximate moderating policy boards. All these developments depend, of course, on humanity evolving greater spiritual awareness.

Apart from its provision of spiritual training and its socio-economic utopia, Ananda Marga also promotes practical initiatives designed to bring about social, educational and cultural change. In each case the assumption is that aspects of Hindu tradition make possible futuristic developments. Consistent with its prosocial orientation, Ananda Marga runs orphanages, retirement homes, disaster relief, free kitchens, cooperatives, drug rehabilitation centres, farms and a global eco-village network of model communities. It also argues for prison reform and the use of meditation to correct criminal behaviour and encourages a culture of self-reliance in medical matters in rural areas and provides a range of yogic treatments for about forty diseases given by Sarkar.[39] Ananda Marga is also engaged in emergency relief. Finally, Ananda Marga aims to promote higher levels of cultural evolution through Renaissance Universal, a universalistic cultural movement based on Neohumanist principles that encourages initiatives in all the arts, including sacred dance literature, music, art and film that seeks to take account of world culture as a whole.[40] This movement promotes a generous transculturalism which accepts but also passes through modernity.

Ananda Marga also promotes *a new system of education*, based on Sarkar's philosophy of Neohumanism, exemplified in teacher training and in over 2,000 kindergartens, schools and institutes engaged in teaching, research and services in some seventy countries, including at Ananda Marga University, and in Ananda Marga Gurukula at Ananda Nagar in Purulia.[41] Neohumanist education is developed through international conferences publications and the Gurukula education network, with a strong emphasis on universalism, the integration of life and cross-curriculum ethics, as well as the deployment of Tantric philosophy of mind, meditation and yoga. It is holistic education emphasizing idealism, moral education and the integration of Western science and Indian philosophy. There is also a pre-school curriculum entitled the *Circle of Love* (1980), which teaches Ananda Marga's cosmogonic theory, monistic world view and meditation techniques. Ananda Marga's integrated global education is more extensive than a view from outside South East Asia might suggest, and educates thousands of people. It is also open to post-humanist conceptions of education that transcend anthropocentrism and speciesism and accord greater status to animals, plants and the earth. In Western countries, the movement is associated with the idea that universities should be concerned with the future.[42] Here again the futurism of the movement has sometimes proved prophetic. Indeed, in several respects Sarkar's vision of neohumanist education arguably prepares the way for changes now emerging across the world.

Once again the range of creativity involved in these contributions is vast. It is possible to minimize the originality of particular contributions and in some cases to stress the presence of traditional elements. Nonetheless, it is difficult to deny that Ananda Marga addresses change in a very large number of areas and may also anticipate a future fusion of ecological and spiritual concerns which movements in West have largely failed to envisage or implement. Sarkar himself was very sensitive to the need for local reforms in South East Asian societies and insisted for example, on the importance of giving women the same rights and opportunities as men, setting up a Women's Welfare Department to support such changes. Ananda Marga's futurism, however, takes it beyond local reforms, important as they are. It means that it is not over-invested in the world at hand and can envisage future developments in technology transforming both the world and the humanity we know.

Postreligious features

Despite its Hindu features, there is a marked, if somewhat surprising, post-religious side to Ananda Marga. Indeed, Sarkar imagined a world after religions or at the very least the dogmatic aspects of religions and his vision challenges the power of pundit, mullah and priest. Apart from its minimalization of doctrine, there is criticism of traditional religions as dogmatic, divisive and not based on scientific philosophy, and a rejection of ritualistic and superstitious forms of Tantra. Meanwhile, the reliance on Tantra suggests that at some levels the core of the movement is not a religion but a spiritual science seeking to unify the individual human being with the Cosmic Consciousness. Accordingly, there is no requirement of religious prayer and members of Ananda Marga may belong to any religion as long as they meditate twice a day and follow the ethical precepts of the Indian disciplines of *yoga, yama* and *niyam*a. The movement also accepts that spirituality should not contradict rationality, and that dogma and superstition are to be rejected. Indian members, however, tend to bond with the more occult side of the movement, and not only its modernist service of humanity dimensions. In some ways, the movement seems to draw out the post-religious tendency always present to some extent in Hindu esoteric practices which tend to make traditional religious observance less central. At the very least the more radical dimensions of the movement illustrate how it escapes from the limits of 'religion' as generically conceived, not only in its embrace of secular activities and concerns, but in its reliance on personal knowledge rather than religious traditions.

Organizational form

Ananda Marga is a multilayered spiritual movement that combines radical futurism with adaptations of Indian tradition. Its most radical elements come from Sarkar himself, and the movement sees itself as continually advancing towards the brilliant future it expects, involving both a revitalized humanity and a new type of ethically advanced society. Unlike Soka Gakkai, it is significantly esoteric, and has strong futurist tendencies which allow it to envisage *overcoming the modern rather than conforming to it*. Like Soka Gakkai, it is crucially dependent on an outstanding transformative figure, but less indebted perhaps to the great thinkers of Europe and China. Despite its association with agricultural farmers in Bengal, it does not seem to be a vehicle for the advance of specific social strata.

Clearly Ananda Marga's Indian hierarchical structures may impose organizational limitations on the movement under conditions of modern social differentiation. Despite its use of media and literature designed to profile its egalitarian features, Ananda Marga practices a modified form of monasticism and relies on monks and nuns for much of its leadership. Again, despite its modernist and futurist aspects, Hindu elements remain, including a guru who manifests both as a human person and as in a transcendent form as Tāraka Brahman, practices that lead to initiation, the repetition of mantras, the wearing of a sacred *yantra* that guarantees protection of the *guru* at all times, visits to holy places, the treatment of Krishna and Shiva as historical figures,[43] an occult physiology of subtle bodies and chakras, stories about the action of luminous bodies and an account of the occult history of Gondwana.[44] Currently members are sometimes divided between those who think that Ananda Marga should structure itself like a religion, and those that think of it as a socio-spiritual movement.

Conclusion

The case of Ananda Marga shows that transformative esoteric spiritual practices can be effectively combined with work for political, social, economic and cultural transformation, a perspective largely lost in major political movements in the West. Ananda Marga's more complex teachings can also be presented as a version of futurism which can be related to the work of futurists such as Fred Polak and Richard Slaughter. A fully universalized version of the movement, an impulse arguably present in Sarkar himself, may still be to come. Ananda Marga's mixture of traditional and futurist perspectives allows members of the movement to speak concretely of place-based futures, of the need for cosmic awareness as well as local ecological concerns, of the need for anticipatory work and the creation of the new, but also the relevance of traditional cultures, where they are still valuable. As a result, Ananda Marga is probably more open to advanced technology and to the transforming power of artificial intelligence than any other spiritual movement in the world, and less committed to preindustrial imaginaries than one might imagine. It is also sensitive to the needs of rural populations and sympathetic to the rise of Asia, while attempting to promote universalist horizons which need to be embraced by concrete creative innovations, including a new global political system and a new global economy.

It is perhaps paradoxical that a movement with so many contributions to reform relies heavily on extrasensory perception and the spiritual teachings of a guru. Clearly much depends on whether the results of such extrasensory perception are confirmed or disconfirmed in the future. Without prejudging this question, it is possible that the advanced spiritual practices the movement promotes are relevant to the movement's creativity across diverse areas and over time. Members of the movement often see the source of the movement's creativity in its Tantric spiritual practices, even though these practices can be represented to contemporary audiences as spiritual pragmatics and karma yoga or service to the world.[45] This is difficult to determine because other movements engaging in Tantric practices are often not as creative as Ananda Marga. Nor are they as futurist. The combination of advanced spiritual practices, contributions to reform and a futurist outlook makes Ananda Marga a more significant example of practical utopianism than the existing scholarship suggests.

5

Brahma Kumaris

Modernism on the Way to Apocalypse

Next, consider the *Brahma Kumaris,* a millenarian Indian spiritual movement focused upon a coming cosmic catastrophe, involving environmental disaster and/or nuclear war.[1] Like Ananda Marga, the Brahma Kumaris accept a Hindu cosmic historicism according to which the world drama passes through cycles made up of the same phases. Unlike Ananda Marga, however, the Brahma Kumaris adopt a shortened timeline version of this historicism that involves imminent apocalypse. Again, unlike the Ananda Marga, the Brahma Kumaris show few signs of being influenced by the Bengali Renaissance, shaped as they are by the quite different cultures of Sind and Rajasthan. Then The Brahma Kumaris are modernists who seek to engage with what is developing in the world, but not futurists because they do not expect the world to last long. Nonetheless, they have embraced modernism as an appropriate comportment during the interim or entry period before the present world ends, where modernism means attempting to be fully up to date and engaged with contemporary developments, as opposed to futurism, which attempts to actively anticipate a different order to come.

In the existing literature the Brahma Kumaris have been construed as a doomsday cult and as a new religious movement.[2] Neither description is that helpful. Certainly the movement should not be reduced to the pre-modern world view with which it began. The movement has changed with the contexts in which it has found itself. It changed dramatically when it moved from Sind to Rajasthan in 1947, a change involving a change of language, custom and culture. More recently it has changed with further as visions and revelations have clarified aspects of its teachings and with the need to address populations outside of India.[3]

Unlike Ananda Marga, the Brahma Kumaris do not have an explicit political dimension, although they do challenge domestic power relations in favour of structures dominated by women. Nor do they make use of esoteric Tantric practices.[4] In effect, the outlook of the movement is available in two versions: a Western optimistic New Age version, and a more cosmological Indian version full of references to Hindu deities and mythical stories. The Western version refers to God as 'the Light' and places a strong emphasis on hope. The Indian version appears to be more oriented towards achieving high status, wealth, health and power in the world to come.

Currently the Brahma Kumaris present themselves as World Spiritual University, as a spiritual movement, as an educational organization, not tied to any specific religion operating through learning centres, and as a service religion, working for a better world.[5] Precise understandings tend to vary from country to country, although most Brahma Kumaris construe their practice as a spiritual path rather than a religion. The Brahma Kumaris embody this presentation in publications, meditation centres and up to date digital products. However, the movement is more esoteric Hindu than this suggests, as the details of the revealed knowledge (*yagya*) to which they have access makes clear.

The context

Founded in Hyderabad by a wealthy diamond merchant, Dada Lekhraj (1884–1969), a devotee of the Vaishnavite Vallabhacharya sect who became a prophet visionary in his sixties, the movement started in 1936 among wealthy women alienated from very patriarchal Indian marriage arrangements, but later became a proselytizing sect before developing into a worldwide ethical movement with modernist features. In their early days, the Brahma Kumaris were an embattled group, a quasi-monastic group who set themselves apart and promoted themselves to the status of Brahmins, many of them young girls from the Bhaibund or merchant caste whom the founder Lekhraj named daughters of Brahma (*Brahma Kumaris*). They seem to have experienced collective visions and had ecstatic experiences consistent with the founder's dramatic interpretation of the contemporary situation. Even at this early stage, the Brahma Kumaris confronted outsiders with a revolutionary social development that challenged the patriarchy and the caste system of Hindu society, including its belief that only men could decide whether to marry, although as yet they had no interest in worldly affairs. Through the benevolence of the founder, young girls who became Brahma Kumaris were able to join a new spiritual family and take on a new name, after which they adopted a world rejecting lifestyle in preparation for their life as deities in the world to come. The idea of encouraging young girls to abandon men, distance themselves from their physical families and pursue lives of celibate purity encountered resistance, and the movement was attacked under Indian law for breaking up families. At this stage, there was no reason to expect the Brahma Kumaris to develop into a global movement with allegedly one million members and 8,000 learning centres around the world. Instead, the movement seemed notable for its expectation that the world would end soon in apocalypse.

When the Brahma Kumaris apocalypse failed to occur, the Brahma Kumaris moved from Karachi to Mount Abu in Rajasthan, and in stages revised their public presentation away from Hindu asceticism, emphasizing instead world-affirming spiritual trainings as ways to achieve success in life. The classic Hindu themes – soul consciousness, remembrance of God, understanding of one's divine origins, spiritual perfection based on transforming the subtle characteristics of the soul in order to reconstitute the divine qualities – remained, but after 1952 there was a new emphasis on 'world service'. This led to a tension between the claim that the present world was beyond redemption in its present form and action to improve the present world. Currently, the original emphasis on world destruction when God again enters the world at the end of the cosmic cycle is less stressed than the prospect of world renewal in which members of the movement co-create a perfect world with God, a change consistent with the fact that many earlier annoucements of an imminent end of the world have proved mistaken, which raises, of course, about the reliability of the sacred messages received through visionaries.

Despite their belief in an immanent apocalypse, outsiders mainly encounter the Brahma Kumaris as a meditation movement through the many courses they offer free of charge, not only on meditation, but on positive thinking, self-esteem, value-based living, stress reduction, holistic health and so forth. These courses are supported by books, music and videos. At this level, the movement can be seen as a New Age organization primarily concerned with self-realization. Those who continue to participate discover that the movement is about both personal transformation and world renewal. Indian teachings, such as the Tree of Life, are held back to later courses. Seekers do a foundation course in which they are gradually introduced to the movement's teachings,[6] including that the world is at a turning point, that a transformation of consciousness is taking place, and that human beings need to act to regain their original soul-based nature.

The outlook of the movement is largely derived from the Vedas and Vedanta. At the heart of the movement is an incarnation of Shiva. According to the Brahma Kumaris, Shiva or the Supreme Soul, the self-luminous incorporeal being, descended into the body of the founder Dada Lekhraj after which he became Prajapita Brahma or Adi Dev, the first deity of the eternal world drama.[7] Lekhraj was called God, and recognized as the chariot who revealed divine knowledge in the form of messages (*Murlis*) each morning, giving his followers reliable knowledge of both history and the cosmos.[8] Consistent with his divine visions, Lekhraj wrote letters revealing his knowledge of future events to national and international leaders, who did not respond. After the death of the founder trance messages continued to be received through a spirit medium. A distinction is made between Shiva's original revelation (*Sakar Murlis*) and later angelic versions (*Avyakt Murlis*). Today the Brahma Kumaris still remain committed to some form of apocalypse, although speculations about when it will occur vary. The year 2036 is sometimes given. They also insist that the catastrophe they envisage should be seen as desirable.[9]

Cognitive materials

The Brahma Kumaris have very extensive cognitive materials that help to reframe the life horizons of those who join the movement, including a vast system of occult lore about four mortal bodies, chakras, auras, the seven rays, occult colours, as well as alternative science, philosophy of mind and philosophy of history. The positive psychology version of the movement's teachings offered to Westerners gradually blends into Indian esotericism, and reference is regularly made to Hindu deities and figures in Hindu mythology such as Lakshmi, Narayan and Saraswati. The Brahma Kumaris cognitive materials abound in residues of Hindu theosophy. Nonetheless, this feature should not be exaggerated to the exclusion of others.

The Brahma Kumaris cognitive materials are creative in at least three respects. First, their cosmic historicism gives them a specific approach to social, economic and cultural change. Unlike most Hindus, they expect such changes to be dramatic and see contemporary social and cultural developments as connected with the cosmic changes to come. Second, their apocalyptical expectations heighten their hermeneutics of current changes, including their interpretations of political events. Third, their access to a rich cosmosophy gives them a qualitative conception of reality as inherently directional and meaningful and this orients them towards purified forms of life and an implicit critique of Western externalism, although this aspect could probably be more deployed by members of the movement than is the case to date.

In addition, the Brahma Kumaris cognitive materials give them *model ideas* about the universe, science, history, biopsychology and the nature of the human being which may be capable of portable elaborations as their reforms to Hinduism are not. These model ideas show their value once they are elaborated in contemporary terms. It remains an open question how far the Brahma Kumaris have achieved such elaborations at this point, but the potential is there, as the Brahma Kumaris have themselves recognized in the case of meditation. The Brahma Kumaris cognitive materials set them apart from their contemporaries as inhabitants of a special cognitive space. They believe that they are better informed about crucial matters than those around them, and also find confirmation of their beliefs in the exemplary lives of those who surrender entirely to Baba.

At the centre of the movement's cognitive materials is *a revealed cosmosophy*, derived from classical Indian texts. This cosmosophy centres on the Supreme Soul, Shiv Baba, who does not create souls, matter or the laws of nature, just as he does not pervade the physical universe, although he does restore souls to their original state of purity. The aim of Brahma Kumaris spirituality is to remember and then unite with Baba. The Brahma Kumaris treat this cosmosophy as *revealed science* and as *revealed philosophy of history*. This cosmosophy is clearly positivity in Hegel's sense and is accepted on authority. Through it the Brahma Kumaris have revealed knowledge about the nature of God and the universe, the soul, space, time, karma and the coming apocalypse. Thus they know that God, matter and the soul are all eternal and uncreated, and the universe is governed by unchangeable natural laws. Then there are three worlds: the corporeal world, the angelic or subtle world and the incorporeal or soul world. According to the Brahma Kumaris, the universe is governed by a cycle of ages: the Golden Age (*Satya yuga*), the Silver Age (*Treta yuga*), the Copper Age (*Dvapara yuga*), the Iron Age (*Kali yuga*) and a diamond or confluence age (*Sangam yuga*) in preparation for the new golden age to come. The eternal world drama lasts only 5,000 years.[10] These phases also correlate with types of human being (*varnas*) and with types of consciousness.[11] The cycle never changes and implies that the world declines from a state of original perfection which is then restored after world destruction. This cosmic cycle is visualized in a diagram known as the *Kalpa* Tree. Reincarnation is central to this drama. Human souls reincarnate, but do not enter other species. The number of reincarnations is relative to the soul's purity, but followers of Baba can be restored to their original status and then reborn as deities in a coming heavenly golden age.[12] In the coming golden age, there will be no armaments or acquisitiveness. Members of the movement will become kings and queens, emperors and empresses. All will enjoy good health, prosperity, education, sport and the arts, and a world government will provide universal justice.[13] At the end of the present transitional age, the supreme soul and the majority of other souls will depart for the soul world, which is only open at the end of the cycle.

On the basis of this divine knowledge, like Ananda Marga, the Brahma Kumaris advance a reformed Hinduism, keeping many doctrines and language, but rejecting caste, and shifting the main emphasis to social and cultural transformation. This is a major shift, with implications for gender as well as social, cultural and gender reform. Even at the level of doctrine and spiritual symbolism the Brahma Kumaris version of Hinduism involves changes. Thus the Hindu Trimurti is remodelled so that the deity Shankar appears as the third deity, and Shiva is placed above the Trimurti as its creator,[14] While God and human souls both reincarnate, and future incarnations of spiritual teachers such as Buddha and Jesus are expected in the next kalpa. Current needs and ancient mythology are easily cojoined. Thus, both Shiv Baba and Brahma Baba have been coming periodically to the corporeal plane to make revelations through one of the senior members or Dadis since 1969, and Lekhraj, as a cosmic being, has given the warnings of an end to come many times before.

The Brahma Kumaris revealed cosmosophy gives members of the movement access both to a cosmic determinism and a cosmic historicism. The stages of the world drama are fixed, but how the next phase works out in detail depends on how human beings act now. Those who have received the revelations from Lekhraj and the *Murlis* are in a special and favoured position. They know what is coming and can read the signs. Accordingly, the Brahma Kumaris manifest an urgent sense of the present, which for Brahma Kumaris is a time for purification in preparation for the world to come. A correct understanding of history is essential in the present life,[15] even though each soul will do exactly the same things in each world cycle.[16]

A specific comportment towards the present follows from this. Individuals must make haste in order to enjoy life in the paradise to come. The present is the time of salvation, when God, who is not omnipresent, incarnates again to impart holy knowledge before the world is destroyed. The violence associated with this does not, however, perturb the Brahma Kumaris, who are to look upon it with disinterest or fact transcending optimism.[17] Again, although it might be thought that their cosmosophy puts them in conflict with the contemporary natural sciences, intellectually inclined members of the movement argue at length for their cosmogony and against claims that the world is much older than 5,000 years and see their cosmosophy as making them sensitive to the weaker points of the scientific cosmology generally accepted in the West.[18]

Brahma Kumaris cosmosophy also involves, at least on one interpretation, a form of philosophical anthropology and a biopsychology that distinguishes the intellect, the conscious mind, the sub-conscious mind and the superconscious mind (*Videhi*) as well as physical, mental, emotional and etheric bodies.[19] The Brahma Kumaris reject the modern identification of the self with the body: the self is the soul, an eternal conscious entity of light located in the corporeal human being in the hypothalamus. Moreover, the soul controls the body. There is a great emphasis on purity, bodylessness and the avoidance of sex lust, and self-transformation is equated, in the Hindu manner, with world transformation.[20] All this gives the Brahma Kumaris a perspective different from the conception of the human being current in most Western societies.

Spiritual practices based on remembrance

Spiritual practices are central for the Brahma Kumaris and provide them with both experiences of personal transformation and access to the absolute reality of the cosmos.[21] The primary focus is on soul consciousness as a direct spiritual experience and those who have profound experience of this often remain with the movement.

The main Brahma Kumaris spiritual practices are *remembrance* and the use of open-eyed Raja yoga to overcome *sanskaras* or negative karma in order to connect the soul to God or the Supreme Soul, understood as a point of living light. This is necessary because human beings have forgotten that they are eternal souls and need to be awakened and brought to self-realization. Through Raja yoga meditation in front of a red light, they perceive the soul, which is eternal and not part of the body, as a non-dimensional point of conscious energy located in the centre of the forehead. In successful meditation an individual experiences being beyond this world and in the company of Shiv Baba. Practising Raja yoga leads to self-sovereignty, and those who attain self-sovereignty in the confluence age will achieve world sovereignty in the golden age.[22] Moreover, Brahma Kumaris believe that Raja yoga meditation impacts on karma and rebirth, and also changes physical nature. If consciousness changes, biological changes will follow.[23] In actual situations of difficulty, the Brahma Kumaris see themselves as spiritual practitioners alleviating suffering. They do not seem to have esoteric practices of the type associated with Tantra, although they have a spiritual practice of divine gazing (*drishti*) in which an advanced practitioner looks on people spiritually, which positively affects others and the environment. However, their focus on the human being as a soul intrinsically linked with God, who is in the soul world, gives their spirituality a radical edge, and they use it to insist that we now need to transcend differences based on race, nationality, religion and gender. Moreover, they see transforming the human being into a being who manifests good wishes and pure feelings as a form of world service.

All this goes with a strict lifestyle characterized by an extreme emphasis on purity. Surrendered members are lacto-vegetarians or vegans, eat only sacred food prepared by other Brahma Kumaris and often live in the same accommodation, with the implication that a pure spiritualized diet is essential for advanced spirituality. In addition, surrendered women wear white clothes as a sign of purity. Daily life begins at 4 a.m. Celibacy is mandated within and outside marriage.[24] As a result, the movement has a quasi-monastic elite at its core who manifest the extreme purity at which the movement aims. In effect, the Brahma Kumaris combine a renovation of Hindu tradition with radical modernism or attempt to be absolutely up to date. On the one hand, they privilege celibacy and negative views about human sexuality. On the other hand, they provide aids and devices to help modern people cope with the strains and anxieties of urban life.

Social, cultural and educational contributions

Like other contemporary spiritual movements, the Brahma Kumaris engage in social and cultural activism, and aim to promote progressive change at all levels of society. These activities are of high quality, and the movement is an active agent for change in many different areas.

In place of temples, the Brahma Kumaris set up Centres for Spiritual Learning. They also run about 4,000 meditation centres around the world. In the West, they run retreat centres, including the Global Retreat Centre near Oxford. In India, the Brahma Kumaris run hospitals and homes for the elderly, work with prisoners, engage in medical outreach and support many community projects. In doing so, they make use of traditional Indian medicine based on vibrations. They also run spiritual museums in the larger Indian cities designed to make the learning available to large and less literate populations.

The Brahma Kumaris also work to promote peace and environmentalism and have developed a range of social initiatives, including values education programmes for schools.[25] They also advance a limited form of social critique based on the conviction that modern civilization is unsustainable and appear to expect a unified world government in the future Golden Age. The Brahma Kumaris are also active as an NGO of the United Nations, organize academic conferences and have also developed environmental initiatives that embrace new technologies, including the development of the world's largest solar cooker. There is also some medical outreach and they have health centres in India. Finally, the Brahma Kumaris have attempted to address the problems of Indian farmers by providing a self-empowerment programme for them, by teaching them traditional and organic farming techniques, and experimenting with the claim that their meditation techniques, allied to other spiritual practices such as singing, music and flying the red and yellow flag of Shiva, can enhance seed growth and germination and the soil and so contribute to sustainable agriculture.[26] Here, as elsewhere, the Brahma Kumaris reassert ancient esoteric teaching – in this case the teaching that consciousness can change the environment – in a para-scientific form and combine it with modernist impulses to promote social and economic change.

Despite their many initiatives and their radically holistic outlook however, the Brahma Kumaris do not have a detailed plan for social and cultural development that is uniquely their own. They believe that a new paradigm of society will emerge, but, unlike the Ananda Marga, they do not have revealed information about how this society should be organized. On the other hand, they do envisage higher forms of social life and attempt to embody less exploitive and more cooperative social relations inside the movement than those found in the society outside.

The Brahma Kumaris are also more organizationally radical than their social origins might suggest. The major social organizational change they promote is the emphasis they place on government by women. In the Brahma Kumaris movement, women are equal to men and given leading roles because of their spiritual qualities,[27] a development with little precedence in Hinduism or, for that matter, in Islam, Judaism or Christianity. They therefore go beyond other movements that aim to end the domination of women by men and a concern for the liberation of women as leaders is central to their charism.[28]

The crucial point here is that this model of governance only by women did not emerge out of Indian secularism or out of the many Indian feminist movements. It arose out of a movement with apocalyptical expectations, originally as a protest against the excesses of Hindu patriarchy in business communities in Sind. Clearly an emphasis on government by women is a development of some importance which can obviously be extended to secular as well as spiritual contexts and to non-Indian societies. Of course, the tendency to opt for exclusive leadership by women is more controversial and may involve conceptions of purity that are less portable. On the other hand, the predominance of women in the movement may enhance the movement's contributions to practical reform.

The Brahma Kumaris may also have the nucleus of a new form of life in their spiritual university cum world headquarters on Mount Abu, which they established in 1950. Inspired by radically non-Western beliefs, the university offers courses and spiritual training. It also publishes books. Its purpose is to help people divinize themselves. Outsiders are encouraged to visit and see the paradise lifestyle which the members of the movement are beginning to develop. Some two and a half million people are said to visit the headquarters each year and there are special Baba meetings for those confirmed in their practice attended by thousands from all over the world. In this way, Mt Abu functions as a concrete utopia for the Brahma Kumaris or a utopia that can be experienced now which models the movement's commitment to a global culture based on soul consciousness and transcending body-based labels such as race nationality, religion and gender.

Postreligious features

Like Ananda Marga, the Brahma Kumaris movement has postreligious features which give some indication of what a future organization of spirituality without religion might look like. Lekhraj himself was critical of the state of modern Hinduism, including the purely formal nature of much religious practice and meat eating by Hindus. Consistent with this, the Brahma Kumaris emphasize that their core doctrine is knowledge which needs to be understood rather than dogma accepted as a matter of faith. Interpretations of other religions are offered, including Buddhism, Christianity and Islam, and there is a tendency to claim that the movement has a supra-religious non-denominational status. In practice, the strong emphasis on Raja yoga as a spiritual practice means that the doctrines of the movement are secondary and can change with context.

The Brahma Kumaris have little ceremonial, although Thursday is a special day on which a food offering is made to Shiv Baba. Likewise, Brahma Kumaris do not practice exorcisms or pray to *Devas*.[29] There will be no need for any formal religions or scriptures or places of worship in the perfect golden age to come. Then the only religion will be the religion of the deities.[30] Here Hindu traditionalism seems to prevail over modernist impulses, but this too may change in the future.

Organizational form

Despite their radical features, the Brama Kumaris may lack some of the organizational forms they need to realize their charisms. This may be surprising since the Brahma Kumaris have their own modern management philosophy which combines sensitivity to social roles, influenced by their cognitive materials, with a sense of the need to adapt to new conditions. They give courses on Self-Management Leadership and have trained bureaucrats and government people in Mexico. Nonetheless, although the movement has radical organizational features, it is still based on a hierarchy of relative spiritual capacities.

The Brahma Kumaris do not seem, however, to have radical ideas about the future organization of their movement. Thus, for example, now that revelation in the form of trance mediumship has ceased, it is unclear who will interpret or revise Brahma Kumaris doctrine, or which features are essential to the movement and which relate only to its early phases. Again, although the movement is gradually becoming more and more modernist in its international literature, in its Indian versions it still has strong recursive elements, including the idea that a state characterized by unity of belief, culture, language and governance will be restored in the golden age. It is possible, however, that over time the movement will reinterpret its apocalyptical beginnings, as Christianity has done. Currently the recursive and the modernist strands of the movement are in tension.

More generally, a recursive comportment pervades the movement. The Brahma Kumaris emphasize remembrance (we have forgotten that we are souls), and remain fixated on the need to remember Shiv Baba. The emphasis on restoration, including the restoration of the deities and deity sovereignty, is very strong. The Brahma Kumaris also show little inclination to engage with contemporary philosophical or theological thought. Efforts are allegedly made to rewrite the movement's early history and to conceal cases of pressured recruitment, sexual abuse, economic malpractice and the persecution of dissidents.[31] The movement has not embraced an autonomous ethics, and a heavy emphasis is placed on obeying God or Shiva. Correct action is to be based on 'godly knowledge', that is, the holy knowledge arrived at by divine visions (*sakshatkar*), although there is also an emphasis on good wishes and pure feelings towards others and a general commitment to *ahimsa* or non-violence. Elements of an India-centred outlook clearly remain. The Brahma Kumaris may embrace world betterment with enthusiasm, but the coming paradise is to be located on the Indian subcontinent, from which all civilizations derive.[32]

On the other hand, the rigidities of the movement are increasingly less prominent,[33] and the movement has already changed from a world rejecting movement into a 'world corresponding' movement working for world improvement which stresses positive psychology, life skills training and Raja meditation as well as various environmental initiatives. It has been suggested that although this may in part reflect the influence of East Indian and Australian members in London who made extensive use of agendas and techniques from outside the movement to win converts.[34] Crucially the theology of the Brahma Kumaris is variable with cultural and temporal context, and recent teaching does not appear to correspond to what was believed or revealed earlier in all respects.

The growth of the movement in purely numerical terms is impressive, but may not be crucial because much of this success amounts to marketing New Age materials and aids to well-being rather than converting people to the movement's world view and ascetic lifestyle. However, this self-presentation is itself a sign of flexibility, as well as an ability to exploit globalization to the movement's advantage. Eventually modernist presentations adopted to convert the outer world may end up refiguring the movement itself. If so, a key issue will be: on which issues do the Brahma Kumaris move beyond Hinduism entirely and on which issues do they use traditional Hindu resources to fashion a new and better modern?

Conclusion

In this chapter I have stressed that the apocalyptical side of the Brahma Kumaris gives little idea of their modernist creativity. The Brahma Kumaris already exemplify a strong form of ordered spiritual life with some possible applications to Western societies. Their modernization of Raja yoga reaches large numbers of people and delivers for some the concrete spiritual experiences they seek. Spirituality for the Brahma Kumaris is a matter of *life enhancing practices*. It is not a devotional extra, as it may be for many Westerners. The existence of fully committed celibate members gives the Brahma Kumaris some of the advantages of monasteries without having to isolate their social ascetics from the general community. They see themselves as demonstrating the relevance of strong meditation and a strict diet for spirituality as well as signalling the possibility of postreligious developments.

The fact that a movement with apocalyptical expectations has adopted modernist methods and values in its self-presentation to Western audiences raises the issue of what is invariant in the Brahma Kumaris outlook and what is not. If it is possible to move out of Hinduism in so many respects, why is it not possible to move out of Hindu apocalyptic as well? No doubt, the Brahma Kumaris will change even further if their apocalypse does not occur. At this stage, like other movements discussed in this volume, they seem to be in transition from a more sectarian and context-bound first phase to a second phase in which they try to translate their message to all cultures. What is striking, however, is the way that a movement which originated in expectations of imminent apocalypse has managed to become a movement working for progressive reforms in much of the world.

6

The Church Universal and Triumphant

The Democratization of Counterfactuality

Introduction

I now turn to two American Christian churches with controversial beliefs, the Church Universal and Triumphant and the Church of Jesus Christ of Latter-day Saints. Both churches are shaped by specific American contexts and are to some extent indebted to occulture. Neither movement is socially radical. Nor do they propose a new form of life. Both, however, break with what theologians and sociologists characterize as the collapse of transcendence in many forms of mainstream Christianity and reassert the possibility that the divine can be motivated to intervene directly in the ordinary affairs of human life. Both rely on strong forms of positivity with surprising results.

The Church Universal and Triumphant is a New Age movement combining Theosophy, esoteric Christianity, Buddhism, Hinduism, Daoism and various perennial currents.[1] The Church has received little serious attention scholarly, except from students of new religious movements, who tend to be interested in why people join or leave, or in the various controversies surrounding the movement.[2] In this chapter, I draw attention to what is creative about the Church, and its contemporary relevance in the context of an extensive rethinking of the relations between counterfactuality and truth. Specifically, I construe the Church as providing *performative counterfactuality*, that is, counterfactual materials to be experienced as a performance such as a play.[3] I do not investigate how far the Church can be seen as genuinely Christian, even though this is very important for its members. Nor do I impose a New Religious Movement framework on the Church. Many features of the Church are not new, and not all of the Church's activities are exclusively 'religious'. Indeed, it has operated several successful businesses. As is the case with other movements discussed, the Church has been attacked for its authoritarianism, and its practice of mind control. It has also been accused of excessive secrecy, of manipulating members, of stockpiling large numbers of weapons and of financial fraud.[4] I do not address these charges here. Instead, I emphasize the creative side to the Church's positivity which suggests that spiritual narratives and symbols without manifest epistemological warrants may function to reorient people's lives in advanced technological societies. The possibility that this involves creativity of an unexpected kind, including a radical democratization of counterfactionality, underlies the discussion which follows.

The context

The Church Universal and Triumphant arose against the background of earlier movements of American popular occultism, including New Thought. Its founder, Mark Prophet (1918–73), a Midwestern businessman with little education from a Pentecostal Canadian background, inhabited an American popular culture in which claims to meet Ascended Masters and to travel with them in Tibet were current.[5] The immediate background was the example of Guy and Edna Ballard who studied the theosophy of H. P. Blavatsky and claimed to receive messages from Ascended Masters. Guy Ballard claimed himself to have met the Comte de St. Germain, and promoted the 'I AM' Activity movement.[6] Mark Prophet belonged to the Self-Realization Fellowship and was associated with the form of Rosicrucianism set up by the Danish-American astrologer Max Heindel. In addition, he studied the teachings of Paramahansa Yogananda and belonged to or attended one of the splinter groups from the I AM movement known as The Bridge to Freedom led by Geraldine Innocente. Mark Prophet's teachings were syncretic, but heavily influenced by Blavatsky's theosophy. From 1951, Prophet sent out letters from the Ascended Masters to a small group of followers. In 1952, he began publishing a series of letters for his students called *Ashram Notes*, dictated by the Ascended Master El Morya from his ashram at Darjeeling, India. In 1958, Prophet set up The Summit Lighthouse as a press, with the task of making the teachings of the Ascended Masters known. After his marriage to Elizabeth Clare Wulf (1939–2009) in 1962, he and Elizabeth ran the organization together until his death in 1973. The Prophets claimed to be the sole living messengers of the Ascended Masters. Their collaboration was a considerable success.

Mark Prophet was a charismatic travelling salesman who became a spiritual teacher, Elizabeth Prophet a New England housewife who went to high school in Switzerland and then studied at Antioch College and Boston University a popular spiritual Before she emerged as a clairvoyant she worked worked as a secretary for the Christian Science Church and the *Christian Science Monitor*. While meditating with Mark Prophet at a public meeting in Boston in April 1962, Elizabeth Prophet realized that she was intended to be a Messenger for the Ascended Masters, and in June 1962 she was visited by the Ascended Master El Morya. Further, both Mark and Elizabeth Prophet received extensive training enabling them to rise to the level of the Christ self.[7] After Mark Prophet's death, Elizabeth Prophet restructured their organization in 1975 as *The Church Universal and Triumphan*t, a term previously used by the founder of Christian Science, Mary Baker Eddy, whose teachings, Prophet had followed for some years previously. The fact that the Church was a further development of existing trends is important and helps define the Church's creativity. Consistent with this, almost all of the Prophet's early followers were former members of the I AM movement or the Bridge to Freedom, while the emphasis on Christianity (completely lacking in Blavatsky's Theosophy) seems to reflect the influence of New Thought, an American spiritual movement which located the divinity within each individual.[8]

Elizabeth Prophet was a gifted writer, orator and media star who appeared on radio and television programmes in many countries. She wrote some fifty or so books, allegedly selling over a million copies, some of which were translated into languages other than English, especially Spanish. Prophet claimed to be able to provide members of her church with the most advanced esoteric teaching on the planet, including reliable means by which to achieve self-realization and become an Ascended Master. She also claimed healing powers herself, and was known in the movement as Guru Ma.[9]

Elizabeth Prophet definitely regarded her teachings as a form of Christianity. Specifically, she claimed to teach the Path of Personal Christhood or union with God through Christ consciousness. Like Mark Prophet, she gave many dictations from saints and sages from both East and West. Her teachings combined elements of 'I AM' movement mysticism, Anglo-American theosophy, and elements of Hinduism, Buddhism, Daoism, Confucianism and Zoroastrianism, as received in popular texts in America.[10] In due course, she claimed more than a thousand hours of direct revelations from a list of Ascended Masters which included Saint Germain, Djwal Kul, Hilarion, Jesus, Krishna, Buddha, Paul the Venetian, Serapis Bey, Sanat Kumara, El Morya, Kuthumi, Meru and many others. She also published weekly dictations from these Ascended Masters as *Pearls of Wisdom*. In addition, her clairvoyance included information about aliens, black magicians and evil coloured rays from which members needed to be protected. After Mark Prophet's death, Elizabeth Prophet placed a greater emphasis on astrology and elaborated a complex theory of evil and hybrid humanity based on interpretations of the Book of Enoch. Indeed, she warned that fallen angels could incarnate in human form to create war and chaos.[11]

Through these and other performances Elizabeth Prophet broke with the modernist minimalism of the mainstream churches and reasserted an extensive and elaborate preternatural world. Further, she did so while seeming to embrace modern technology and media, as if the radically old was compatible with the radically new. Her synthesis provided her followers with practical occultism in their living rooms, while encouraging them to expand their cultural horizons radically in order to assimilate personalities and traditions from different religions and parts of the earth. My interpretation here goes against the dismissal of Prophet and her teachings in much of the literature. Prophet combined a charismatic seer, a potpourri of teachings and personalities from many different traditions, with a very competent deployment of print and digital technologies. She also grasped that positivity could have an important role in a spiritual organization in advanced technological societies.

Prophet's Church Universal and Triumphant has passed through several phases and many locations. In its ecclesiastical form it has some of the features associated with a Christian church. There are twelve tenets of faith including material on the Divine Mother and the Age of Aquarius, nine sacraments and seven rituals to communicate the seven rays of the Christ. Seekers are first to become a Keeper of the Violet Flame, and then become a communicant of the Church when they have reached the eighth lesson or above in good standing. Eventually they fuse with the Holy Christ Self with the assistance of the Ascended Masters, at which point they will receive the full initiations received by Jesus Christ. Finally, they may take part in the ritual of the Ascension. Seekers are to understand themselves as becoming Christ and Buddha, who are the sponsors of the Church. The Church is not, however, yet another theosophical Christian church.[12] Most theosophical churches have been middle class, have attracted educated people including writers and artists, and have had restricted popular appeal. Many members of the Church Universal and Triumphant hold university degrees and others are intelligent spiritual seekers. It does not, however, mainly recruit from people with a background in High Church Anglicanism or in Greek or Russian Orthodoxy. Again, the Church prioritizes democracy as much as hierarchy, which most theosophical churches do not. Those who join may come to see themselves as an elite, but the Church does not primarily recruit from elite audiences.

Cognitive materials

The Church Universal and Triumphant provides its members with an abundance of cognitive materials designed to confer upon them an elevated status at odds with their workaday lives. The Church remobilizes many historical materials with a gnostic tendency, but does not appear to have its own philosophical ideas. Those who join the Church are encouraged to purify their lower bodies and unite with a Higher Self, an individualized presence of Christ and an I AM presence. They are to awaken the light within, and are given detailed instructions about angels, karma, reincarnation, the three causal bodies, diet, the seven rays and the crystals and Chohans attached to them, the duties of a disciple or chela, chakras, alchemy and astrology.[13] The goal of life, members learn, is to grow in self-mastery, to balance karma and to become one with God by achieving Ascension.

Like other esoterically oriented Christian groups, the Church teaches that the Bible, as commonly received, is incomplete, and does not contain all the authentic scriptures. Specifically, the Church believes that the *Book of Enoch*, a book excluded from the orthodox canon, is authentic.[14] It also looks outside the canon for authentic spiritual teaching in many traditions, and holds that new teachings may be expected to come forth from progressive revelation.[15] The ethos of the Church is immanentist (the divine falls within the ontological order), and, despite a doctrine of grace, tends to be strongly Pelagian in its emphasis on self-help and human action. The Church also provides detailed technical information about astrological time cycles.[16] In this way, both members' needs for mythology and their desire for quasi-scientific technical details are accommodated. Other controversial claims are made, including the disclosure that Jesus spent seventeen years in the East mastering the Hindu and Buddhist scriptures and becoming an adept.[17]

Although the Church understands its materials to be received from the Ascended Masters through the Holy Spirit, it also makes use of materials already extant, including Helena Roerich's *Leaves of Morya's Garden*, especially in the lessons given by Summit University.[18] In effect, the Church offers members access to a treasury of esoterica. Thus, it provides its members with *revealed cosmosophy* or an enchanted interpretation of the universe and its evolution designed to accelerate their spiritual progress. In doing so, it addresses pathologies associated with the collapse of spiritual cosmology in mainline Christianity. This revealed cosmosophy cannot be reconciled with the contemporary natural sciences. The details are mainly of Hindu origin. Thus, members learn about the cosmic egg, the solar *logoi*, the great central sun, the seven root races, the five secret rays, as well as specifics about angels, gods and elementals. The implication here is that external religion without such mediating cosmosophy is unable to transform human beings to the point of Ascension. In the Church Universal and Triumphant, by contrast, members learn how to actively work with the esoteric cosmos, including how to help the elementals and how to prevent earthquakes.[19] There is also a rehabilitation of alchemy, understood as the science of the soul that Jesus and St. Germain teach involving the ability to create matter.[20] Much of this material can be construed as projective imagination and/or fantastic, where both are technical terms and not derogative. That is, it provides imaginative contents or features thrown onto the world or events and material imagination realized in portable cultural forms as opposed to personal subjective fantasy.

As in the related case of Anthroposophy, members appear to find such occult lore of great interest and may claim to have esoteric experiences themselves as a result of being exposed to it. Thus the Church makes much of the life and achievements of the Count of Saint Germain, as the I AM movement did before it.[21] According to the Church, Saint Germain is an Ascended Master known as the Lord of the Seventh Ray. Over the centuries, however, it is taught that St. Germain was embodied as the prophet Samuel, Saint Joseph, Saint Alban, Merlin, Roger Bacon, Christopher Columbus and Francis Bacon before he became a mysterious figure at the time of the French Revolution. The Church also assists members to locate themselves in various maximalist narratives. From the founding of the organization up until the mid-1980s, a major theme was the bringing in of the golden age of Aquarius and the establishment of a new mystical Camelot in America. In effect, the Church offers an immersion in magical and mystical lore to people with no previous experience of such materials. Through them, the Church achieves a major social shift by communicating a range of esoteric materials to wide audiences. It thereby achieves what might be called a middlebrow elitist effect, whereby members become aware of materials available in highbrow literature or in ancient languages.

The outstanding feature of the Church Universal and Triumphant is that the Church provides a vast range of esoterica, *from which members are free to choose*, even though some materials are more central than others. This raises crucial questions. First, there is the question of whether the Church adopts a radically postmodern stance and takes the counterfactual character of the materials it provides as irrelevant. Most members of the Church do not see it this way and regard the diverse strands of esoterica provided as coming from the Ascended Masters. More intellectual types may take a more performative view.

Materials from the past which have helped people transform themselves are to be treated with reverence and respect, whatever the literal truth of the teachings or narratives they contain. To be fair, this is a standard view taken by Hindu and Buddhist intellectuals and has considerable precedent in the Catholic view of popular piety as well. If the materials the Church provides are construed as performative, then it is fair to observe that they sit easily enough with the self-help books and texts on sacred psychology that the Church also offers.

Spiritual practices

The Church Universal and Triumphant provides its members with a range of powerful spiritual practices, including some based on Agni yoga. Elizabeth Prophet taught a spiritual practice, the giving of 'dynamic decrees', which is deemed especially powerful when practised on a daily basis. Decrees are a form of affirmative prayer by which members can command God to make certain conditions prevail[22]:

> The decree, as we use it, is the most powerful of all applications to the Godhead. It is the command of the son or daughter of God, spoken in the name of the mighty I AM Presence and your Christ Self, for the Light to descend from the Unformed to the formed – from the world of Spirit to the world of Matter. The decree is the means whereby the kingdom of God becomes a Reality here and now through the power of the spoken Word.[23]

Prophet taught that her followers must command God to enter into their being if they would experience Him in their consciousness. With dynamic decrees her followers were given accelerated and effective forms of prayer (also involving visualizations) by which they could change themselves and the world for the better.[24]

The aim of giving decrees is to purify the body and the chakras to hold more spiritual light as a means for personal and world transformation. According to the Church Universal and Universal decreeing is the most powerful of all applications to the Godhead. It provides actual techniques for forcing spiritual powers to attend to church members' concerns. Indeed, according to Prophet the God presence and the Masters' momentum of perfection needed to be invoked *before praying* in order to transmute what impedes the penetration of God's light and to realign the energy patterns so that the four lower bodies can be chalices of the Holy Spirit.[25] Prophet explained this in classic theosophical terms as drawing the light of God down upon the earth from the great central sun of the universe. Further, decrees were important because the cosmic powers could not intervene unless human beings asked for their help. The emphasis on giving decrees also meant that a form of spiritual activity is needed *before* the symbolics of external religion could work to transform the spiritual bodies of the human being. The giving of decrees appears to have originated with Emma Curtis Hopkins, a former disciple of Mary Baker Eddy, although a number of different New Thought movements and teachers used the practice in various forms. However, there are also parallels with the practice of commanding deities in Enochian magic.[26] The use of decrees in the Church Universal and Triumphant included decrees in rhythmic verse form. There was also, however, a decidedly Western dimension to the enterprise required of the church member in order to pray effectively, in the stress on the hours each day to be devoted to the work, and in the belief that better technology would make greater achievements possible, regardless of the ability and background of the members themselves.

The giving of decrees can be construed as a revolt against the passivity of traditional Christianity and a strong assertion of the will to command the spiritual powers, in marked contrast to the passive supplications of traditional Christian prayer. Decrees may also relate to the better management of political affairs:

> In the name of Jesus the Christ, I call to the heart of Almighty God, to the heart of beloved Alpha and Omega, Helios and Vesta, the Great Central Sun Magnet, all the forces and beings of the elements, the mighty Elohim, the archangels, and the chohans of the rays. I call to the entire Spirit of the Great White Brotherhood and the World Mother, the Seven Holy Kumaras and Lady Master Venus. I Call to Mighty Victory, Saint Germain, the Great Divine Director, beloved Guru Ma, Lanello and K-17, beloved Archangel Michael and your legions of Light, beloved Mother Mary:
>
> We demand and we implore your intercession this day. We declare in the name of the living Christ the end of World Communism. We demand the arresting of the spiral! We demand the removing of the cause and core. We demand the binding of the seeds of Lucifer and the fallen ones. We demand the binding of the seed and the egg of the dragon and the serpent and the beast. And we demand the binding of the false prophet, the great whore, and the Antichrist in the four quadrants of Mater.
>
> We demand that Light go forth from our I AM Presence and causal bodies this day! We demand that that Light be met and multiplied by the action of the Cosmic Christ and the great incoming avatars. We demand the halting of

abortion and the abortion of avatars … We demand the cleaning up of this government of the United States and the cleaning up of all governments of the world … …

We demand the reversing of the tide of all Communist forces and spy activities in America, all infiltration and germ warfare, and the release of viruses upon the American people. We demand the reversing of hatred, that darkness, that infamy. We call to the hosts of Light! We call to Mother Mary! We demand action this day! We expect action this day! We demand it! We expect it! We determine it! We invoke it! We call it forth![27]

Once again, the Church provides an almost unmanageable surplus of spiritual resources and members are able to decree not only in the name of I Am, but in the name of Holy Christ Self, Beloved Prince Oromasis and Diana, Aries and Thor, Neptune and Luara, Virgo and Pelleur, Beloved Omri-Tas and the World Mother. Decrees were also associated with action to combat both psychic and physical evil and seen as part of a developing theology of evil.[28]

Prophet also promoted the use of the violet flame, the seventh-ray aspect of the sacred fire, allegedly derived from Saint Germain, as the most perfect fire in the universe, a high frequency energy by means of which negative karma could be burned away and the causes behind old age, disease and death could be removed. Followers were encouraged to think of themselves as Keepers of the Flame, to learn how to expand the three-fold flame within the secret chamber of the heart and to become gods.[29] Every member of the Church has a threefold flame in their heart and could ascend to be a realized Master. According to Prophet every flame could burn away bad karma, increase extrasensory perception and mitigate the danger of earthquake, flood, fire or even nuclear war. It could also erase past mistakes and help with psychological and medical problems. When invoked and visualized in the giving of dynamic decrees, this seventh-ray aspect of the sacred fire transmutes the cause, effect, record and memory of negative karma and misdirected energy that results in discord. Those who correctly call forth the violet flame daily, experience transformation, soul liberation and spiritual upliftment. Through the violet flame Prophet gave members technology to transform their lives and their destiny using their own will power. She also broke free of the traditional Christian aversion to direct contact with the divine. Instead she appealed to a tangible spiritual fire and to the direct intervention of spiritual beings in worldly affairs.

By encouraging such practices the Church Universal and Triumphant opens up new perspectives on the relationship between imagination, spiritual practices and plasticity. Moreover, it does so with social strata not over familiar with such imagination or practices. There is not much evidence, for example, that members were concerned when Prophet announced that she had fulfilled the conditions for Ascension, but had decided to remain in embodiment as a bodhisattva or when she accepted the roles of Guru, Mother of the Flame, World Mother, Messenger and Vicar of Christ, the latter role conferred on her by Christ himself. In the same way there is no unambiguous evidence that members were concerned to learn that Mark Prophet came to earth with Sanat Kumara from Venus, had been Noah, Iknaton, Aesop, Origen and Lancelot in previous lives, and gave staff members of the organization access to his causal body, to use a theosophical term, for forty days after his Ascension.[30] Here, as elsewhere, the Church deploys claims that fall outside of traditional canons of true and false.

What is new here is the scale on which compensations[31] are provided, and the ultra-flexible approach to appropriating other traditions, a form of ecumenism, albeit of an unusual kind. Consistent with this, Elizabeth Prophet provided her public with Mother Mary and rosaries for Catholics,[32] Mary Magdalene for women,[33] Kabbalah for those inclined to Judaism, mantras for those sympathetic to Buddhism, Krishna for Hindus, Afra for Afro-Americans,[34] Lanto for Chinese, astrology and the chakras for the New Age, alchemy for those with natural science interests and courses on soul mates for those beginning their romantic lives. She explained how to know the future from the cycles of the cosmic clock.[35] The Church also provides material culture versions of esoteric spirituality[36] on a grand scale making available a multi-faith home altar and religious cards, candles, crystals, videos, DVDs among other 'products' including The Chart of Your Divine Self.

Political, social, economic, educational and cultural contributions

The Church Universal and Triumphant does not promote a specific socio-economic utopia. In contrast to many New Age leaders, however, Prophet was genuinely concerned about political and social issues and encouraged individual members of the Church to be active in a range of political and social causes. However, she had no plans for a global ecological civilization or for an integration of different races and peoples and tended to propagate conservative, ultra-patriotic and populist views. On the other hand, Elizabeth Prophet claimed to be able to give prophecies about the future and the power of prophecy extended, she claimed, into political matters and she did not hesitate to give decrees for political causes, including the defence of Taiwan.[37] Prophet also flirted with economic conspiracy theories, and claimed that many world leaders and financial circles were led by reincarnated fallen angels, and that an international elite were planning to construct a world corporate state.[38] On the other hand, the Church was opposed to nuclear power and supported both organic farming and alternative medicine. It also looked forward to a future golden age when concern with the transformation of consciousness would prevail over material pursuits.[39]

The Church also has an involvement in education, especially spiritual education. The Church runs Summit University, originally a series of twelve-week residential intensives held at the organization's headquarters, but now expanding through internet courses and attendance courses offered in multiple languages in many different countries.[40] It also promotes popular spiritual education through its publications. There are also teaching centres, providing classes and daily worship. The Church has also established a Montessori school and a Four Winds Centre for organic food and diet. All this shows that the Church is prepared to innovate organizationally in order to attract a public shaped by digital media for whom the traditional sermon or the scholarly tome may be less appealing.

Given the Church's emphasis on performative counterfactuality, the issue about whether the Church is Christian may be definitional. The Church understands itself to be Gnostic Christian, although Jesus is a Master rather than the cosmic Logos. Jesus came to earth as a volunteer with Sanat Kumara and has had many embodiments since, including one as the emperor of Atlantis with his twin flame the Lady Magda, after which they went with two million subjects to the land which was later to become Southern India, where half of them made their Ascensions.[41] These are not ideas entertained by the traditional churches, but the point at issue is really what role do such teachings play in the lives of those who receive them? Clearly, they cannot be entirely separated from resort to spiritual practices that members find to be effective.

What is striking about the Church Universal and Triumphant, however, in contrast with other theosophical Christian churches, is *the movement away from conceptions of spirituality that prioritise belief in formal propositions.* By embracing performative counterfactuality as opposed to spiritual materials grounded in historical documents or supported by detailed arguments, the Church suspends the traditional Western obsession with correct beliefs and allows a plenitude of stances more commonly found in Hinduism as well as a surplus of extraordinary narratives and sacred figures to choose from. Once this is understood, new perspectives open up. Precisely because the Church does not engage with professional levels of theological culture, it is able to experiment freely for a restoration of enchantment in many different areas. Because no one knows exactly what a Church member has to believe or whether there are any external evidences that suggest that Church teachings are true, members are at liberty to develop their own spiritual mix, always remembering the goal of Ascension with the help of Christ and Buddha.

All this amounts to a democratization of esotericism and counterfactuality more generally. The Church Universal and Triumphant has created a literature of easy-to-read esoteric books which can be read for personal benefit or pleasure. Apart from internet lessons, popular publications are sold in New Age bookshops and monthly lessons are mailed out to members. There is also a global online radio programme. Here the Church may be compared perhaps with AMORC, a Rosicrucian organization which mails out *fin-de siècle* occultism to popular audiences in return for money. Unlike the Church Universal and Triumphant, AMORC reveals its secrets in hierarchically ordered grades and students must progress through them in a strict order. In contrast, the Church Universal and Triumphant allows its public choice, although there are hierarchical distinctions between members of the Violet Flame and others.

The Church Universal and Triumphant offers popularized esotericism in a form which reverses the standard social logic governing esoteric movements.[42] Whereas traditional esotericism was often secretive and associated with underground movements and secret societies, the occultism of the Church Universal and Triumphant is accessible and for purchase online. The Church makes democratized esotericism available to all. It combines media religion with traditionalist syncretic revival. In bookshops Prophet's paperbacks sit easily with other self-help texts, despite their unconventional cognitive contents. The Church provides its teachings in popular forms – books, audiobooks and DVDs – and claims to have sold vast numbers of copies, often 50,000 copies of a single book. This suggests that the Church, through its Summit Lighthouse gateway, may be the most successful theosophical publisher in history reaching a wide audience of independent-minded people. This can only mean that the audience found the Church's publications helpful, partly because the contents in such publications were new to them,[43] but mainly because they provide them with access to transformative spiritual experiences. Prophet grasped that older forms of occulture condemned and abandoned by the mainline churches helped ordinary people to have significant spiritual experiences, however those experiences are sometimes interpreted. This point is easier to comprehend in the light of developments in contemporary medicine and cognitive science which emphasize plasticity and the causal influence of the mind on both the body and what is experienced.

All this means that the Church Universal and Triumphant exhibits substantial creativity, although not creativity of the absolutely new Romantic kind. The relation between the Church's popularization of esotericism and occulture is less clear.[44] Much of the material culture generated by the Church relates to occulture or a cultural undergrounds and 'rejected knowledges', including astrology, angelology, reincarnation, magic rays, crystals and similar matters.[45] There are parallels between the popular movie quality of much that is related about the Masters and the occult residues found in popular culture, film, TV, video and popular music. There are also intensities, however, not found in occulture.

The Church is also exceptional, although not unprecedented, in the degree to which it relies on digital technology to deliver its teachings. The Church provides occult information to mass audiences through publications and the internet without any attempt to control its diffusion by levels of initiation at least in the initial stages. The establishment of Summit University shows how effective an initiative aimed at non-elites can be, with the University offering courses on the sacred scriptures of East and West, how to gain self-mastery through the science of the spoken Word, the purification of the aura and the chakras, alchemy as the science of self-transformation, the cycles of karma and past lives, hatha yoga and the macrobiotic diet.

Postreligion

In addition, although this is not obvious at first sight, the Church Universal and Triumphant can be seen as exhibiting some of the features of postreligion. The Church raises the possibility of a form of spirituality beyond traditional notions of true and false. Such a spirituality marks a profound cultural shift to which the mainline churches sometimes seem oblivious. Mainstream Christians increasingly recognize that many elements of the New Testament may be described as mythological in a non-reductive sense, but this is different from embracing fictional materials without reservation or taking up materials which fall completely outside classical conceptions of the credible and are unaccompanied by minimum epistemological warrants. The story of the Resurrection has always been a challenge, but the accounts in the New

Testament include accurate historical details and people alleged to be witnesses. The Church Universal and Triumphant sometimes gestures in this direction, alleging some historical basis, for example, for the claim that Jesus travelled to India. For the most part, however, counterfactual material is asserted with no regard for its intrinsic incredibility. That the success of the Church may be based in part on such a shift is little noted in the existing literature and is a matter of some importance. Embracing fantastic and projective imagination as such may be more radically postmodern that the Church's critics realize.

Organizational forms

Like other movements discussed, the Church Universal and Triumphant may lack some of the organizational forms needed for its development after the death of its seer. There are tensions between its *fin-de-siècle* esoteric elements and its traditional church form, and it is possible that just as the Church attracts followers in parts of the world where its cognitive materials and practices are new, so it will also lose them over time.[46] Since Elisabeth Prophet's death the Church has rechristened itself as a body of *pioneers in practical spirituality*, concerned to bring liberation to souls everywhere who seek spiritual freedom. It still claims to provide a worldwide resource for the teachings of the Ascended Masters, but now it emphasizes that the aim is to spread the message of 'spiritual universality'. Currently the Church aims to attract those who sense their innate divinity and claims to respect the right of members to choose their own beliefs. There is, however, no longer a source of revelational authority now that the movement's seer has passed and it seems likely that previous authoritative teaching by Elizabeth Prophet will be seen as less authoritative over time. Indeed, the Church is now governed by a board of directors and a council of elders. On the other hand, the Church is succeeding in marketing itself as Summit University, which serves as a concrete utopia for those who find it online, from which they can draw endless spiritual treasures.

Conclusion

The case of the Church Universal and Triumphant shows that a movement which provides people with massive counterfactuality provides a challenge both to the prejudice against counterfactuality displayed by some strands of the

Enlightenment and to the related bias against positivity. These strands of the Enlightenment held that positivity should be rejected in so far as it involved counterfactuality. The Church Universal and Triumphant takes the opposite view. Yet it has grown into a global movement from modest beginnings. This suggests that the extensive counterfactuality the Church provides may meet spiritual needs that more mainline forms of Christianity do not.

7

The Charismatic Latter-day Saints

Introduction

In this chapter, I construe the Church of Jesus Christ of Latter-day Saints as a charismatic spiritual movement with many creative features. Many see the Church as quintessentially American,[1] although the eminent Latter-day Saint historian Richard Bushman construes Mormonism as a religion estranged from American society.[2] Others construe the Church as a new world religion, distinct from Christianity, or at least significantly different from it.[3] Evangelical critics sometimes take this as a reason to dismiss the Latter-day Saints entirely. Others see Mormonism as a movement beyond Christianity, as Christianity was beyond Judaism.[4] The British scholar of Mormonism, Douglas Davies, argues that Latter-day Saints have an alternative religious tradition based on the transcendence of death.[5] In the last fifty years, some Latter-day Saint intellectuals have sought to reconcile the Church with Reformed Christianity. Other intellectuals have noted strong resemblances between the Church and the Catholic and Orthodox traditions.[6] My approach to the Latter-day Saints is relatively independent. However, I do not hesitate to judge their creativity to be outstanding.

Against the spirit of much of the scholarly literature, I emphasize the charismatic nature of the movement, that is, its dependence on personal experiences of revelation. I also suggest that the Latter-day Saints are more spiritual than most outsiders suspect. The movement also has an unusual temporal structure at its heart, a structure that can mean that a narrowly contextual reading will not be entirely adequate because as a restoration movement the Church both looks back to ancient Israel and to quasi-Biblical tribes in America, and also looks forward to a Last Judgement and Zion still to come. There is also a tendency in some of the literature to underplay the fact that the Latter-day Saints regard their Church as the Church of Christ restored after centuries of apostasy, and take their Christianity absolutely seriously. The creativity of the Latter-day Saints has also been occluded, I suggest, both by a prejudice against positivity and counterfactual belief and by subsuming the Church under generic conceptions of religion which imply that religion is otherworldly and mainly about beliefs. The charismatic nature of the movement is also underrated because of a tendency to assume that visions and revelations reported by the Saints did not occur, whereas the evidence is that they did most certainly occur as human experiences, just as Latter-day Saints have charismatic experiences of revelation in the course of their ordinary lives. As Bushman explains:

> From an early age, children are told to listen to the spirit. When we are in doubt about our lives-what course to take, what we believe, what dangers threaten us-we consult the Spirit. Long before children understand the intricacies of doctrine, they are told to listen to Heavenly Father whispering to them ….. The discipline of spiritual listening lies at the heart of the Church's organization and teaching. We see it working every day of our lives.[7]

Much of the literature on the Latter-day Saints plays down the fact that the Latter-day Saints are a people formed by multiple and continuing revelations, including modern revelation. The originality of the Saints largely consists, I suggest, *in their access to new positivity, including future positivity*, a phenomenon scarcely known in Christianity since the time of Montanus (fl. second century) who was excommunicated for receiving new revelations from angels. The Latter-day Saints are exceptional because they allege not only that revelation should guide human beings over a vast area, but that such revelation which prevailed in their view in the time of the apostles, has now been restored. This link between Latter-day Saint creativity and positivity is little noted in the literature, mainly because prejudice prevents many from assuming that positivity can be original, creative and culturally important, while contemporary revelation, whether personal or communal, is ruled out in advance.

It may seem controversial to construe the Latter-day Saints as a creative spiritual movement. The Saints insist that they are a church, indeed the true church, while outsiders often represent them as materialistic and money obsessed rather than spiritual. I do not deny that the Saints are a church. In this chapter, however, I offer an alternative reading to highlight their extensive creativity and its potential social importance. In the present context, construing the Latter-day Saints as a church, although entirely appropriate in other contexts, can lead us to overlook just how innovative the Saints actually are, and also to underestimate the extent to which the nature of their movement is occluded by a generic conception of religion. Specifically, a generic conception of religion may lead us not to connect the success of the Latter-day Saints in allegedly secular affairs with their development of doctrines which outsiders may regard as counterfactual. It will not do to characterize the Latter-day Saints as religious delusionists who just happen to have strong families and become economically successful. Instead, we need to ask whether a movement based on open revelation may have certain advantages. Having innovative doctrines provides the Latter-day Saints with a mark of distinctiveness, while continuing revelation means that the interpretation of these doctrines may change over time with alterations in political, economic and cultural circumstances. At the same time, the fact that the Church is wealthier than most nation states should not be ignored since it provides an initial indication that Latter-day Saint success is not confined to or explained by what is popularly thought of as religion.[8]

Finally, although I find vast evidence of Latter-day Saint creativity, I do not interpret this creativity as Romantic creativity. On the contrary, when the Latter-day Saints achieve creativity – in cosmosophy, in historical narratives, in theological doctrines, in political, social and cultural developments and in education – their creativity is of a different kind. What they generate is not absolutely new, but a matter of reviving older beliefs and practices, further developing existing resources, or projecting older cultural repertoires into new contexts or cultural spaces. In many practical contexts their creativity manifests in an *enhanced 'ordinariness'*. Latter-day Saints appear to accept ordinariness and raise it to a higher power. They do not build palaces, lay out world-class gardens or open the world greatest art galleries. Even when they become wealthy, they are not prone to aristocratic display or opulence. Most of their culture is militantly middlebrow, and their charisms tend towards improvement, amelioration and the better management of daily life. This had led some to downgrade Latter-day Saint creativity. However, this is wrong headed because the novelty achieved by the Latter-day Saints often does not depend on whether a particular development has been on the earth before, but on *the difference it makes when it is realised under modern conditions*. Baptising the dead was not historically new when the Latter-day Saints unexpectedly revived it in the nineteenth century, but its revival was new in a Christian church context.

The context: Positivity restored by a modern prophet

The Church of Jesus Christ of Latter-day Saints is one of the fastest growing spiritual organizations in the world with about seventeen million members. From early on it was characterized by a commitment to mission manifested in the mission to the American Indian and the British mission, and now has the most successful missionary expertise on the planet. According to Mormon sources, 50,000 missionaries convert around a quarter of million people every year, although success rates are only very high in less developed parts of the world, including countries in South America, Africa and the Pacific. In a century and a half the Church has changed from a movement of low status rural whites[9] into a global religion, attracting a diversity of populations. The success of the Church can be attributed to its charismatic features, its positive innovations and its excellent organization exemplified in the strong focus on the family (including the mandating of the family home evening), in the organization of the Church into wards and stakes, in the establishment of priesthood councils and Sabbath schools, and in the welfare organizations which help members of the Church to become prosperous. The Church also has a social welfare dimension through the Relief Society and extensive service organizations.

Although Latter-day Saints insist on the unity of faith and reason and that the glory of God is intelligence, the Church is more charism-based and thaumaturgic than this suggests, and appeals to direct spiritual experience in confirmation of its claims. Missionaries standardly invite potential *converts to seek their own spiritual witness of the truth of the Book of Mormon,* and insist that no one should be baptised unless they have some witness of its truth. Further, every member of the Church has a duty to gain that witness for themselves. In Latter-day Saint teaching every normal person can receive revelation in the course of their daily lives, and an effort is made to seek revelation before a person is called to a leadership role in the Church, although such revelation is expected to confirm and not displace the Church's teachings.

The Church of Jesus Christ of Latter-day Saints derives from Joseph Smith (1805–44), who is sometimes described as a modern prophet. Joseph has not received the recognition he deserves, partly because secular prejudices have prevented many scholars from grasping the charismatic reality which manifested in his life and his revelations. To do justice to the Latter-day Saints, however, the scandal of a *modern* prophet must be faced. It is not adequate to treat Joseph, as Alexander Campbell did, in the nineteenth century, and as the distinguished historian of Jacksonian democracy Robert Remini has done, as the product of his context and his times.[10] Joseph can be said to have transcended the contexts which shaped him, and his revelations were not part of American civil religion. It is also not satisfactory to reduce Joseph Smith to the rural esotericism, with which he was certainly familiar.[11] As a young man Joseph was immersed in folk magic, familiar with dealing with under-ground spirits, and professionally engaged in digging for buried money and other treasures.[12] He knew ceremonial magic, and the family possessed esoteric parchments. He may have known of the Kabbala through his Hebrew teacher Alexander Neibaur. Certainly, he lived in a world in which reports of theophanies, angels and magical events and the use of seer stones were not uncommon. In this world many people hoped that Christianity would be restored. There were also contemporary suggestions that the American Indians were the lost tribes of Israel. Joseph undoubtedly was shaped by these contexts. None of them, however, leads us to expect the charismatic explosions that occurred in Joseph's life when in 1827 he received gold plates written in reformed Egyptian from the angel Moroni.[13]

Nor would they lead us to predict the complex thought found in Joseph's writings and sermons. Perhaps the best way to understand Joseph is to see him as a prophet in an historical sociological sense,[14] a perspective which invites comparative studies—that is, as a man who was seen by his followers as a covenantal prophet, a restorer of past worlds, a translator and a healer, as well as a person who predicted future events. It is clear that he was also an inspired orator, a social utopian and, at least at times, an organizational genius. Once Joseph is understood as a prophet in this sense, it is not surprising that the intentional content of his revelations transcended the folk religious forms in which they were given. But this is not to explain the striking fact that, unlike other thinkers of the period who attempted to revive primitive Christianity, Joseph attempted to restore aspects of the ancient religion of Israel, including polygamy and a form of temple worship.

For Latter-day Saints the crucial question is whether Joseph was or was not a prophet of God. This, however, narrows the interpretative range unduly, especially when the person of Joseph Smith is surrounded with charismatic awe, an awe intensified, in an almost Shi'ite way, by his murder in 1844, which Latter-day Saints construe as martyrdom. Understandably Latter-day Saints want to insist that there really is evidence that Joseph received gold plates. However, it is not helpful, I suggest, to concentrate too much on narratives about the gold plates. The nature and origin of the gold plates may never be resolved.[15] In many ways, what is striking is the ordinariness of the details of the story, such as the fact that some 116 pages of the manuscript of Joseph's 'translation' of the gold plates were stolen and never returned. Arguments from context, however, explain the form, but not the originality of Joseph Smith's revelations, as the case of his contemporary James Strang (1813–56) makes clear.[16] Nor is it sufficient to note that the early Latter-day Saints were millenarians, convinced that the heavens were again open and the Second Coming was not far off, since such expectations were not uncommon in Joseph's context.[17]

Cognitive materials in the context of a restoration

Consistent with their goal of restoring the true Christianity, Latter-day Saints provide members with a wealth of cognitive materials, including *The Book of Mormon,* a collection of 138 divine revelations to Joseph, Brigham Young and later leaders of the Church known as *Doctrine and Covenants,* and *The Pearl of Great Price,* which itself includes the Book of Moses that Joseph claimed had been removed from the Book of Genesis as well as various other texts 'translated' by Joseph from other languages.[18] Then there are the retranslations of the Bible that Joseph made, including some 3,700 revisions to the King James version. There are also texts of uncertain provenance, such as *The Book of Abraham, The Lectures on Faith,* the *Journal of the Discourses* 1854–1886 and *The History of the Church.*[19] There is also a vast amount of archival material, some of which is being published as *The Joseph Smith Papers.* Latter-day Saints also accept texts which the traditional churches reject, including the *Book of Enoch,* which they receive in a Smithian version.[20]

The most important of these Latter-day Saint cognitive materials, the *Book of Mormon* and *The Book of Moses,* are only now receiving the detailed scholarly attention they deserve. A work of 531 pages translated by Joseph Smith, a man of twenty-three years with only little formal schooling, *The Book of Mormon* gives detailed accounts of two distinct civilizations that rose and fell in the Americas, and also narrates the coming of Christ to the New World shortly after His Resurrection. Each of the three main characters (Nephi, Mormon and Moroni) has their own style and perspective. There is also a displaced time perspective, such that peoples before Christ are Christians and Nephi in the sixth century BCE has a vision of the life of Christ.[21]

The Book of Mormon can be read as scripture in the sense of writing which elicits a changed relationship between the reader and the divine.[22] It can be seen perhaps as an eruption of utopian function whereby Old Testament lore, American Indian history and American geography are reconciled in a narrative which brings Bible events close to home.[23] Claiming to be Mormon's abridgements of earlier texts, it provides detailed and complex narratives through which we learn that the Jaredites came to America after the fall of the Tower of Babel circa the third millennium BCE and that three other Israelite groups came in the sixth century BCE aided by a magic compass. Given the wealth of detail, the variety of voices and style, the changes of perspective and the large number of characters, it is not an exaggeration to state that the imagination involved is stupendous. Moreover, as Terryl Givens argues, the *Book of Mormon* is a disruptive text that reconfigures traditional religious paradigms and fractures and decentres standard Biblical themes.[24] To appreciate the book the intricacy of its detail needs to be carefully explored.[25] The Book of Moses is much less well-known, but contains many Latter-day Saint themes that are not present in mainstream Christianity: a weeping God, human pre-existence and a literal Zion.

Latter-day Saints also have *revealed cosmosophy*,[26] or an enchanted account of the universe which they derive from their sacred texts according to which there is no creation *ex nihilo* and neither matter nor intelligence can be created or destroyed. Joseph himself intended to restore the centrality of cosmosophy as part of the restored Gospel, as Hugh Nibley argued,[27] and his revelations included ideas about a multiverse of millions of worlds, each of which is ruled by a dominant God and some of which are inhabited. According to Latter-day Saint cosmosophy, the universe is dynamic and radically pluralistic, although subject to laws. Evil is an eternal part of the cosmos, for which God is not responsible. Further, everything is natural and material, a claim which led nineteenth-century Latter-day Saints to trumpet Latter-day Saint materialism against the immaterialism propagated by the Christian Churches.[28] There is no supernatural in the sense of a level of reality not bound by natural law. All spirit is matter, matter and spirit differing only in degree, and all spiritual entities are material entities, albeit invisible and more refined.[29] Similarly, all miracles are natural events. This seems to imply that there is more than the physical world, but that this more is in the universe. Finally, there is a spiritual birth in the premortal world before the physical birth of an individual on earth, and life on earth only makes sense with reference to premortal and postmortal worlds. In the premortal world, individuals were the actual children of real spirit parents.[30]

Latter-day Saint cosmosophy combines metaphysical immanence and thaumaturgic imagination. The metaphysical immanence dimension means that there is no ontological separation of the divine from the universe. Hence the Father and the human being are of *the same species*. Again, humans can become angels, and angels can become humans. On the other hand, thaumaturgic and mythological teachings are reasserted under conditions of modernity, but interpreted as intra-ontological and naturalistic. Such phenomena occur in the universe. Hence Latter-day Saints can accept that Michael and Jehovah participated in the creation of the earth under the leadership of the Elohim, that there was a war between members of the Council of the gods when Lucifer and Jehovah fought over the plan of salvation, and that translated beings exist who are more powerful than mortals and are temporarily not subject to death.

It is more difficult to characterize how the Latter-day Saints read these materials. In some cases, they are received almost as sacraments, and treated as sacred. In other cases, there is a matter of fact attitude to them, as if they contained ordinary historical facts that others happen not to know. It is also fair to note that many Latter-day Saint texts may not as yet have had their full impact. Even the current focus on *The Book of Mormon* only dates from the time of President Benson (1985–94), which is as surprising as the fact that Joseph himself did not preach from it.

Again, some writers claim that Latter-day Saints have *a distinct philosophy* revealed to them in their scriptures. This philosophy is often identified as a form of materialism, as opposed to the immaterialism dominant in the Christian tradition. Latter-day Saint scriptures teach that spirit is a form of matter and so hold out, on their view, the prospect of a world view consistent with current science. Earlier Latter-day Saint thinkers took this to be a brilliant demonstration of the superiority of the restored Gospel, and many Latter-day Saint intellectuals still assume that materialism is an essential part of the restoration. Thus far, however, Latter-day Saints have not shown that their materialism involves technical advances over other varieties. Moreover, some Latter-day Saints have noted that it is not clear that Mormonism does involve materialism in a physicalist sense, since the eternal laws Latter-day Saints posit can hardly be material and the matter they posit is invisible. Consistent with a recognition of these complexities, some Latter-day Saints are now attempting to come to terms with recent developments in European philosophy, including French and German philosophy, as received in the United States.[31] Nonetheless, the bias against traditional Christian immaterialism is still in place, and this has implications for Latter-day Saint anthropology.[32]

Again, some writers claim that the Latter-day Saints have *a distinct ethics*, although others assimilate their views to well-known ethical positions such as Kant's deontology, utilitarianism or natural law.[33] Some argue from the fact that the natural and the spiritual are not separated to an environmental ethics. The Church, however, has shown no particular insight into contemporary moral evils and there has been a tendency for Saints to embrace military action and nationalism with enthusiasm, although they also have subsidiary pacifist traditions. Latter-day Saints are known for their integrity in business but are only now recognizing the need to address the rights of minorities, although it seems unlikely that major ethical advances are hidden in their sacred texts. In practice, Latter-day Saints have been flexible over time, shifting, for example, from allowing polygamy to banning it, and from a general condemnation of contraception to an acceptance of it. Their ethical positions are voluntarist and derived from church authorities, not elaborated argument.

The fact that the Latter-day Saints have so many cognitive materials is well-known, but the cognitive character of these materials is less well appreciated. It is not widely understood that the Latter-day Saint sacred texts have led some Saints to find a complex cosmosophy, an original philosophy and even an alternative ethics in them. It is also important to note that the Latter-day Saints, to a greater degree than other movements I have discussed, elaborate a wealth of doctrinal innovations based on or in response to their cognitive materials. These innovations include one or more alternative conceptions of God, a Latter-day Saint Christology, a different conception of grace, a revised conception of sin, a distinctive conception of salvation, an expanded understanding of revelation based on a reassertion of religious literality, a non-standard conception of faith, a different conception of Church, a different account of creation, compensations for the inadequacies of modern secular life and a detailed account of life after death.[34] Here I note only that these innovations may be read intentionally as countermoves against Western nihilism and the somewhat dehydrated understanding of Christianity prevailing in many of the mainline churches. Latter-day Saint theological innovations relocate Christianity in a cosmological scheme. In doing so they confront the mainline churches with a spiritual naturalism which contradicts parts of the secular culture of modernity, hence raising the crucial question of whether that culture can provide the basis for a future ecological civilization or whether it is indeed tending to nihilistic decline, as Nietzsche predicted.

I also suggest that Latter-day Saint theological innovations embody *model ideas* that may be portable to other contexts such as that revelation should be considered open and not closed, that sacred geography and sacred place may need to be re-spatialized in advanced societies, that sexuality and family life can be embedded in a wider scheme of cosmic meaning, that sacerdotal roles can be successfully extended to everyone, that sacral concerns and economic activity can be successfully integrated, that advanced technocratic societies require more and not less communal organization and more and not less sacralization if they are not to decline, all systematically related to a new understanding of the universe. On this view, Latter-day Saint theological innovations may also be relevant to understanding why twentieth-century attempts at political and social reform have often failed as well as to attempts to develop a more sustainable global society in the future.

Spiritual practices

The Latter-day Saints also have many spiritual practices. Spiritual practices are sometimes thought to be less important for Latter-day Saints, but this is not the case. On the contrary, it is the efficacy of their spiritual practices that leads many Latter-day Saints to continue with the Church. Some of these spiritual practices are designed to achieve *organized community spirituality* rather than individual spiritual development. Here the American character of the movement can be misleading. Latter-day Saints are individualistic in many contexts, but not in their spiritual life. Rather they are practical workers trying to build Zion as a spiritual community. Latter-day Saints are committed to 'strong religion' that requires heavy commitments of time, in the case of bishops up to forty hours a week. Consistent with this, their lives are structured by multiple exoteric practices, that is, practices that do not require transfigured inner states or exceptional clairvoyant powers. Latter-day Saints pray, have dietary practices, tithe, attend church and work in the temple. They are a people set apart, a characteristic developed even in clothing such an undergarments. Nonetheless, although there is the weekly sacrament meeting as well as the anointing of the sick, and a strong emphasis on making and keeping covenants, the charismatic dimension of the Latter-day Saints is quiet, and often a matter of personal or communal experience. Latter-day Saints mostly do not see visions as Joseph did, although popular Mormonism was long pervaded by thaumaturgic features.[35] There are no unambiguously esoteric practices, and very few reports of personal plasticity in the sense of major changes to the body or the mind, in sharp contrast to members of Ananda Marga or the Church Universal and Triumphant. Latter-day Saints do, however, report charismatic experiences in response to prayer.

Latter-day Saints are also unusual in developing spiritual practices that *sacralize ordinary life beyond contexts normally considered religious.* This manifests most clearly in their distinctive approaches to sexuality and to care for the dead. Latter-day Saints have *an innovative approach to family-creating sexuality.* At one level, this is a matter of Joseph's attempt to promote a spiritually causal positive view of sexuality, including not only plural marriage, but the attribution of sexual activity to the gods as well as to human beings after death.[36] On this interpretation, the gods literally sire the spirit populations of the worlds they govern,[37] and Jesus created many worlds for the Father before incarnating as Jesus of Nazareth and will create future worlds for himself and populate them with his spiritual children. That is, Latter-day Saints *include sexuality within the divine activity*, and affirm the cosmic significance of distinctive sexes and concomitant sex roles. They regard the body and its purification as essential to godliness, although they do not sacralize sexuality in non-family creating contexts. Here the Latter-day Saint valorization of family-creating sexuality can be read as a critique of Augustinian Christianity, with its tendency to associate concupiscence with sin, as well as a massive re-valorization of the family as the basic religious unit, not the individual. Moreover, and under certain conditions the family can endure in eternity. Latter-day Saints seek to secure strong families by weekly family meetings and visitation of families by other families. The intentional meaning here may be that marriage and sexuality have cosmological effects, a notion more familiar to the ancient Canaanites than to modern Americans.

It is important to note that the Latter-day Saint positive evaluation of sexuality has spiritual aspects. Latter-day Saints charisms manifest in Latter-day Saint women. This partly qualifies the widespread criticism of Latter-day Saint patriarchy and opens up the possibility of future roles for women in the Church as queens and priestesses. In the nineteenth century the Church was unusual in educating women and allowing them the vote in elections. There are now hundreds of thousands of Mormon women preaching, teaching and ministering in different contexts. It is also possible that the Latter-day Saints possess a charism for the reformation of male psychology which they have not yet adequately developed. Latter-day Saint writers sometimes suggest that male psychology is positively modified by polygamous arrangements, a view also advanced in some Muslim contexts,[38] which outsiders seldom share. Significantly, polygamy, practiced by the Church until 1904, was primarily abolished for political and not theological or moral reasons.

Latter-day Saints also prioritize care for the dead. Indeed, they transform the population that may be saved by *extending baptism to the dead*, a practice supported by the fact that Christ preached to the dead and the fact that such a practice may be found in the ancient Church.[39] In providing for salvation for the dead Latter-day Saints allow an operation of utopian reason against death and the tendency in Protestant Christianity to concentrate almost exclusively on those who have not yet died. They also reassert the relevance of the dead to the lives of the living. Latter-day Saint teaching here goes beyond what is made public, but the notion that the dead can speak to the living gains in depth when it is remembered that Moroni spoke to Joseph as a resurrected living being who had died 1400 years earlier. For Latter-day Saints the dead, some of whom are in spirit prison, can be baptised by a Church member going through baptism in their stead, although the dead are free to accept or reject baptism on their behalf. Here Latter-day Saints characteristically combine a reassertion of pre-modern enchantment with contemporary technology, locating the names of the dead by means of their unsurpassed genealogical services. In the same way, they now construe salvation as encompassing all living things including pets.

Consistent with this unusual focus on the dead, Latter-day Saints also *give temples a central place in their spiritual lives,* an institution lost in Christianity, with obvious exceptions such as the Templars, for almost 2,000 years. In doing so they re-valorize the importance of sacred space, the idea of temples as places where revelations from the divine occur and the ancient conception of a place where it is possible to access and impact upon invisible spiritual worlds. Joseph intuited that the Temple was fundamental to ancient Judaism and he interpreted this centrality in literal cosmological terms.[40] Latter-day Saint temples add a mystery religion or sacred depth dimension to Latter-day Saint spirituality They also raise the issue of a possible return to ancient religious practice since Joseph implied that he would also restore the Jewish temple ceremonies. The Latter-day Saint temple, however, is not the temple of ancient Israel, but a mixture of Jewish, Christian and Masonic themes, with architectural features that aspire to feudal greatness, hence the frequent use of castle turrets.

Prioritizing temple work, including sealings of marriages and ancestors, temple ceremonies and garments, goes with a recovered theology of the temple, and with forms of architecture based on the recovery of sacred space. These achievements partly reflect the fact that some of Joseph's early followers were Masons, just as the ceremonies and architecture of the early temples were influenced by Royal Arch Free Masonry.[41] Consistent with this, Latter-day Saint temple ceremonies send Church members on a spiritual quest to obtain the mysteries of godliness, modelling themselves on Adam and Eve. They reinforce the sense of a people apart who are able to make covenants and relate individual lives to the mysteries of the universe by dramatically retelling the story of the Fall. Mormon temple culture allows Latter-day Saints to maintain camaraderie based on secret temple ceremonies, and, on some interpretations, doctrines. Temples embody and manifest sacred truths. They enable Church members to attempt to overcome the corruptible elements in their lives and to make sacred oaths. Joseph himself talked up the causal efficacy of the temple, declaring that 'We need the temple more than anything else.'[42] Moreover, Latter-day Saints expect that direct communication with God and the spirits of the dead will be possible in the holiness of the temple. They also hold that entry to the highest heaven may depend on Temple endowments and on receiving secret signs and tokens to give to the angels who bar the way. Moreover, men and women need to be eternally married in order to become gods and become co-creators in eternity because marriage covenants and temple sealings are binding in the world to come.

In summary, Latter-day Saint spiritual practices are designed to locate spirituality in community, including the community of the dead and the future community of the eternal family. They are not designed to transform bodies, minds or spirits in the present life.

Political, social, economic, educational and cultural contributions

Given their reputation as conservatives, it may seem counter-intuitive to suggest that Latter-day Saints model elements of major social and cultural reforms derived often enough from their positivity. Latter-day Saint positivity requires them, however, to engage in creative forms of social and cultural activism. To take the case of political theory, Joseph himself developed a theory of governmental authority which combined seventeenth-century communitarianism and natural right philosophy with theo-democracy in Nauvoo and tried to establish a theocracy in which there was no separation of church and state and a system of church courts.[43] He also received revelations associating Zion with an egalitarian redistribution of wealth[44] and a communitarian social and economic order.[45] Further, Joseph received revelations about a new cooperative economic system, which he took to be a restoration of the United Order of Enoch, under which members of the church were to deed all their property to a bishop of the church, who would then hold it for them as stewards. Cooperation was also evident in the precedent of the Mormon Corridor when a cooperative system and common ownership allowed Mormons to build a farming community in the desert. Once again it is fair to comment that the Latter-day Saints have fallen away from their early social and economic radicalism. However, this may change and there are some signs of the Saints renewing their early alternativism. For example, some Latter-day Saints currently discover liberation theological themes in the *Book of Mormon*'s insistence on the need to eliminate poverty.[46]

The Church is also heavily involved in education and encourages its members to adopt an ethic of lifelong learning and to achieve the maximum education possible. It has a highly effective system for training missionaries, including excellent language education. It also runs Brigham Young University as well as providing spiritual education through the instruction provided to school children and its many educational publications and the Church Educational System. There also is a vast periodical literature providing religious instruction and news about the Church. It is true that Latter-day Saint educationists mostly makes maximal use of established methods and are not educational avant-gardists. It is also fair to note that some of the education provided on the Church's website would seem to be fundamentalist suggesting, for example, that some Biblical characters were hundreds of years old. On the other hand, the emphasis on lifelong education in many different areas has radical implications for a different level of culture in the long run.

The Church also has *an arts ministry*, exemplified in folk realist art and sculpture,[47] a music ministry exercised through the Mormon Tabernacle choir, a long tradition of well-performed theatre, a marked enthusiasm for dancing as well as cinema, excellent jazz groups and performing troupes.[48] Better known is the fact that the Latter-day Saints have impressive *material culture* that allows the Church to display its wealth in an apparently religious form.[49] The church is much more culturally open in its practical concerns than one might expect, and this is evidenced in the best ecumenical education in the world for the general public, outreach to Islam at an intellectual level, including translating many major Arabic texts, and in a well-funded effort to preserve and celebrate Polynesian culture at the Polynesian Cultural Center in Hawaii. Once again it is fair to suggest that the Church has more models for cultural transformation than it has been able to realize at this stage.

Organizational forms

Like the other spiritual movements discussed, the Latter-day Saints work with a mixture of original and inherited organizational forms some of which have their problems. There is a problem, for example, about who decides who is a Latter-day Saint and who is not. There are many different types of Latter-day Saint, including progressive and cultural Latter-day Saints, members of the Reorganized Church of Latter-day Saints now known as the Community of Christ, as well as many secessionist groups, including fundamentalist groups and groups who continue to practise polygamy. The centralized and secretive nature of the leadership of the Church is also an issue. There is a First President and the Quorum of the Twelve Apostles all of whom are deemed prophets, seers and revelators. It is not clear how these leaders are held accountable, and there is evidence that the Church controls Church history and Church records, and sometimes makes misleading changes in different editions of major works such as the *Book of Mormon* and the *Doctrine and Covenants*.[50] It also issues its own translations of the Bible, including Joseph's improved translations and Mormonized notes, and restricts access to controversial documents such as Joseph Knight's biography held in the Church vaults. There seems to be no institutional way of criticizing the leadership's conduct in these areas, partly because Joseph's conception of prophecy did not include the right of others to prophesy against his revelations. Joseph expected others to prophesy, but he left no mechanism for resolving cases in which prophecies conflict, except submission to those entrusted with the leadership of the Church. The Church provides no means by which individual Mormons can reject the authorized teachings of the current leaders of the Church, even though it is possible to suggest that previous leaders were seriously mistaken.

The Church also has a history of erroneous identifications, including the exclusion of blacks from the priesthood,[51] many of which were divine revelation until they were changed. The same applies to a lesser extent to the identification of the American Indians as the lost tribes of Israel, and the many decades in which the Church identified the peoples in the *Book of Mormon* with ancient South American civilizations, even to the point of including coloured photos of ancient American sites in popular editions of the Book of Mormon. For over a century the Church identified the American Indians as Lamanites and dealt with them on this basis, including preparing a *Lamanite Handbook,* although there is no evidence that they came from the Middle East. There is also some evidence that the Church turned Joseph's cosmological priesthood into an ecclesiastical priesthood and forbade women to perform exorcisms and healings which Joseph allowed.[52] It is also fair to note problems associated with patriarchy, gender essentialism and sexual abuse in Latter-day Saint families, and a tendency to scapegoat sexual minorities, although the Church has recently made efforts to modify its record in this area.[53] The Church now allows gay people to be baptised, and it seems likely that a post-heterosexualist theology will emerge eventually.[54] All this, however, only confirms that the Latter-day Saints have not always found organizational forms adequate to their positivity.

As is well known, Latter-day Saints combine the angel and the beehive: a mixture of preternatural *luxus* and *this worldly activism,* of hostility to mystery and transcendence with a hierarchical Church structure, an emphasis on intellectual freedom with submission to divinely guided Church leaders.[55] Critics charge that the Church deploys arbitrary interpretations of Old and New Testament texts,[56] shows a blindness to the spiritual traditions seen as superseded by the Restoration and lacks a developed political economy, despite the revelations Joseph received about Zion. It is also fair to say that the Church finds it difficult to critique American exceptionalism, and that there can be a problem about the exalted status attributed to Joseph, whose revelations have to be accepted because they are revealed. Finally, the Church still struggles to deal with Joseph's personal frailty evident in the financial failures of the Kirtland period and, on one view, in his sexual choices.

Conclusion

The creativity of the Latter-day Saints is complex because many Latter-day Saint revelations are designed to restore what was lost, and so are often recursive. Nonetheless, Latter-day Saint creativity can be both radical and extensive, partly because it is not bound by the Bible as commonly received, by the history of the traditional churches, by or by past statements by church authorities. Because fresh revelations are expected, Latter-day Saint creativity can include utterly novel developments. Against this, it might be argued that most Latter-day Saint innovations are only 'creative' in a generous sense. Read as utopian indications, however, the innovations of the Saints may sometimes point to developments missing in contemporary Western cultures. These indications include the location of spiritual events in the universe, the integration of sexuality with spirituality, the valorization of economic success in a horizon that includes extensive spiritual work, the care for the dead and the strong commitment to family life. The Latter-day Saints also tend to close much of the distance between the sacral and the secular,[57] and so illustrate one of the themes of this volume: the need not to contrast the secular and the sacral too sharply and to look instead for how the one inhabits the other.

8

Conclusion

This volume has approached a large theme – the need to think beyond both generic religion and the secular. It has done so by applying a disaggregative approach to six spiritual movements on the hypothesis that many elements found in these spiritual movements can be studied in their own right. This disaggregative approach has revealed that many of these movements have features that fall outside generic religion, just as many of them have more secular features than one might expect and are active in what might be deemed worldly enterprises.

Once generic concepts of religion and dualistic conceptions of the religious and the secular are treated with caution or even bracketed for certain purposes, it becomes clear that these movements are more creative than is generally supposed, and that they may generate both indications of what is lacking in contemporary Western societies, and also models of possible alternative arrangements to those found in those societies. The degree to which this is the case varies with each movement and each issue, and it is fair to suggest that being creative in many different areas may sometimes not be as important as embodying a crucial challenge to existing arrangements in one respect. It is also important to remember that the creativity involved is not Romantic and includes cases in which these movements reinvigorate and strengthen older cultural materials, and further develop existing social possibilities. Intellectually all these movements depend on positivity, but to different degrees and with different consequences.

Having marshalled considerable evidence for the degree of creativity displayed in these movements, it remains for me to evaluate, however tentatively, their relevance to political, social and cultural reform. Before I do so I need to introduce a note of caution. It is not possible to prove that these creative developments are relevant to political, social and cultural reform in an absolute sense, especially since these movements are sometimes better at signalling what is lacking than at specifying how the lack should be filled. The term 'reform' is also not without its ambiguities. It suggests possible changes for the better, but in concrete cases reform can be in the eye of the beholder. Nonetheless, it is sometimes possible to thematize reform in terms of organizational learning, as cases such as sanitation and hospital administration show. On the other hand, much depends on whether the proposed arrangements would be better in specific real-world contexts. Then there is the issue of better for whom? These movements tend not to address this issue in adequate detail. On the contrary, they tend to suggest that the changes they advocate would benefit humanity in general, which may or may not be the case. Finally, it is crucial to recognize that identifying the need for reform and proposing an arrangement that might help achieve it should be seen as possible contributions to a causal series that may lead to change in the future. Actually realizing the change, however, may depend on other factors and may involve intervention by other causal agents.

The delicate issue here is how not to undervalue the emergence of utopian intentionality which suggests that existing arrangements might be changed and also proposals for concrete arrangements which suggest one way in which change might be achieved, while recognizing the difficult and tangled paths actual reform takes. The view I adopt stresses the importance of both utopian intentionality and concrete utopian proposals, while insisting that less utopian elements will be needed for real changes to occur. Utopian intentionality and concrete utopian proposals are not in themselves enough. Real-world changes may be characterized by anti-utopian features, and not the perfectionist set of outcomes many of these movements envisage.

The movements discussed in this volume have different strengths and weaknesses. Some provide structured organization and multiple activities for members to the point where the sense of belonging to a meaningful community matters more than ideology. Others win members by providing them with significant spiritual experiences. Having apparently experienced spiritual realities, members often seem to decide that the ideational framework has some basis in truth. All of the movements discussed possess positivity which is not subject to epistemological or scientific constraints, just as many of them transcend in some respects any religious-secular dualism. All these movements combine democratization and a degree of elitism. All offer indications about how human spirituality might be managed in advanced societies and some of them profile spiritual republicanism and/or non-sectarian spirituality. All respond to modernity in ways that signal what may be lacking in contemporary Western societies. Many explore alternative organizations of social, economic and cultural life.

As the studies in this volume show, the contributions of these movements are by no means distinct from their beliefs and practices accepted on the authority of spiritual traditions, that is, their positivity. In most cases their positivity is the major source of their creativity. To this extent, these movements suggest that the Enlightenment critique of positivity is one-sided, and that more attention needs to be paid to the cultural productivity of forms of organization traditionally labelled 'religious'. On the other hand, none of these movements theorize their own positivity in contextual terms or understand it in rigorously comparative terms, although doing so would help them to explain what they have received in more rational ways. This means that the major problems exposed by Hegel in the nineteenth century have not been successfully resolved, including the epistemological standards that need to be met before accepting that something is the case and the need to limit the political, ethical and social hegemony of organizations advancing claims that do not meet these standards. In so far as positivity may have great value, it may not be useful to shield it from rational analysis by giving it the status of revelation. Many strands of the Enlightenment were inclined to assume that no revelation could ever take place, so that arrangements and practices based on positivity were without a rational foundation and probably harmful. The studies in this volume do not assume that revelation cannot occur. Rather they suggest that a form of revelation can be found in all these movements, provided we understand such language to refer to the fact that new contents appear in cultural history. Again, these studies do not assume that the positivity found in these movements is entirely without warrant, although they do suggest that the degree of warrant varies from specific example to specific example and deserves more rigorous elaboration by these movements.

All of these movements have charismatic aspects and allege that certain individuals possessed spiritual gifts, but none of them claim current supernatural powers, although both the Christian churches border at times on such claims. Instead, in several cases there is a definite tendency to re-centre on practical spirituality and social activism (the Bahá'ís, Soka Gakkai, the Brahma Kumaris, Ananda Marga) as opposed to traditional ritualistic practices. Again, although all of these movements have utopian features, it is striking that none of them assumes that human beings are currently perfect. Nor do they claim that utopian results are achievable now under conditions which allow of scientific testing. Like utopian communities, they provide rewards and benefits for members, but with the partial exception perhaps of the Brahma Kumaris, do not insist on rigid bonding or on complete separation from the outside world even for elite members. In the same way, attending to the concrete utopianism of these movements, yields many fresh perspectives, but does not explain why most of them do not go so far as to advance a comprehensive socio-political vision. In societies dominated by economic, social and cultural developments, these movements are themselves shaped by such developments and do not find it easy to reconfigure them.

On the other hand, all these movements address issues unsolved in Western societies and provide instances of both utopian intentionality, and examples of concrete utopianism in the form of possible alternative arrangements. Moreover, although this is little discussed in the scholarship, these movements are directly relevant to the failed reformed efforts of Western socialism and Communism. Most of these movements make the crucial move of allying personal spiritual transformation with proposals for reform in many different areas. This is of potential historic importance because the socialist and Communist movements of the twentieth century failed to do this. The overwhelming assumption of secular reform movements in the twentieth century was that a better world could be built with people as they are. Of course, given the reformed institutions and arrangements proposed, it was often expected that a new socialist humanity would appear, and Soviet propaganda insisted it had already done so. Nonetheless, the reform of humanity did not need to come first. In contrast, the Baha'is, Soka Gakkai and Ananda Marga all emphasize personal transformation *before* wider political, social, economic, educational and cultural reform.

All these movements promote and model possible reforms in a wide range of areas, including spirituality, philosophy, governance, administration, education, economics, international relations, nutrition, agriculture, medicine, the arts and media. In doing so, these movements suggest that:

- contemporary Western anthropology is too restrictive and neglects fundamental needs of the human being;
- more powerful spiritual practices can strengthen individuals and change their consciousness and experience over time;
- contemporary Western social life lacks the strong prosocial and mutualist features it arguably needs;
- contemporary economic arrangements need to be radically reformed in some respects;
- positive changes to nutrition, diet and health are possible;
- agriculture may be redeveloped along organic and participatory lines;
- the contemporary sciences need to be supplemented with qualitative perspectives in certain respects.

All these movements advance such perspectives in the public sphere, while accepting that enclaves or sacred spaces may be needed to combat nihilistic and externalist features of modern social and economic life.

The studies in this volume have paid close attention to the *cognitive materials* these movements possess. They have done so because these materials tend to have been under-valued in the existing scholarship, partly because many scholars assume that materials presented as based on positivity are likely to be irrational and mythological, as well as possibly dangerous. In contrast, I have sought to show that such cognitive materials often contain *model ideas* that are capable of further development. Thus many of these movements provide *revealed cosmosophy* or an enchanted conception of the universe which functions as compensation for the difficulties and ambiguities of a meaningless universe, even though the relevance of such cosmosophy to those outside the movement remains unclear. This cosmosophy allows members to imagine a spiritual universe which is not the physical universe that immediately appears and to feel at home in a structure that is both meaningful and wondrous without abandoning modern scientific cosmology. Several of these movements also provide *revealed science*. In doing so, they imply that the passive reception of the natural sciences in the West is to a degree harmful and that qualitative perspectives on the universe may be needed if human beings are to order their lives and their societies in fruitful ways. Finally, as Appendix 1 makes clear, Latter-day Saints have generated a vast number of doctrinal innovations, some of which may be of wider significance than their articulation in the context of one spiritual movement might suggest.

Several of these movements have cognitive materials that contain model ideas in the area of *philosophy*, albeit admixed in several cases with cosmosophy. Model ideas in philosophy sometimes appear in grandiose philosophical systems and only reveal their theoretic power when they are reinscribed in other discourses. Consistent with this, both the Brahma Kumaris and Ananda Marga advance philosophies of mind that are imbricated with older philosophical systems, but potentially of wider purport. In addition, and with more originality, Ananda Marga proposes a new philosophy, neohumanism, elements of a philosophy of language and a new form of science that integrates physical and mental sciences, an integration largely lacking in the natural and human sciences as they are currently organized. Again, and perhaps surprisingly, the Latter-day Saints flag the possibility of a new philosophy based on materialism, as an alternative to the immaterialism embraced by the mainline churches, although this alternative arguably remains under-developed, despite the efforts of the Society for Mormon Philosophy.

Two of these movements advance new ethics: pan-species universalist ethics in the case of Ananda Marga and value creation ethics in the case of Soka Gakkai. In both cases, they make crucial shifts which are now directly relevant to humanity: from humanist ethics to an ethics of life in general in the case of Ananda Marga, and from anteriorist ethics to ethical openness in the case of Soka Gakkai. Two of these movements, Ananda Marga and the Brahma Kumaris, advance a form of cosmic historicism which may be able to be reconstructed as a philosophy of history if the cosmic historicism is interpreted very liberally, as it currently is by Ananda Marga. In applying their ideas to historical change, these movements arrive at two different stances towards modernity: futurism in the case of Ananda Marga and modernism in the case of the Brahma Kumaris. Only Ananda Marga is radically futurist and envisages technological changes to human beings, plants and animals, a prospect now before us with which better known spiritual movements have arguably failed to come to terms. Both movements, however, encourage the expectation that the current world may change in significant respects either because a radically different future arrives (Ananda Marga) or because the present world ends (the Brahma Kumaris).

Several of these movements directly address the lack of a coherent philosophical anthropology in the West, where social and cultural theory have developed in isolation from the natural sciences, and where the need for a metaphysical account of personhood is understood by professional philosophers and theologians, but not necessarily by anyone else. They do so by reasserting older anthropologies and /or new biopsychologies. This is very much the case with the renovated traditional Indian anthropology found in Ananda Marga, while the Brahma Kumaris reassert the Indian view that the real human being is the soul, not the body, a view they articulate in terms of a specific account of what the soul is and where it can be found. In a more radical vein, Soka Gakkai makes an advance which bears upon many recent post-humanist discussions in promoting a form of cosmic humanism which is Buddhist in inspiration but clearly of wide purtenance.

It is important to note that the valuable aspects of these cognitive materials tend to be made known as a result of interpretative commentaries and thematizations provided by leaders of these movements, and also by the sometimes formidable intellectuals and scholars who join these movements. These intellectuals generate literature that attempts to relate them to recent scholarship and intellectual trends in the wider world. This literature is often richer than much of the scholarship suggests and supports my claim that the cognitive materials provided by these movements should be taken seriously. I do not, of course, suggest that the interpretations and thematizations such scholars propose should be accepted uncritically or read without regard to their frequent apologetic intent.

All of these movements insist on the need for *spiritual practices* that require individuals to exert disciplined effort in order to achieve moral and physical regeneration, and many of them hold out hopes for emergent cognition, perception and transformed dreaming. The range of spiritual practices they require members to engage in varies from movement to movement. Spiritual practices are important both because they may provide members with powerful spiritual experiences and because they may go to the relative absence of developed spiritualities in Western societies. Precisely because such practices may be portable or at least translatable into less confessional terms, they may provide some of what is chronically lacking in political and social movements in the West.

I do not show in these studies that the spiritual practices I discuss have this potential, although well-known research on monastic practices and forms of meditation and mindfulness establishes the point to some degree. To differentiate different cases, I distinguish between esoteric practices that are alleged to change the minds and bodies of members and are often associated with emergent capacities, and exoteric practices, which mainly aim at the formation of the self as well as to community and identity formation. I suggest that the practices these movements promote go to possible ways of strengthening mental health and well-being in Western societies and also to spirituality which has a definite communal character. Once again, I am interested in the utopian intentionality of these practices. I do not analyse or advocate any specific spiritual practice, although there is a well-known medical basis for taking seriously both meditation and community dancing. I also note that experiences of the effectiveness of spiritual practices may be a motive for some members accepting the cosmosophies these movements also provide.

The *contributions* made by these movements to a very large number of areas are more substantial than much of the literature implies. Many of these movements are ethically activist, and advance innovative approaches to education, media, popular culture, social reform, economics, agriculture, health and nutrition. These innovations are often either portable or suggestive of possible alterations to current organization and practice. Some of these movements are actively involved in trying to help refugees, prisoners, drug addicts and the mentally ill, while struggling to modernize their own operations in other respects. None engage at an advanced level with the contemporary sciences, although some of them attempt to do so. None of these movements, with the partial exception of Soka Gakkai through its Toda Institute, has a developed approach to international relations. Three movements (Brahma Kumaris, Soka Gakkai, the Bahá'ís) see themselves as heavily involved in *work for peace*, but only Soka Gakkai has had a major international impact by opposing Japanese rearmament and nuclear weapons through its political party, the Komeito. Other movements also produce publications and media materials or even, in the case of the Brahma Kumaris, ten million signatures for peace.

In the same way, several of these movements agitate for *political, social, legal and economic reform*. None of these movements has made an uncontestable contribution to political reform, although several of them engage with political reform at various levels. Several of these movements campaign for global citizenship and global governance. Soka Gakkai works for these goals through the United Nations and Ikeda's annual peace proposals. The Bahá'ís are pioneers of a global civilization which they envisage in radically prosocial terms. To this end, they promote various forms of concrete utopianism aiming at the reform of political, social and economic and cultural life. Drawing on their philosophy of history and their evolutionary conception of religions as vehicles for the education of humanity, they reframe religion as education for lifelong learning to promote the cultural and social development of humanity. Their political and legal institutions and organizational and administrative forms, provide models of reformed arrangements which are not based on hierarchy, exclusion, conflict or competition. The Bahá'ís also advocate specific changes to achieve global governance, including political arrangement without parties, campaigning or mimetic rivalry. Again, while several of these movements are recognized as NGOs by the United Nations, only the Bahá'ís agitate for a universal language, a universal court of arbitration, a world currency and a world military force. The Bahá'ís also promote the ideal of a unification of humanity that will include and reconcile all peoples, races, religions and genders and the overcoming of all national, religious, racial and economic divisions. Only one of these movements, the Bahá'ís, are involved in legal reform and in their case there are tensions between more traditional legal regimes and more modern approaches.

Ananda Marga, in contrast, advances reform proposals which are much more systematic. It has a developed political and economic utopia, Prout, based on a South East Asian perspective and a strong preference for localism allied to a sense of place. Ananda Marga proposes a new cooperative economic system designed to transcend both capitalism and communism for which spirituality is central. It is also envisages the transcendence of the Western domination of the world, while fully embracing future technologies in the context of a radically transhumanist futurism. Ananda Marga's utopia remains, however, largely unrealized even in Bengal. Surprisingly, the Latter-day Saints may perhaps have the capacity to make a major contribution to political and social thought on the basis of revelations to Joseph about a possible new political and social order involving the redistribution of wealth and a cooperative economic system. However, as yet they have not done so.

These movements also make contributions to *social reform*, including specific microsocial advances such as an emphasis on group work and mentors in the case of Soka Gakkai, and the development of learning circles and educational institutes in the case of the Bahá'ís. Indeed, the radically prosocial reforms advocated by the Bahá'ís have resulted in actual alternative procedures and processes, concrete examples of development projects inspired by prosocial principles, as well as the promotion of egalitarian family life, inter-racial marriage and non-sectarian spirituality. Major initiatives for the emancipation of women are proposed by Ananda Marga as well.

Several of these movements also provide detailed models for *alternative organizations of the economy and agriculture*. Most of these movements contend for some form of economic reform, but only Ananda Marga has a fully developed economic utopia. The Bahá'ís, however, are clear that economic life must be reformed on spiritual and moral principles. Two movements, the Brahma Kumaris and Ananda Marga, promote agricultural utopianism and three of these movements, Ananda Marga, the Brahma Kumaris and the Bahá'ís, make contributions to cooperative economics.

Educational reform is also central to many of these movements. Soka Gakkai and Ananda Marga both develop new pedagogies of international importance. Models for alternative holistic education are provided by Soka Gakkai, Ananda Marga and in another way by the Church Universal and Triumphant. The Church Universal and Triumphant stands for a form of educational reform by making previously arcane knowledges available on the internet and engaging in extensive cultural education of those associated with it, something also found in the literature and cultural activities of Soka Gakkai. These innovations would not be necessary if citizens in most societies already received adequate cultural education or were not barred from certain types of learning by economic considerations. Because pedagogic practices are highly portable, Ananda Marga has been able to export its educational utopias to several parts of South East Asia.

Several of these movements are also working for *medical reform*, often in developing societies, sometimes coloured by revivals of traditional medicines. Ananda Marga and the Brahma Kumaris are both active in this area, while the Latter-day Saints also possess revealed knowledge about diet and health. Outsiders tend not to take such knowledge seriously, even though Latter-day Saints live longer than most other Americans.

Many of these movements also make contributions to *cultural reform*. All these movements generate cultural productivity of greater significance than might be expected, albeit sometimes admixed with revivals of older cultural practices. Specifically, they contribute to the arts, including poetry, novels, theatre, dance, sculpture and painting. Two movements, the Bahá'ís and the Latter-day Saints, make major contributions to sacred architecture. There is also evidence of musical creativity, including Sakar's 6,000 songs and the songs of the Brahma Kumaris.

Again, all of these movements contribute, albeit in very different ways, to *spiritual or religious reform*. The reform of spirituality and religion more generally is proposed by all these movements and most of them suggest that reliance on more powerful spiritual practices can replace an obsession with propositional beliefs. The Latter-day Saints are especially radical in their expectation of personal revelation, while Soka Gakkai makes a contribution by seeking to reframe and humanize religion so that it comes to mean meeting the needs of people and finding solutions to the problems of humanity.

All of these movements accept the need for some form of *religious reform*. Strikingly, only the Brahma Kumaris insist on an ordered lifestyle for surrendered members, just as only Ananda Marga has monks and nuns. The Latter-day Saints also contribute to possible religious reform by having no trained clergy, no theologians in a strict sense and no agreement about how their doctrinal innovations should be interpreted. They are also active in dialogue with Islam. Ecumenism is a fundamental concern for the Bahá'ís, although their claim to supersede Islam makes it difficult to pursue in practice. The Bahá'ís, however, open up the horizon of a unification of all so-called religions on the basis of a new religious relativism. In the immediate term, they argue that the various religions should all work together. They also attempt to revalue all Indigenous religions. Here their approach may gain more acceptance over time than initial responses might suggest.

All these movements exemplify to some extent a movement beyond historical religion towards forms of postreligion. Many of these movements raise the possibility that powerful spiritual practices can displace the role played by allegedly religious doctrines over previous centuries. In the case of the Brahma Kumaris, for example, it is the successful practice of Raja yoga which matters, rather than belief in the movement's conception of apocalypse. The same probably holds for the efficacy of decrees in the case of the Church Universal and Triumphant. Both Soka Gakkai and the Bahá'ís can be seen as anticipating a post-creedal spirituality, while the Bahá'ís are open to all spiritual traditions, including all Indigenous religions, which they alone of these movements work actively to rehabilitate. Some of these movements promote spiritual pluralism and inter-religious syncretism, but only the Bahá'ís fully adopt interpretative pluralism, although there are elements of religious republicanism in Soka Gakkai. Indeed, despite its origin as a narrow sect, Soka Gakkai combines cosmic humanism with spiritual republicanism in original ways. Some of these movements also develop alternatives to traditional houses of worship. Significantly the Brahma Kumaris now present themselves as World Spiritual University and run retreat centres, the Church Universal and Triumphant presents itself as Summit University Press, while Ananda Marga and the Bahá'ís run spiritual learning centres.

The Church Universal and Triumphant also has a radical side which has largely been overlooked. This is the Church's shift from propositional doctrines to performative spirituality for which truth claims about propositional content may not be central, possibly on postmodern premises, as well as the democratization of esotericism and counterfactuality more generally. Here again what emerges as a new feature of a spiritual movement may anticipate or cohere with a wider change in advanced cultures. Like the Church Universal and Triumphant, the Church of Jesus Christ of Latter-day Saints can seem more conservative than the other movements discussed. However, the two Christian churches are both creative in their own particular ways. The Church of Jesus Christ of Latter-day Saints advances a mass of innovative doctrines with utopian intentional meanings, including new accounts of creation, salvation, the church, grace, life after death. These innovations locate salvation in the universe and within the limits of a spiritual naturalism. The Latter-day Saints also provide new hope in the American context for eternal family life, progression and exaltation. They also deploy organizational excellence to achieve a communal as well as an individual spirituality, a precedent which may be relevant to future spiritual reform.

There is also what might be called a post-secular side to many of these movements. Some of these movements challenge the exteriorism of modern secularism. The Latter-day Saints, for example, pose a major challenge to Western secularism in their care for the dead and their revival of temples as sacred sites achieving a recovery of sacred space in the midst of the secular desert. Some of these movements directly challenge secularization as an adequate basis for civilization and propose instead sacralized time and space. Here the Latter-day Saints are outstanding with their care for the dead and their revival of temples as sacred and enclosed spaces where mysteries are enacted. The Baháʼí temples are also beautiful and open to all, as opposed to mystery sites where secret doctrines are taught and secret rituals and covenants are sealed.

The relevance of these movements to reform in the area of *organizational form* is more contestable. As we have seen, several of these movements have developed new organizational forms and arrangements. All these movements, however, tend to have problems of leadership succession and generational change, often because they tend to cling to older organizational forms and arrangements which limit their achievements.

All this suggests that a balance needs to be drawn between recognizing the large number of reform proposals made by these movements and the smaller number of areas in which they have achieved concrete reforms on the ground. Ananda Marga and the Brahma Kumaris have achieved on the ground reforms in parts of India in areas such as education, medicine and agriculture, while the Latter-day Saints have achieved concrete reforms in some areas of Latter-day Saint life, including in the areas of welfare provision in the state of Utah, and in the crucial area of family life in Latin America and the Pacific. It would be misleading, however, to suggest that proposals that are not realized are without value. In some cases, such proposals may depend on additional developments in the wider world to bring them to general attention. Scientific advances, for example, could make Ananda Marga's microvitas part of ordinary life, just as such advances are already spreading attitudes worldwide to non-human sentient life that are compatible with the visionary philosophy Sarkar proposed under the title Neohumanism. In the same way, it is possible that ethical changes already underway will lead to a greater reception over time of Makiguchi's ethics of value creation, as promoted by Soka Gakkai. Indeed, there are already many areas such as euthanasia where traditional ethical stances based on an allegedly anterior natural order are being replaced by more value creative approaches.

Again, several of these movements are arguably relevant to the contemporary project of a prosocial ecological civilization. Even on a minimalist account, these movements show that an ecological civilization will need to address personal and social ecologies as well as natural ecologies, and that there is merit in holistic approaches which bring different aspects of life into interaction, even if the way that this is done may be contestable. It is also fair to note that three of these movements (Soka Gakkai, Ananda Marga and the Bahá'ís) actively promote the ethical and organizational ideal of a global ecological civilization, although only the Bahá'ís provide detailed institutional and administrative arrangements by which to get there. The Bahá'ís are also exceptional in their rejection not only of discriminations based on race, class and gender, but also of hierarchy in all organizational forms. Ecological concerns are central to Soka Gakkai, Ananda Marga and the Bahá'í, but not to the two Christian churches discussed. Ananda Marga stands out here with its concretely realized global eco-village network.

This is not to deny that these movements may have features that set limits to their relevance to political, social and cultural reform, despite their own good intentions. All these movements might be characterized as conservative in some respects. Both the Church Universal and Triumphant and the Latter-day Saints have obvious conservative features, not least in the areas of economics and politics. There is also a conservative side to the Bahá'ís, who are more tied to Middle Eastern models than their more modernist members suggest. Soka Gakkai too has a conservative Japanese side, including an authoritarian chain of command of which Westerners are often unaware. Both the Brahma Kumaris and Ananda Marga are also more conservative in India than their global outreach suggests. Again, all of these movements have problematic political features, including leadership not subject to explicit rational controls and/or opaque governance. All these movements claim to be compassionate and contemporary minded, but no movement cooperates extensively with any other. It is also fair to conclude that many of these movements have not found as yet the best organizational forms by means of which to give their good intentions real-world effect in the longer term.

None of this detracts from the main upshot of these studies: the uncovering and revaluing of the creativity of six spiritual movements which has been underestimated in the past. To find not only creativity, but creativity potentially relevant to reform in these movements may seem controversial as long as these movements are mainly seen as irrational and possibly dangerous. Such a view may have merit, depending on the case. However, once the degree of creativity found in these spiritual movements is recognized, then an argument can be made for a disaggregative approach in other cases as well.

Appendix

Latter-day Saint Doctrinal Innovations

Introduction

The Latter-day Saints have generated a vast number of innovations of doctrinal innovations from their cognitive materials. I discuss these in some detail in this appendix. Attending to Latter-day Saint doctrinal innovations is not the same as studying the beliefs of individual Latter-day Saints. Depending on the example, the general church membership may have only a limited knowledge of such innovations and/or may not understand them in way that they are understood by Church intellectuals. Indeed, it is clear that there are significant differences between the way these doctrines have been received by believers generally in various periods and the way they have been thematized by intellectuals professionally concerned with such matters. Of course, this holds true for the Catholic, Orthodox and Protestant churches as well.

Firstly, the Latter-day Saints have one or more *alternativist conceptions of God*, conceptions that differ significantly from the theistic conception the Christian Church developed when it adopted Greek philosophy and the notion of a timeless perfect being.[1] These conceptions take time to unravel and are not always central to more popular understandings of the teachings of the Church. Latter-day Saints hold that God the Father is a real person, and in some sense cosmologically immanent as well as transcendent, even perhaps the maximal exemplification of laws and qualities applying to all intelligences. Latter-day Saint scholars distinguish between 'the Godhead', 'God' and 'gods', and are not agreed among themselves on how these terms should be construed. On sophisticated accounts, the Latter-day Saint Godhead is a unity of persons, and a locus which can be occupied by different personages worshipped as one.[2] This interpretation allows some Latter-day Saints to be neo-polytheists, while others are monotheists who admit plurality within the divine. On a very literal interpretation there are three Gods, entirely separate and distinct hierarchically ranked centres of will, 'other' to each other. On this account, the Father is an exalted man, who once lived as a mortal on an Earth. He has a glorified body of flesh and bones as tangible as a human being's body.[3]

The central claim that God has a body is bound to remain controversial, even when it is spelt out in genealogical terms.[4] Thus, the Father Himself had a Father, and each Father also had a Father. Moreover, both the Father and the Son have glorified bodies of flesh and bones. Christ, like the Father, is a physical being. He was not begotten of the Holy Spirit, but was a man subordinate to the Father. The Holy Spirit is less clearly characterized. It is said that the Holy Spirit has only a spiritual body,[5] although the Holy Spirit also has the form of a man, and is a spirit son of the Father.[6] Alternatively it is sometimes suggested that the Holy Spirit is feminine. Faced with these unusual teachings, Latter-day Saints have justification to subtleties, such as Brigham Young's reference to the God 'with whom we have to do', and later suggestions that God may have His attributes as the eternal Father contingently, or only be omnipotent in dimensions of which we have knowledge. Others suggest that the Father is material but not corporeal.

In the context of worship, Latter-day Saints use the term 'God' for an all-powerful and eternal being on whom we can rely, although, following a revelation to Joseph, the term 'gods' is used for the Council of Gods called together by the head god' to create the world.[7] Gods in this sense are lower-level divinities, like 'the gods' mentioned in the Old Testament.[8] Latter-day Saints, however, also use the term 'gods' for human beings who through *apotheosis* are being made divine (D&C 76:58). In this sense, Latter-day Saints teach that all human beings may become 'gods'. Nonetheless, Latter-day Saint scholars insist that in the Latter-day Saint scriptures humans are always subordinate to the Father, the Son and the Holy Ghost, and are never pictured as worthy of worship. Indeed, Blake Ostler has written at length against modalist interpretations of Mormon theism and in favour of a social Trinitarianism closer to Christian orthodoxy. Nonetheless, the Saints themselves accept that it is difficult to reconcile Joseph's plural theology with the councils of Nicaea and Chalcedon.[9]

In effect, Latter-day Saints have at least two distinct theological traditions: a less orthodox tradition, based on the teachings of Joseph Smith and Brigham Young,[10] and a more orthodox tradition, based on the directions of recent Church leaders, exemplified by President Benson, with the great majority of Saints following the latter.[11] According to the less orthodox tradition, Latter-day Saints worship a finite temporal God who is subject to time and space, although some contest this by referring to Alma 40:8 in *The Book of Mormon*. On this account, God is not the uncaused first cause of classical theism, a perfect being characterized by aseity, incorporeality and metaphysical simplicity, but a complex, progressive, co-existent finite being who operates within the constraints of natural law. He did not create all things. Nor is He absolutely transcendent or independent of the universe. Instead, God is located in space and time. Nor is He absolute or omniscient in all respects (there are limits to His knowledge of future contingents), all-powerful or impassable. Rather God has a range of very human attributes and suffers (Moses 7:44).[12] On this view, the world will never be finished, and the future is as real for God as for his children. The totality of reality has always existed.[13]

The more orthodox tradition, in contrast, attempts to reconcile Joseph's plural theology with a view of the Latter-day Saint God as the one eternal God of the universe.[14] In this context, some Latter-day Saint scholars now argue that Joseph did not mean to teach polytheism or the existence of deities with distinct spheres of sovereignty. On this view, Latter-day Saints accept plurality within the Godhead, but not polytheism. In more recent times, the Church has tended to assimilate Mormonism to Protestant neo-Orthodoxy, as theorized by Protestant theologians such as Karl Barth. The main emphasis then falls on *The Book of Mormon,* read as a neo-Protestant text. The plural theology is not abandoned (it still appears in the *Doctrine and Covenants* and in temple ceremonies), but it receives less emphasis in presentations to non-believers. It is also construed as consistent with Protestant neo-Orthodox Christian theology by Church apologists, such as Robert Millet and Stephen Robinson, who accept only what is canonical and current Church doctrine.[15] Earlier Church teaching, including the explicit teaching of Church Presidents as well as the *Lectures on Faith* (1835), approved by Joseph, but probably written by Sidney Rigdon, is finessed. Given these uncertainties, some Latter-day Saint writers are now attempting to rethink the Church's theology in radically contemporary terms.[16] The fact that the Saints have no agreed creed, and do not agree among themselves on the meaning of central terms,[17] has its positive side, however, and has helped the Saints develop new versions of major Christian doctrines.[18]

The Latter-day Saints also have their own *Christology.* For Latter-day Saints Jesus was Jehovah, and actively involved in the events of the Old Testament.[19] Then, while Latter-day Saints emphasize that Jesus Christ reveals who God is, they interpret this to mean that the Father is like the man Jesus, whereas orthodox Christianity takes the man Jesus to be the icon of the invisible God. Latter-day Saint scholars are divided between those who make Jesus an androgenous divine being, and those who regard him as a divine *man* who exerts power, sweats blood in the garden of Gethsemane and was sexually active, both while on earth and in the spirit world.[20] On the latter view, Jesus acquires activist characteristics as the son of an immortal father and a mortal mother, and he cannot be killed unless he consents to his fate. As a cosmic being Jesus is the creator of this world, and also of many other worlds. There are also references to seeing the pre-mortal body of Christ. Latter-day Saints tend to insist that Jesus is of the same species as ourselves and refer to Jesus as our elder brother. On the other hand, Jesus is pre-existent and active in the Old Testament. There are also hints of a universal Christology for which Jesus radiates as an energy in all things.[21] All this sits strangely with the less orthodox older view that Jesus and the Father are both physical beings made up of flesh and bones, and the Father lived on 'a world like this' before he became God. The Holy Spirit, in contrast, is a personage but does not have a physical Body. Understandably the Trinity is a complex topic for Latter-day Saints, although they seek to avoid tri-modalism.[22]

Latter-day Saints also have *a different conception of grace*. Godhead is a gift of grace, not given by human nature, and grace heightens God's knowability. Latter-day Saints also have *a revised conception of sin*. For Latter-day Saints human beings are ultimately good, and responsible for their own sins, not Adam's. Hence there is no need to baptise little children. Joseph himself taught that human beings were eternally existent, inherently innocent and infinitely perfectible. Accordingly, Mormon scholars interpret the Fall as a happy event, although they now allow more of a role for personal sin than formerly, and no longer always reject original sin entirely. They do, however, reject predestination, and do not emphasize the imputed righteousness versions of the atonement.

Latter-day Saints also have *a distinctive conception of salvation*. They posit three heavens and only observant Mormons will be admitted to the highest celestial heaven. Nonetheless, God will save many holy men and women outside the Mormon faith, and all will have a chance to hear and accept the Gospel, and the morality of their lives will matter, not the formal correctness of their theological beliefs. Unlike traditional Christians, they teach salvation by works, although exaltation requires grace. Latter-day Saints also argue for a stronger version of free will or free agency than that found in Augustine. For Latter-day Saints free will is the power to do otherwise, and this strong libertarianism is central to their theology and ethics, which are characterized by optimism about daily life. Latter-day Saints are also largely free of the traditional Christian dualism. They are epistemological optimists, and devoted more than many other Christians to the natural sciences.[23] Latter-day Saints introduce *a new level of salvation known as exaltation*, in which human beings become 'gods', and acquire the glory of the Father. In this context, they emphasize *eternal progression*, and an eternal life for families who have received the Temple ordinances. More recently exaltation has been assimilated by Latter-day Saint writers to *theosis* or becoming like God in the tradition of the Orthodox churches.[24] However, Latter-day Saints understand this to mean that individuals can quite literally come to acquire the attributes of the Father. They speak of an *apotheosis* as a result of which humans share *the same divinity* as the divine persons. On the Latter-day Saint view, human beings can become divine *in the same sense* as Christ.[25] Accordingly, Joseph expanded the notion of Godhead so that human beings could possess the divine attributes and participate in God's own power, knowledge and glory.[26]

Latter-day Saints also have *an expanded understanding of revelation* based on a *reassertion of religious literality*. In contrast to conceptions of revelation based on symbolism and the sublime for which the literal sense of religious claims is often uncertain, Latter-day Saints believe that God gives exact directions to Church members, including, in stories in the *Book of Mormon*, directions for war and hunting. Further, the words of Genesis are to be taken literally. The originality of all this is easily missed. As Terryl Givens observes, there is a lack of a clear distinction between transcendent and phenomenal which collapses the sacral distance at the heart of Western religion, and results in a rendering physical and literal of what the Christian Churches had tended to make otherworldly.[27] Indeed, there is an eruption of the everyday into the holy, evident in elision of any strong distinction between body and spirit. Even if this eruption is not quite a new religious imagination, it implies a continuity between the natural and the divine. Consistent with this, revelation can be practical and mundane. Thus, Latter-day Saints have *a revealed law of health*, based on dietary indications and the proscription of hot drinks (in effect alcohol, coffee and tea),[28] as well as *a revealed system of Church administration* through which they have institutionalized their founding charisms.

Then, unlike other Christians, Latter-day Saints claim to possess modern revelation. For them revelation is continuing and the heavens are open. Post-Biblical revelation has occurred in the life of Joseph and can occur again in the future when according to the *Articles of Faith* God will reveal many great and important things pertaining to his Kingdom. For Latter-day Saints God is again speaking from Heaven, as in Biblical times. Thus, the church leader Bruce R. McConkie claimed to have heard the voice of the Lord in the upper room of the Salt Lake temple telling President Kimball that Afro-Americans could be priests. Here the innovation in doctrine is creative because it frees the Saints from being tied to historical revelations in the past, as Jews, Christians and Muslims tend to be. Latter-day Saints also assume that revelation can encompass almost anything, and include in revelation not only covenantal mysteries, but practical advice about the management of human life, including the need to have a store of food in every house. Their notion of revelation is dialogical, in the sense that what is revealed responds to questions asked. This means that for the Latter-day Saints, as for the Bahá'ís, there is a degree of relativism at the heart of revelation.

Again, for Latter-day Saints personal revelation is normal. At an individual level there is the expectation that everyone can receive revelation, when and as they need it. At a communal level, instances of revelation are qualified by the awareness that there is further revelation to come. It follows that the authority of the Bible is limited, and that theological doctrines can change as the community learns, especially since the bulk of gold plates are still to be revealed and translated. Joseph himself taught that the Bible was not perfect or complete, but a stepping stone to future revelations, and this allows Latter-day Saints to free themselves from the traditional Christian conception of the Bible as a quasi-infallible text to which Christians should unfailingly refer for guidance. On this view, it is possible for Latter-day Saints to understand prophecy as binding, but also as continuing, fallible and specific.

Latter-day Saints also have *a non-standard conception of faith* as the power by which God acts, a part of the capacity for reason which He has shared with humans.[29] God commands by virtue of the faith He has in Himself, and the chaos responds in faith to Him. For Latter-day Saints, faith is a positive attribute of a divine being, not a condition lower than knowledge. However, despite the existence of the *Articles of Faith*, Latter-day Saints lack a coherently formulated and stable set of beliefs which one must accept in order to be saved.[30] Further, although the Church has doctrines, there is no developed Latter-day Saint creed. Consistent with this, Latter-day Saints do not hold heresy trials, and are not anxious about the opinions of individuals on secondary matters, although they do hold apostasy trials and excommunicate those who go beyond the limits. Overall, there is a surprising diversity of views, and a tendency to regard many matters as 'still open' because not the subject of specific revelation, even though a much narrower range of positions are raised in Church services. There is no determinate revelation explaining what Latter-day Saint doctrines and practices mean.

Latter-day Saints also have *a different conception of Church*. Unlike Protestants, Latter-day Saints associate the Church with the restoration of the fullness of the Gospel after historical Christianity succumbed to the apostasy of Hellenization. Unlike many other Restorationists, however, Latter-day Saints hold that the Church existed from the creation.[31] Since the Church is eternal, there is little sense among Latter-day Saints that ancient practices might be inappropriate to current evolutions of consciousness. Latter-day Saints believe that their Church is the Ancient Church restored after apostasy.[32] Some Latter-day Saint scholars now argue, however, that their religion is closer to Qumran than to Hellenized Christianity. They also explore parallels with the Old Testament *pseudepigrapha*, including the Apocryphon of Ezekiel, with the Jewish Christianity rejected by St Paul, with Gnostic texts long excluded from the Christian canon, and with the theosophical and cosmological religion of early Egyptian Christianity.

The Latter-day Saint Church is hierarchical and has married bishops with the power to hear confession and as well as three levels of priesthood, Aaronic, Melchizedek and Patriarchal, with powers to bless, lay on hands and give communion. Latter-day Saints have a laicist approach to priesthood and the priesthood is exercised by all adult males. There is no separate clerical caste. As a result, the Church has a less dualistic laity than other churches. Women, however, have no direct role in the Church's ecclesiastical hierarchy, although under the direction of President Russell M. Nelson it is now taught that men and women may equally receive the priesthood power, and it seems likely that further revisions to patriarchy will be made in the future.

The Latter-day Saints also have *a different account of creation*. There is no creation *ex nihilo*. Rather the present physical creation is a copy of an earlier spiritual creation. Human beings are as spirits before birth,[33] and there are spirits in the universe waiting for bodies. According to Joseph, God the Father resides near the planet Kolob, the central dynamo from which the rest of the galaxy receives its light and power, and there will be a death and resurrection of the earth, when the earth will receive its celestial glory.[34]

Other original aspects of Latter-day Saint theology can be construed as *compensations* for *the inadequacies of modern secular life*, concrete innovations that respond to unaddressed needs in modern cultures. Thus, the Latter-day Saints provide *a detailed account of life after death*. This account, possibly of Swedenborgian derivation, details three heavens (celestial, terrestrial and telestial) and also includes a milder conception of hell. Latter-day Saint positivity here is consistent with the Church's emphasis on eternal progression from premortal existence to the state of glory, a state restricted to those sealed by the priesthood. For Latter-day Saints, the reality of these destinations is confirmed by spiritual experiences of both the prenatal and the postmortal spirit worlds. Moreover, it is reinforced by special garments worn in the Temple and after Temple endowment and for burial. After death the individual has no body, but still progresses and interacts with others. At the resurrection the matter of their earthly body and spiritual matter are united in a new perfect body. Those who reach the highest stage after death will experience *exaltation* and become gods. That is, they will receive all the attributes of the Father. The mixture of ecclesiastical legalism and mysticism here goes beyond the Masonic background with which it is sometimes associated.

Because Latter-day Saint theology changes, it is not seen as a problem that President John Taylor (1808–87) tended to adopt neo-orthodox Protestant theology, including the satisfaction model of atonement, even though President Brigham Young had rejected it. Likewise, the twenty-six-volume *Journal of Discourses* is not currently taken as a source of authoritative doctrine. Latter-day Saint miracles are also less common than they were in the nineteenth century, when reports of Joseph's healings, stories of hundreds of people of hearing rushing wind and seeing angels at the dedication of the Kirtland Temple, descriptions by eye-witnesses of the transformed visage of Brigham Young and accounts of the Miracle of the Gulls were standard, although there is still a preternatural hush associated with Joseph and the present apostles.[35] From a Latter-day Saint perspective, all this is consistent with the Church's reliance on contemporary dialogical revelation for direction rather than on historical documents or past statements by Church leaders.

Conclusion

The doctrinal innovations of the Latter-day Saints deserve more attention than they have received, especially as sources revealing utopian intentionality. Much of the literature passes over these doctrines in some embarrassment or else devotes attention to whether such innovations can be reconciled with the Bible or with Evangelical Christianity. My discussion restores these innovations as examples of serious cultural productivity, to which those concerned with political, social and cultural concerns might well pay attention, not least because these innovations may contain model ideas. At the very least Latter-day Saint doctrinal innovations imply that the immanence-transcendence distinction needs to be rethought, that the relationship between religion and science needs to be recast in more cosmological terms, that immaterialism may be an inadequate basis for Christian theology, that traditional Christianity has failed to take seriously the humanity of Jesus Christ, that personal revelation should play a greater role in Christian spirituality and that there is a case for admitting continual revelation, however that is to be construed.

Glossary of Technical Terms

Adventist	Expecting the coming of the end of the world or a new prophet
Apotheosis	Elevation to divine status
Charismatic	Used here in a theological sense emphasizing personal experience of revelation or the divine
concrete utopia	Technical term from Ernst Bloch, a partial realization of utopia in real life or human experience
cosmic historicism	Doctrine that history reflects cosmic patterns and always passes through the same phases
cosmic humanism	A humanism that identifies the human being with the universe
cosmosophy	An enchanted account of the universe; here a contrast term to cosmology
counter-factual	Relating to states of affairs not found in ordinary life
disaggregative	An approach that breaks up into elements or features
dualist	Dividing into two separate and often opposed parts
esoteric	Arcane or secret, not open to public view
exoteric	Open to public view, externally visible, not secret
fantastic	Material imaginary as opposed to subjective fantasy without a realization in the real world
fictionality	The characteristic of being fictional especially without a negative valorization of this characteristic
futurist	Expecting a very different world still to come
generic concept of religion	An approach that assumes that different instances of the religious fall under a single concept or genus
hermeneutics	A method or principle of interpretation
historical sociology	Application of sociological categories to historical materials
intentional meaning	What is objectively intended regardless of the intentions of the particular actors concerned, for example, a dam is a way of holding back water
Messianism	Mentality that expects a Messiah
model ideas	Thought experiments with portable features relevant to other contexts
moderate naturalism	Version of naturalism that avoids strong reductionism and recognizes the need for second as well as third person standpoints

modernist	Attempting to keep up with contemporary developments
nominalism	tendency to treat items as particular and arbitrary versus realism which assumes that there are recurrent features reflecting structural constraints
occulture	Technical term for trends in occult undergrounds or fringe popular culture
Pelagian	Theological term, tending to assert human goodness and free will
Performative	Having the character of something performed such as a play
philosophical anthropology	Philosophical account or doctrine of the human being
positivity	Term from Hegel, doctrines and practices accepted on the authority of spiritual traditions as opposed to doctrines and practices founded on reason
postreligious	Coming after historical religion in a way that drops some of the latter's features
postsecular	Coming after the secular in a way that asserts the value of the sacred while accepting the need for secularity in political and economic life
preternatural	Beyond the natural, often with the implication that the phenomena are part of the ontological order rather than supernatural
projective imagination	Imaginative contents or features thrown onto the world or events
prosocial	Conduct or behaviour benefiting other people or society as a whole
social holism	The attempt to account for social order by properties other than those attributable to individuals
spiritual republicanism	An approach privileging the autonomy and agency of the individual in spiritual matters
Tantra	Hindu and Buddhist practical methods to realize the divine
Teleological	Tending to an end that can be specified in advance
Thaumaturgic	The working of magic or miracles
Theosophy	Doctrines that imply that the spiritual world can be known by natural means
tri-modalism	Doctrine that the divine exists in three separate modes
utopian intentionality	The possibility of construing something as relevant to utopia, for example, a piece of music or a building or a social experiment
veridiction	True according to a particular authority rather than independently true

Notes

Chapter 1

1. For an attempt to theorize reform in terms of immanent critique, see Rahel Jaeggi, *Critique of Forms of Life*, trans. Ciaran Cronin (Cambridge, MA: Harvard University Press, 2018).
2. See, for example, R. T. McCutcheon, *Manufacturing Religion: The Discourse on Sui Generis Religion and the Politics of Nostalgia* (New York and Oxford: Oxford University Press, 1997); T. Fitzgerald, *Discourse on Civility and Barbarity: A Critical History of Religion and Related Categories* (New York and Oxford: Oxford University Press, 2007); D. Dubuisson, *The Western Construction of Religion: Myths, Knowledge, and Ideology*, trans. William Sayers (Baltimore: The Johns Hopkins University Press, 2003). Cf. Christopher R. Cotter and David G. Robertson eds., *After World Religions: Reconstructing Religious Studies* (New York: Routledge, 2016).
3. For discussion, see W. Hudson, *The Marxist Philosophy of Ernst Bloch* (London and New York: Macmillan, 1982) espec. chs 2 and 3, *The Reform of Utopia* (London: Ashgate, 2003) and 'Bloch and a Philosophy of the Proterior' in P. Thompson and S. Žižek eds., *Ernst Bloch and the Privatisation of Hope* (Durham and London: Duke University Press, 2013) ch. 1; *The Reform of Utopia* (London: Ashgate, 2003); *Australian Religious Thought* (Clayton: Monash University Publishing, 2016).
4. See W. Hudson, *The English Deists: Studies in Early Enlightenment* (London: Pickering and Chatto, 2009) and *Enlightenment and Modernity: The English Deists and Reform* (London: Pickering and Chatto, 2009).
5. Here my work is indebted to the pioneering perspectives of Eileen Barker. See E. Barker ed. *New Religious Movements* (Lewiston, NY: Edwin Mellen Press, 1982) and ed. *Of Gods and Men: New Religious Movements in the West* (Macon, GA: Mercer University Press, 1983) and *The Making of a Moonie: Choice or Brainwashing?* (Oxford and New York, NY: B. Blackwell, 1984).
6. Among a vast and varied literature, see I. Hexham, and K. Poewe, *New Religions as Global Cultures: Making the Human Sacred* (Boulder, CO: Westview Press, 1997); P. B. Clarke, *New Religions in Global Perspective: Religious Change in the Modern World* (London: Routledge, 2005); Christopher Partridge ed., *New Religions: A Guide: New Religious Movements, Sects and Alternative Spiritualities* (New York: Oxford University Press, 2004); D. Daske and W. Ashcraft eds., *New Religious*

Movements: A Documentary Reader (New York: New York University Press, 2005); G. D. Chryssides and M. Z. Wilkins eds., *A Reader in New Religious Movements* (London: Continuum, 2006); Carole Cusack and Alex Norman, eds., *Handbook of New Religions and Cultural Production* (Leiden: Brill, 2012); Olav Hammer and Mikael Rothstein eds., *The Cambridge Companion to New Religious Movements* (Cambridge: Cambridge University Press, 2012); David Morgan, *The Embodied Eye: Religious Visual Culture and the Social Life of Feeling* (Berkeley: University of California Press, 2012); Paul Oliver, *New Religious Movements: A Guide for the Perplexed* (London and New York: Continuum, 2012); G. D. Chryssides and B. E. Zeller eds., *The Bloomsbury Companion to New Religious Movements* (London and New York: Bloomsbury, 2014); J. R. Lewis and J. A. Petersen eds., *Controversial New Religions* (Oxford: Oxford University Press, 2014); J. R. Lewis and J. Tolefsen eds., *The Oxford Handbook of New Religious Movements* (Oxford: Oxford University Press, 2004 and 2016) 2 vols; W. Michael Ashcraft, *A Historical Introduction to the Study of New Religious Movements* (London: Routledge, 2018).

7   Some of the sharpest discussion is to be found in journals such as Culture and Religion; *Nova Religio: The Journal of Alternative and Emergent Religions*; Alternative Spirituality and Religion Review; *Journal for Cultural and Religious Theory; The Journal of Contemporary Religion;* and the International Journal for the Study of New Religions. Some of the literature focuses on the notion that members of these movements are new believers, which gives priority to their alleged beliefs. See D. V. Barrett, *The New Believers: A Survey of Sects, Cults and Alternative Religions* (London: Cassell, 2001). Occasionally a study takes these beliefs seriously in their own terms. See, for example, M. F. Bednarowski, *New Religions and the Theological Imagination in America* (Bloomington: Indiana University Press, 1989).

8   See, for example, Hexham, and Poewe, *New Religions*; Clarke, *New Religions in Global Perspective* and Lewis and Petersen, *Controversial New Religions*.

9   See L. T. Sargent, *Utopianism: A Very Short Introduction* (Oxford: Oxford University Press, 2010).

10 For a classic study, see R. M. Kanter, *Commitment and Community: Communes and Utopias in Sociological Perspective* (Cambridge: Harvard University Press, 1972).

11 I. Kant, *Die Religion innerhalb der Grenzen der bloßen Vernunft* (Königsberg: Friedrich Nicolovius, 1793) trans. as T. Asad, *Reason within the Limits of Reason Alone* (New York: Harper and Row, 1960), trans. T. M. Greene and H. H. Hudson 76. The translation is unsatisfactory (*Grenzen* are borders or boundaries, not limits) but its defects are not relevant here.

12 G. F. Hegel, 'The Positivity of the Christian Religion', in *Early Theological Writings*, trans. T. M. Knox and Introduction and fragments trans. Richard Kroner (Chicago, IL: Chicago University Press, 1948), 67–181.

13 Cognitive science is increasingly used to offer a rational construal of practices previously regarded as irrational or esoteric. See, for example, *Aries: Journal for the Study of Western Esotericism,* 17, no.1 (2017) Special Issue: Esotericism and the Cognitive Science of Religion; Egil Asprem, *The Problem of Disenchantment: Scientific Naturalism and Esoteric Discourse,* 1900–1939 (Leiden: Brill, 2014) and Egil Asprem with Kennet Granholm eds., *Contemporary Esotericism* (Sheffield: Equinox, 2013). Related implications follow from conceiving of the mind in terms of embodied action. In the longer term these developments may lead to thinking differently about counterfactuality in general.

14 For older but classic discussion see Scott Atran, *In Gods We Trust: The Evolutionary Landscape of Religion* (New York: Oxford University Press, 2002) and Justin L. Barrett, 'Counterfactuality and Counterintuitive Concepts', in *Behaviour and Brain Sciences* 27, no. 6 (2004): 731–2.

15 Here René Girard's work much discussed, as is his association of the sacred with sacrifice. See R. Girard, *Violence and the Sacred,* trans. P. Gregory (Baltimore: Johns Hopkins University Press, 1977) and J. Meszaros and J. Zachhuber eds., *Sacrifice and Modern Thought* (Oxford: Oxford University Press, 2013).

16 D. Scott and C. Hirschkind, eds., *Powers of the Secular Modern: Talal Asad and His Interlocutors* (Stanford: Stanford University Press, 2006).

17 See G. Agamben, *The Highest Poverty: Monastic Rules and Forms-of-Life,* trans. Adam Kotsko (Stanford: Stanford University Press, 2013).

18 T. Asad, *Formations of the Secular: Christianity, Islam, Modernity* (Stanford: Stanford University Press, 2003) and T. Asad, *Genealogies of Religion: Discipline and Reasons of Power in Christianity and Islam* (Baltimore: Johns Hopkins University Press, 1993), and, in response, Scott and Hirschkind, eds., *Powers of the Secular Modern: Talal Asad and His Interlocutors.*

19 For detail on how Calvinism reorganized much of Protestant Europe, see Menna Prestwich, ed. *International Calvinism 1541–1715* (Oxford: Clarendon Press, 1986).

20 Ernst Bloch suggested ways in which cognitive materials from the past could be made relevant to contemporary developments. He showed, for example, that the sermons of Thomas Münzer could be made relevant to contemporary efforts to build a socialist society, that Pufendorf's work on natural law was relevant to the contemporary attempt to develop a Marxist theory of natural law, and that the thinkers he associated with the Aristotelian Left, including Averroes, Avicenna, Almarich of Bena, Avicebron and David of Dinant, provided crucial model ideas for a contemporary open materialism based on developing potentiality (*dynamei on*). See E. Bloch, *Thomas Münzer als Theologe der Revolution* (Munich: Kurt Wolf, 1921); E. Bloch, *Christian Thomasius: Ein deutscher Gelehrter ohne Misere* (East Berlin: Aufbau Verlag, 1953) and *Avicenna and the Aristotelian Left,* trans. Loren Goldman and Peter Thompson (New York: Columbia University Press, 2018).

21 See B. Latour, *On the Modern Cult of the Factish Gods* (Durham: Duke University Press, 2010). There is also a literature asserting that religion is largely fictional and that this fictionality may be empowering. See C. M. Cusack and P. Kosnáč eds., *Fiction, Invention and Hyper-reality: From Popular Culture to Religion* (London: Routledge, 2017) and F. Laruelle, *Christo-Fiction: The Ruins of Athens and Jerusalem*, trans. Robin Mackay (New York: Columbia University Press, 2015).
22 Bryan Turner emphasizes the need to think contemporary religion and globalization together and also the degree to which the state is enmeshed with religion in many societies. See B. Turner, *The Religious and the Political: A Comparative Sociology of Religion* (Cambridge: Cambridge University Press, 2013).
23 For more technical discussion of thought experiments in analytical philosophy, see T. Williamson, *The Philosophy of Philosophy* 2nd edition (Hoboken, NJ: Wiley, 2022).
24 My use of the term *model* here is coloured by the mathematical conception of a model as enabling the systematic description of something, the study of its elements and their effects, and the prediction of future behaviour.
25 For a major reassertion of fictionality in non-religious theology, see the controversial work of the French philosopher François Laruelle, *Christo-Fiction*.
26 For work on fictionality and religion, see Cusack and Kosnáč, *Fiction, Invention and Hyper-reality*.
27 Bohumil Fořt, *An Introduction to Fictional World Theory* (New York: Peter Lang, 2016), 201; Lubomir Doležel, 'Possible Worlds of Fiction and History', in *New Literary History* 29, no. 4 (1998): 785–809. A number of distinguished literary scholars have worked on fictionality, transfictionality and narratology. See, for example, Alice Bell and Marie-Laure Ryan eds., *Possible Worlds Theory and Contemporary Narratology* (Lincoln and London: University of Nebraska, 2019).
28 L. Doležel, *Heterocosmica: Fiction and Possible Worlds* (Baltimore: Johns Hopkins University Press, 1998). His semantics approach differs from the possible worlds theory of the American philosopher David Lewis, although Lewis's sophisticated modal logic approach is more influential in some of the later literature.
29 M. A. Davidsen, 'Fiction-based Religion: Conceptualising a New Category against History-based Religion and Fandom' in *Culture and Religion* 14, no. 4 (2013): 378–95.
30 C. M. Cusack, *Invented Religions: Imagination, Fiction and Faith* (Farnham, Surrey: Ashgate, 2010) and S. Sutcliffe and C. M. Cusack eds., *The Problem of Invented Religions* (London and New York: Routledge, 2016).
31 A. Possamai, *Sociology of Religion for Generations X and Y* (London: Equinox, 2009) and A. Possamai ed. *Handbook of Hyper-Real Religions* (Leiden: Brill, 2012).

32 See E. P. Pritchard, *Theories of Primitive Religion* (Oxford: Oxford University Press, 1965).
33 On Simmel, see D. P. Frisby, *Simmel and since: Essays on Georg Simmel's Social Theory* (London and New York: Routledge, 1992) and D. P. Frisby and M. Featherstone eds., *Simmel on Culture: Selected Writings* (London: Sage, 1998).
34 See M. Mann, *The Sources of Social Power: Volume 1, a History of Power from the Beginning to AD 1760* (Cambridge: Cambridge University Press, 1986); *The Sources of Social Power: Volume 2, the Rise of Classes and Nation States 1760–1914* (Cambridge: Cambridge University Press, 1993); *the Sources of Social Power: Volume 3, Global Empires and Revolution, 1890–1945* (Cambridge: Cambridge University Press, 2012) and *The Sources of Social Power: Volume 4, Globalizations, 1945–2011* (Cambridge: Cambridge University Press, 2012). Also J. A. Hall and R. Schroeder eds., *The Anatomy of Power: The Social Theory of Michael Mann* (Cambridge: Cambridge University Press, 2006).
35 See, among several books, Toby E. Huff, *The Rise of Early Modern Science Islam, China, and the West*, 3rd edn. (New York: Cambridge University Press, 2017). Huff explains failures to solve organizational problems in terms of the presence or absence of specific organizational forms.
36 Process sociology of the type influenced by Norbert Elias (1897–1990) may also offer some insights here. For figurational or process sociology, see J. Goudsblom, *Sociology in the Balance: A Critical Essay* (Oxford: Blackwell, 1977); F. Dépelteau and T. S. Landini eds., *Norbert Elias and Social Theory* (Basingstoke: Palgrave Macmillan, 2013).
37 The Russian philosopher Alexander Bogdanov (1873–1928) pioneered a universal organizational science applying to physical, mental and social phenomena and dealing with the organizational principles underlying all systems at the beginning of the twentieth century. See his, *Essays in Tektology: The General Science of Organization*, trans. George Gorelik (Seaside, CA: Intersystems Publications, 1980); Russian 1922. For discussion, see McKenzie Wark, *Molecular Red: Theory for the Anthropocene* (London: Verso, 2015) and Arran Gare, 'Aleksandr Bogdanov's History, Sociology and Philosophy of Science' in *Studies in History and Philosophy of Science Part A* 31, no. 2 (2000): 231–48. His ideas are now being revived in the context of current attempts to construe the universe as a self-organizing system.
38 Cf. Kanter, *Commitment and Community*. Kanter analyses her communes in terms of their organization rather than primarily in terms of their beliefs.
39 Christopher Partridge, 'Occulture Is Ordinary' in Egil Asprem with Kennet Granholm eds., *Contemporary Esotericism* (Sheffield: Equinox, 2013), 113–33. And *The Re-Enchantment of the West: Alternative Spiritualities, Sacralization, Popular Culture and Occulture* (London: T & T Clark International, 2004) 2 vols.
40 See Cusack and Norman, eds., *Handbook of New Religions and Cultural Production*.

Chapter 2

1. Although the background to the emergence of claims to new revelations is Islamic, there may also be Christian influences. Cf. Christopher Buck, *Paradise and Paradigm: Key Symbols in Persian Christianity and the Bahá'í Faith* (Albany, NY: State University of New York Press, 1999).
2. Denis MacEoin, *The Messiah of Shiraz: Studies in Early and Middle Babism* (Leiden: Brill, 2008).
3. Denis MacEoin, *The Sources for Early Bábí Doctrine and History: A Survey* (Leiden: Brill, 1992).
4. For the wider background, see E. G. Browne, *Materials for the Study of the Bábí Religion* (Cambridge: The University Press, 1918) and H. M. Balyuzi, *Edward Granville Browne and the Bahá'íFaith* (Oxford: George Ronald, 1970). For biography, see H. M. Balyuzi, *Bahá'u'lláh: The King of Glory* (Oxford: George Ronald, 1980) and H. M. Balyuzi, *'Abdu'l-Bahá: The Centre of the Covenant of Bahá'u'lláh* (Oxford: George Ronald, 1971). Cf. Nabil-i-A'zam, *The Dawn-Breakers: Nabíl's Narrative of the Early Days of the Bahá'í Revolution*, trans. Shoghi Effendi (Wilmette, IL: Bahá'í Publishing Trust, 1932). For the conflation of Babism and Bahai'ism in some later Bahá'í writing, see Denis MacEoin, 'From Babism to Bahai'ism' in C. M. Cusack and D. Kirby eds., *Sects, Cults and New Religions: Critical Concepts in Sociology* (Milton Park, Abingdon: Routledge, 2014), 139–74 vol. 1, ch. 7. Bahá'í writers tend to emphasize the extraordinary character of the Bab's revelation and how his break with Islam prepared for Bahá'u'lláh. See Todd Lawson, *Gnostic Apocalypse and Islam: Qur'an, Exegesis, Messianism and the Literary Origins of the Babi Religion* (London: Routledge, 2011).
5. Bahá'í theology construes all the founders of religions as Manifestations in this sense. For a reliable overview, see M. Momen, *Bahá'u'lláh: A Short Biography* (Oxford: Oneworld, 2007).
6. Momen, *Bahá'u'lláh: A Short Biography*.
7. Farida Fozdar, 'The *Baha'i* Faith: A Case Study in Globalization, Mobility and the Routinization of Charisma' in *Journal for the Academic Study of Religion* 28, no. 3 (2015): 274–92.
8. See 'Abdu'l-Bahá, *Paris Talks*, 4th edn. (London: Bahá'í Publishing Trust, 1969); *The Promulgation of Universal Peace* (Wilmette, IL: Bahá'í Publishing Trust, 1982); *The Secret of Divine Civilization* (Wilmette, IL: Bahá'í Publishing Trust, 1975) and *Some Answered Questions* (Wilmette, IL: Bahá'í Publishing Trust, 1985). See also Balyuzi, *'Abdu'l-Bahá: The Centre of the Covenant of Bahá'u'lláh*.
9. Shoghi Effendi also became a spiritual teacher in his own right. See Shoghi Effendi, *Bahá'í Administration: Selected Messages 1922–1932* (Wilmette, IL: Bahá'í Publishing Committee, 1953); *God Passes By*, rev. edn. (Wilmette, IL: Bahá'í Publishing Trust,

1974); *The Promised Day Is Come*, 3rd edn. (Wilmette: Bahá'í Publishing Trust, 1980) and *The World Order of Bahá'u'lláh*' (Wilmette IL: Bahá'í Publishing Trust, 1991). For discussion, see Edward Granville Browne, 'Introduction' in Myron Phelps ed., *Abbas Effendi: His Life and Teachings*, 2nd rev. edn. (New York: G. P. Putnam's Sons, 1912), xi–xxx and M. Bergsmo ed. *Studying The Writings of Shoghi Effendi* (Oxford: George Ronald, 1991).

10 W. Hatcher, *Logic and Logos: Essays on Science, Religion and Philosophy* (Oxford: George Ronald, 1990) and M. Sergeev ed. *Studies in Bahá'í Philosophy: Selected Articles* (Leiden: Brill, 2015). Cf. Julio Savi, *The Eternal Quest for God: An Introduction to the Divine Philosophy of 'Abdu'l-Bahá* (Oxford: George Ronald, 1989).

11 'Abdu'l-Bahá, *The Secret of Divine Civilization*.

12 The works of Bahá'u'lláh alone amount to some 15,000 items, most of which are as yet untranslated. The canon of authoritative Bahai writings is also quite wide. Bahá'ís consider the writings of the Báb and Bahá'u'lláh to be divine revelation, and the writings of 'Abdu'l Bahá and the writings of Shoghi Effendi provide normative interpretations of the faith. They also accept that the Universal House of Justice directs the affairs of the community and legislates where there is no legislation already in the scriptures.

13 Bahá'u'lláh', *The Kitáb-i-Aqdas. The Most Holy Book* (Haifa: Bahá'í World Centre, 1992) and *The Kitáb-i-Íqán: The Book of Certitude*, trans. Shoghi Effendi (Wilmette, IL: Bahá'í Publishing Trust, 1974). For Bahá'u'lláh's sacral concept of justice, see 'Bahá'u'lláh's Paradise of Justice: Commentary and Translation' by Christopher Buck and Adib Ma'sumian Austin in *Baha'i Studies Review* 20 (2014): 97–134.

14 See Bahá'u'lláh, *The Call of the Divine Beloved: Selected Mystical Works of Bahá'u'lláh* (Haifa: Bahá'í World Centre, 2019). For discussion, J. Savi, *Towards the Summit of Reality: An Introduction to the Study of Bahá'u'lláh's Seven Valleys and Four Valleys* (Oxford: George Ronald, 2008).

15 Roland Faber, 'Bahá'u'lláh and the Luminous Mind: Bahá'í Gloss on a Buddhist Puzzle' in *Lights of Irfan* 18 (2017): 53–106.

16 Some writers like to say that Bahá'ís theology is Manifestation theology, not speculation about God. Nonetheless, the Bahá'ís have a more detailed account of God than this suggests, including an account of God in the unmanifest. See Bahá'u'lláh, 'A Tablet of Mirzá Husayn 'Ali Bahá'u'lláh of the Early Iraq Period: The "Tablet of All Food"' trans. Stephen Lambden. *Bahá'í Studies Bulletin* 3, no. 1 (June 1984): 4–67.

17 J. R. Cole, 'The Concept of Manifestation in the Bahá'í Writings' in *Bahá'í Studies* 9 (1982), accessed at https://bahai-library.com/cole_concept_manifestation

18 See J. S. Hatcher, *The Divine Art of Revelation* (Wilmette, IL: Bahá'í Publishing Trust, 1998).

19 For a sophisticated interpretation, see Udo Schaefer, *Heilsgeschichte und Paradigmenwechsel: Zwei Beiträge zur Bahá'í Theologie* (Prague: Zero Palm Press, 1992).
20 J. McLean, 'Prolegomena to a Bahá'í Theology', in *Journal of Bahá'í Studies* 5, no. 1 (March–June 1992): 25–67 and J. McLean ed. *Revisioning the Sacred New Perspectives on a Bahá'í Theology* (Studies in the Bábí and Bahá'í Religion, vol. 8) (Los Angeles: Kalimat Press, 1997).
21 Bahá'u'lláh, *The Proclamation of Bahá'u'lláh to the Kings and Leaders of the World* (Haifa: World Centre Publications, 1967).
22 Bahá'u'lláh, *Gleanings from the Writings of Bahá'u'lláh*, trans. Shoghi Effendi (Wilmette, IL: Bahá'í Publishing Trust, 1952), CIX, 215. Cf. Shoghi Effendi, *The Faith of Bahá'u'lláh: A World Religion* (Wilmette: Bahá'í Publishing Trust, 1980).
23 *'Abdu'l-Bahá on Divine Philosophy*, compiled by Elizabeth Fraser Chamberlain (Boston, MA: Tudor Press, 1918), 56.
24 J. Hatcher, *The Purpose of Physical Reality: The Kingdom of Names* (Wilmette, IL: Bahá'í Publishing Trust, 1987) and *The Arc of Ascent: The Purpose of Reality II* (Oxford: George Ronald, 1994). Cf. John and William Hatcher's theocratic interpretation of Bahá'í law in *The Law of Love Enshrined: Selected Essays* (Oxford: George Ronald, 1996).
25 Bahá'u'lláh, *Gleanings*, 184 and Abdu'l-Bahá, *Tablets of Abdul Baha Abbas*, Vol. 1 (Chicago, IL: Bahá'í Publishing Society, 1919).
26 'Abdu'l-Bahá, *Some Answered Questions*, 177. Cf. Bahá'u'lláh, *Gleanings and The World Order of Bahá'u'lláh; God Passes By; The Advent of Divine Justice* 3rd edn. (Wilmette, IL: Bahá'í Publishing Trust, 1971); *Guidance for Today and Tomorrow* (London: Bahá'í Publishing Trust, 1953); *The Promised Day Is Come*, and *Citadel of Faith: Messages to America 1947–1957* (Wilmette, IL: Bahá'í Publishing Trust, 1980).
27 'Abdu'l-Bahá, *Some Answered Questions*, ch. 29.
28 See Farshid Kazemi, 'Mysteries of Alast: The Realm of Subtle Entities ('*Alam-I dharr*) and the Primordial Covenant in the Babi-Bahá'í Writings' in *Bahá'í Studies Review* 15, no. 1 (2009): 39–66. Kazemi shows that the primordial covenant of Shi'ism is reinterpreted in the Babi and the Bahá'í writings. The writings also refer to occult elements (*dharr*) by which God addresses humanity. Cf. Robin Mihrshahi, 'Ether, Quantum Physics and the Bahá'í Writings' in *Australian Bahá'í Studies Journal* 4 (2002/2003): 3–20.
29 See Keven Brown, 'A Bahá'í Perspective on the Origin of Matter' in *Journal of Bahá'í Studies* 2–3 (1990): 15–44.
30 U. Schaefer, 'The New Morality: An Outline' in *Bahá'í Studies Review* 5, no. 1 (1995): 65–81; *Bahá'í Ethics in Light of Scripture: An Introduction Doctrinal Fundamentals*, Vol. 1 (Oxford: George Ronald, 2007) and *Bahá'í Ethics in Light of Scripture: Virtues and Divine Commandments*, Vol. 2 (Oxford: George Ronald, 2009).

31 *Bahá'í Marriage and Family Life: Selections from the Writings of the Bahá'í Faith* (Wilmette, IL: Bahá'í Publishing Trust, 1997).
32 See Bahá'u'lláh, the Báb and 'Abdu'l-Bahá, *Bahá'í Prayers* (Wilmette, IL: Bahá'í Publishing Trust, 2018).
33 The esoteric background of the movement in the works of the Shayktite Adventist Shaykh Ahmad Ahsá'í (d. 1826) who influenced the Bab, is finessed and modernized in the Bahá'ís writings, including the influential Tablet of the Universe by Bahá'u'lláh's son and successor, 'Abdu'l-Bahá.
34 M. Momen, 'Power and the Baha'i Community' in *Lights of Irfan* 19 (2018): 209-32.
35 In 1996, the Universal House of Justice set up the Training Institute and still more institutions are to come.
36 Michael Karlberg, 'Western Liberal Democracy as a New World Order?' in Robert Weinberg ed., *The Bahá'í World 2005-2006: An International Record* (Haifa: World Centre Publications, 2007), 133-56, available at https://www.bahai.org/documents/essays/karlberg-dr-michael/western-liberal-democracy-new-world-order. Cf his *Beyond the Culture of Contest: From Adversarialism to Mutualism in an Age of Interdependence* (Oxford: George Ronald, 2004).
37 Hatcher and Hatcher, *The Law of Love Enshrined: Selected Essays*.
38 Sen McGlinn, *Church and State: A Postmodern Political Theology* (Leiden: by the author, 2005) book one. McGlinn rejects older theocratic views and reads Bahá'u'lláh' and 'Abdu'l-Bahá as prophets of postmodernism (p. 2). He emphasizes that Bahá'ís distinguish between religion and politics and that the task of religion is only to advise. According to McGlinn Bahá'í political theology recognizes religion and politics as two sovereignties, but also maintains that religion should be established and have a critical role (p. 244). His views have been rejected by the Bahá'í World centre.
39 Shoghi Effendi, *The Unfoldment of World Civilisation* (New York: Bahá'í Publishing Committee, 1936). Cf. *Directives from the Guardian* Gertrude Garrida, compiler (New Delhi: Bahá'í Publishing Trust, 1973).
40 Karlberg, *Beyond the Culture of Contest: From Adversarialism to Mutualism in an Age of Interdependence*.
41 Effendi, *The Unfoldment of World Civilisation*, 152-3.
42 On Bahá'í social thought, see Effendi, *The World Order of Baha'u'llah* 152-3 and Nader Saiedi, *Logos and Civilization: Spirit, History and Order in the Writings of Bahá'u'lláh* (Bethesda, MD: University Press of Maryland, 2000).
43 Among many works, see Arthur L. Dahl, *The Eco Principle: Evolution and Economy in Symbiosis* (Oxford: George Ronald, 1996); W. S. Hatcher, 'Economics and Moral Values' in *World Order* 9, no. 2 (1974/5): 14-27; John Huddleston, *The Search for a Just Society* (Oxford: George Ronald, 1991); John Huddleston, 'The Economy of a World Commonwealth' in *World Order* 9, no. 4 (1975): 37-43 and John

Huddleston, 'Principles of Economic Justice' in C. Lerche ed., *Toward the Most Great Justice: Elements of Justice in the New World Order* (London: Bahá'í Publishing Trust, 1996): 137; Paul Hanley ed. *The Spirit of Agriculture* (Oxford: George Ronald, 2005); H. Badi'i, *The True Foundation of all Economics (A Compilation)* 2nd, rev. ed. (Canada: Webcom, 1996); Janak Palta McGilligan, *The Barli Development Institute for Rural Women: An Alternative Model of Women's Empowerment* (Oxford: George Ronald, 2012); Holly Hanson Vick, *Social and Economic Development: A Bahá'í Approach* (Oxford: George Ronald, 1989).

44 For sensitive work on religious dialogue, see M. Momen ed. *The Bahá'í Faith and the World Religions* (Oxford: George Ronald, 2005); M. Momen, *Buddhism and the Bahá'í Faith* (Oxford: George Ronald, 1994); *Islam and the Bahá'í Faith; An Introduction to the Bahá'í Faith for Muslims* (Oxford: George Ronald, 2000); *Hinduism and the Bahá'í Faith* (Oxford: George Ronald, 1990); *The Phenomenon of Religion* (Oxford: Oneworld, 1999). Cf. U. Schaefer, *Beyond the Clash of Religions: The Emergence of a New Paradigm*, 2nd edn. (Stockholm: Zero Palm Press, 1998).

45 See R. Faber, *The Garden of Reality: Transreligious Relativity in a World of Becoming* (Lanham: Lexington Books, 2018) and *The Ocean of God: On the Transreligious Future of Religions* (London: Anthem Press, 2019). Cf. M. Sergeev, *Theory of Religious Cycles: Tradition, Modernity and the Bahái Faith* (Leiden: Brill, 2015).

46 For an overview, see W. Momen and M. Momen, *Understanding the Bahai Faith* (Edinburgh: Dunedin Academic Press, 2006).

47 Michael Karlberg, 'The Press as a Consultative Forum: A Contribution to Normative Press Theory' in *Bahá'í Studies Review* 16 (2010): 29–42.

48 John Walbridge, *Sacred Arts, Sacred Space, Sacred Time* (Oxford: George Ronald, 1996) and J. Badiee, *An Earthly Paradise: Bahá'í Houses of Worship around the World* (Oxford: George Ronald, 1992).

49 L. Johnson, *Reginald Turvey Life and Art* (Oxford: George Ronald, 1986); B. Leach with R. Weinberg ed. *Spinning the Clay into Stars: Bernard Leach and the Bahá'í Faith* (Oxford: George Ronald, 1999); Arthur L. Dahl, *Mark Tobey, Art and Belief* (Oxford: George Ronald, 1984).

50 Shoghi Effendi, *God Passes By*, 281.

51 R. Diessner, *Psyche and Eros: Bahá'í Studies in a Spiritual Psychology* (Oxford: George Ronald, 2007).

52 *Tablets of Abdu'l-Bahá*, vol. 3.

53 McGlinn, *Church and State: A Postmodern Political Theology*, 128.

54 Bahá'u'lláh, *Epistle to the Son of the Wolf*, trans. S. Effendi (Wilmette, IL: Bahá'í Publishing Trust, 1953).

55 P. Lample, *Revelation and Social Reality: Learning to Translate What Is Written into Reality* (West Palm Beach, FL: Palabra Publications, 2009) and *Creating a New Mind: Reflections on the Individual, the Institutions and the Community* (West Palm

Beach, FL: Palabra Publications, 1999). Contrast A. Taherzadeh, *The Revelation of Bahá'u'lláh* 4 vols. (Oxford: George Ronald, 1974–1987).

56 M. Momen, 'Relativism: A Basis for Bahá'í Metaphysics' Studies in Honor of the Late Hasan M. Balyuzi in M. Momen ed. *Studies in the Babi and Bahá'í Religions*, vol. 5 (Los Angeles: Kalimát Press, 1988), 185–217. Cf. Momen ed. *The Bahá'í Faith and the World Religions*.

57 M. Warburg, *Citizens of the World: A History and Sociology of the Bahá'í s from a Globalisation Perspective* (Leiden: Brill Academic, 2006).

58 F. Stetzer, *Religion on the Healing Edge: What Bahá'ís Believe* (Wilmette, IL: Bahá'í Publishing Trust, 2007).

59 U. Schaefer, 'Infallible Institutions?' in S. Fazel and J. Danesh eds., *Reason and Revelation: New Directions in Bahá'í Thought* (Los Angeles: Kalimat Press, 2002), 3–37.

60 Bahá'ís believe that the Book of Revelation foretells the coming of Bahá'u'lláh. They also accept the interpretation of the book's symbolism Bahá'u'lláh provided in his *Book of Certitude*. See John Able, *Apocalypse Secrets: Baha'i Interpretation of the Book of Revelation* (self-published, 2011).

Chapter 3

1 Some of these earlier forms were associated with Japanese nationalism and militarism, as the founders of Soka were not. See G. Clinton Godart, 'Nichirenism, Utopianism and Modernity: Rethinking Ishiwara Kanji's East Asia League Movement' in *Japanese Journal of Religious Studies* 42, no. 2 (2015): 235–74.

2 Levi McLaughlin, *Soka Gakkai's Human Revolution: The Rise of a Mimetic Nation in Modern Japan* (Honolulu: University of Hawai'i Press, 2019).

3 For studies, see N. S. Brannen, *Soka Gakkai: Japan's Militant Buddhists* (Richmond, VA: John Knox Press, 1968); Christopher S. Queen, and Sallie B. King, eds., *Engaged Buddhism: Buddhist Liberation Movements in Asia* (Albany: State University of New York Press, 1996); K. Murata, *Japan's New Buddhism: An Objective Account of Soka Gakkai* (New York: Weatherhill, 1969); J. A. Dator, *Soka Gakkai, Builders of the Third Civilisation: American and Japanese Members* (Seattle: Washington University Press, 1969); J. White, *The Sokagakkai and Mass Society* (Stanford: Stanford University Press, 1970); R. Causton, *Nichiren Shoshu Buddhism: An Introduction* (London: Rider, 1988); D. A. Métraux, *The Soka Gakkai Revolution* (Washington and Lanham, MD: University of America Press, 1994); B. Wilson and K. Dobbelaere, *A Time to Chant: The Sōka Gakkai Buddhists in Britain* (Oxford: Oxford University Press, 1994); D. Machacek and B. Wilson eds., *The Sōka Gakkai Movement in the World* (Oxford: Oxford University Press, 2000);

P. E. Hammond and D. W. Machacek, *Soka Gakkai in America: Accommodation and Conversion* (Oxford and New York: Oxford University Press, 1999); Jacqueline I. Stone, 'Nichiren's Activist Heirs: Sōka Gakkai, Risshō Kōseikai, Nipponzan Myōhōji' in C. Queen, C. Prebish and D. Keown eds., *Action Dharma: New Studies in Engaged Buddhism* (London: Routledge Curzon, 2003), 63–94; R. H. Seager, *Encountering the Dharma Daisaku Ikeda, Soka Gakkai, and the Globalization of Buddhist Humanism* (Berkeley: University of California Press, 2006) and Ulrich Dehn, 'Soka Gakkai' in Birgit Staemmler and Ulrich Dehn eds., *Establishing the Revolutionary: An Introduction to New Religions in Japan* (Vienna, Zurich: Lit Verlag, 2011), 201–20.

4 See David Snow and Nick Machalek, 'The Sociology of Conversion' in *Annual Review of Sociology* 10 (1984): 167–90.

5 Most members of the movement have little awareness of the esoteric background to Nichiren's Buddhism, and esoteric practices play no part in the contemporary movement. See L. Dolce, 'Criticism and Appropriation: Nichiren's Attitude towards Esoteric Buddhism' in *Japanese Journal of Religious Studies* 26, no. 3–4 (Fall 1999): 349–82.

6 The movement has changed over time from the Soka Kyoiku Gakkai Value-Creation Education Society propagating Nichiren Buddhism among educators, to the Soka Gakkai, promoting Buddhism among all Japanese people, to Soka Gakkai International, promoting Nichiren Buddhism throughout the world. While stressing his debt to his mentor Josei Toda, the founder of the movement after the war, Ikeda has actually moved Nichiren Buddhism away from Toda's aggressive conversion campaigns that claimed that all other religions were false and Toda's traditional insistence that the *gohonzon* has the power to produce changes in the universe. Instead, Ikeda insists on the religious competence of every individual and reads a universalistic prophethood of all believers into Nichiren.

7 See, for example, Ikeda's dialogue with Gorbachev, Mikhail Gorbachev and Daisaku Ikeda, trans. R. L. Gage, *Moral Lessons of the Twentieth Century: Gorbachev and Ikeda on Buddhism and Communism* (London: I.B. Tauris, 2005).

8 Olivier Urbain has argued that Ikeda's contributions can be construed as addressing issues of humanistic psychology, communicative rationality and cosmopolitan democracy. See his *Daisaku Ikeda's Philosophy of Peace* (London: I. B. Tauris, 2010).

9 There have been controversies, however, about his sexual conduct in the tabloid press in Japan and in 1957 he was imprisoned for fifteen days for violating the electoral law. He was detained before the trial and eventually cleared of all charges after numerous court appearances.

10 Ikeda remains loyal to the legacy of his teacher Josei Toda, although there is now little mention of Toda's zealotry, or of the fact that Japanese joining Soka Gakkai

were compelled to renounce other religion as 'evil' and to cleanse their dwellings of all statues, books and devotion items associated with them.

11 Soka Gakkai is still controversial in Japan, but I do not discuss controversies about Soka Gakkai in this chapter. See Seager, *Encountering the Dharma and Murata, Japan's New Buddhism*. For global citizenship, see Jason Goulah, 'Daisaku Ikeda and the Soka Movement for Global Citizenship' in *Asia Pacific Journal of Education* 40, no. 1 (2020): 35–48.

12 Nichiren seems to have identified himself as Jogyo Bosatsu, the leader of the bodhisattvas to appear in the age of Mappo, which he believed had begun in his lifetime.

13 Ikeda's radicalism brought him into conflict with the clergy of the traditionalist Nichiren Shoshu sect and in 1991 the high priest of the sect broke completely with Soka Gakkai and the former Taiseki-ji temple in Tokyo was razed to the ground. Bitter accusations and counter-accusations followed. The priesthood was accused of being corrupt, while Soka Gakkai was accused of persecuting members who tried to leave the sect. Subsequently, the Protestant reformation strand in the movement became more pronounced and Soka Gakkai became independent of any priesthood. Henceforth weddings and funerals were performed without clergy. Recently there has been a marked opening to dialogue with all other religions as well.

14 See Vinicio Busacchi, *Philosophy and Human Revolution: Essays in Celebration of Daisaku Ikeda's 90th Birthday* (Newcastle: Cambridge Scholars Publishing, 2018).

15 E. Boulding and D. Ikeda, *Into Full Flower Making Peace Cultures Happen* (Cambridge, MA: Dialogue Path Press, 2010), 135.

16 Nichiren Daishonin, *The Writings of Nichiren Daishonin* (Tokyo: Soka Gakkai, 1999*)*, vol. 1, 1126.

17 D. Ikeda, M. Kiguchi and E. Shimura, *Buddhism and the Cosmos* (London: Macdonald, 1985).

18 Ibid., 143.

19 There are parallels here with Indian systems that posit a ground field of the law of nature which can be enlivened by meditation. This ground field is the common source of physical and spiritual excitations and is identified with pure consciousness.

20 See D. Ikeda, *Unlocking the Mysteries of Birth and Death: – and Everything in between* (Santa Monica: Middleway Press, 2003).

21 Ibid.

22 See Tsunesaburō Makiguchi, *Education for Creative Living. Ideas and Proposals of Tsunesaburo Makiguchi*, trans. A. Birnbaum, D. M. Bethel ed. (Ames: Iowa State University, 1989), 56–7. For Makiguchi more generally, see D. M. Bethel, *Makiguchi the Value Creator: Revolutionary Japanese Educator and Founder of Soka Gakkai* (New York and Tokyo: John Weatherill Inc, 1973).

23 See Makiguchi, *Education for Creative Living*.
24 Jason Goulah, 'Daisaku Ikeda's Environmental Ethics of Humanitarian Competition: A Review of His United Nations Peace and Educational Proposals' in *Peace Studies Journal* 3, no. 1, (2010): 1–23.
25 See Majid Tehranian and Daisaku Ikeda, *Reflections on the Global Civilisation: A Dialogue* (London: I.B. Tauris, 2016).
26 The problem remains, even though Soka Gakkai has separated itself formally from the party it supports and involves the disadvantage that Soka Gakkai cannot easily critique the corruption of the Japanese political system while allowing President Ikeda to be in effect a part of it, despite its corruption.
27 Makiguchi may have been influenced by John Dewey, although this is uncertain. He was also indebted to Christian educators such as Inazo Nitobe and Kanzo Uchimura. Nonetheless, his emphasis on the creation of value had original overtones, and he was critical of the American pragmatists for conflating value with truth (Bethel, *Makiguchi The Value Creator*, 59). Cf. Jim Garrison, 'Nichiren Buddhism and Deweyan Pragmatism: An Eastern-Western Integration of Thought' in *Educational Studies (Ames)* 55, no. 1 (2019): 12–27.
28 See Hazel Henderson and Daisaku Ikeda, *Planetary Citizenship: Your Values, Beliefs, and Actions Can Shape a Sustainable World* (Santa Monica: Middleway Press, 2004).
29 See T. Makiguchi, *Zenshu* (Tokyo: Daisan Bunmei-sha, 1983), vol. 6, 285, quoted in D. Ikeda, *Soka Education: A Buddhist Vision for Teachers, Students and Parents* (Santa Monica: Middleway Press, 2001), 13–14.
30 Makiguchi advocated an entire alternative pedagogy in his major work, 'The System of Value-Creating Pedagogy' in *Complete Works of Tsunesaburo Makiguchi* [In Japanese], (Daisan Bunmeisha, 1930), Vols 5, 6–7 and in his study, 'The Geography of Human Life' in *Complete Works of Tsunesaburo Makiguchi* [In Japanese] (Tokyo: Daisan Bunmeisha 1903), Vols 1, 23, he paid special attention to geography that he believed could unify the curriculum. Responsibility for learning was to be placed in students' own hands. He emphasized the importance of beginning with the actual life of the child in the local community and advocated that schooling be reduced to half a day. Education was the task of the family and the local community as well as the school. Teaching methods were to be based on actual situations in schools and not on the ideas of intellectuals. It was to enhance the powers of intuition and discovery of students, and not to transfer passive knowledge. Students were to take responsibility for their own learning and to become alert, informed and responsible members of society. For discussion, see D. M. Bethel ed. *Education for Creative Living. Ideas and Proposals of Tsunesaburo Makiguchi,* trans. A. Birnbaum and D. M. Bethel (Ames: Iowa State University, 1989) and W. Hudson, 'Daisaku Ikeda and Innovative Education' in O. Urbain ed. *Daisaku Ikeda and Dialogue for Peace* (London: I. B. Tauris, 2013), 99–112 ch. 6.
31 *The Writings of Nichiren Daishonin*, vol. 1, 832.

Chapter 4

1. Buddha Prakash, 'The Hindu Philosophy of History' in *Journal of the History of Ideas* 16, no. 4 (1955): 494–505. I am indebted in this chapter to the excellent comments provided by two leading Ananda Marga scholars, Sohail Inyatullah and Marcus Bussey.
2. For a contemporary interpretation, see Shaman Hatley and Sohail Inayatullah, 'Karma Samnyasa: Sarkar's Reconceptualisation of Indian Asceticism' in K. Ishwaran ed., *Ascetic Culture: Renunciation and Worldly Engagement* (Leiden: Brill, 1999), 139–51.
3. See Subrata Dasgupta, *Awakening: The Story of the Bengal Renaissance* (London: Random House, 2011). For the Bengali context more generally, see J. T. O'Connell, 'Bengali Religions' in Mircea Eliade ed., *The Encyclopedia of Religion*. Vol. 1 (New York: Macmillan Publishing, 1987), 100–9.
4. Helen Crovett, 'Ananda Marga and the Use of Force' in *Nova Religio: The Journal of Alternative and Emergent Religion* 12, no. 1 (2008): 25–56 and N. P. Sil, 'Anatomy of Ānanda Mārga: Hindu Anabaptists' in *Asian Culture Quarterly* 16, no. 2 (1988): 1–18. More generally, see James R. Lewis, *Violence and New Religious Movements* (New York: Oxford University Press, 2011).
5. See N. P. Sil, 'The Troubled World of the Ananda Marga: An Examination' in *Quarterly Review of Historical Studies* 27, no. 4 (1988): 3–19; 'Anatomy of the Ananda Marga' and 'The Odyssey of the Ananda Marga: A Comparative Study' in *Journal of Asian and African Studies* 48, no. 2 (2013): 229–41.
6. P. R. Sarkar, *Discourses on the Mahábhárata* (Kolkata: Ánanda Márga Pracáraka Samgha, 1991).
7. P. R. Sarkar, *Varńa Vijináná-The Science of Letters* (Ananda Nagar: Ananda Marga Publications, 2000) and Subhāsha Sarakāra, *Prabháta Samgiita: A Literary and Philosophical Appreciation* (Ananda Nagar: Ananda Marga Publications, 2010). Many of Sarkar's works are hard to obtain and/or published by Ananda Marga. See, however, P. R. Sarkar, *The Electronic Edition of the Works of P. R. Sarkar*, Version 6.0, compiled by G. Dhara and Acyutānanda (Kolkata: Ānanda Mārga Publications, 2001).
8. For basic introductions, see Ś. Ānandamūrti, *Ānanda Mārga Philosophy in a Nutshell*, parts 1–4, trans. Vijayānanda and Vishvarūpānanda (Kolkata: Ānanda Mārga Pracāraka Samgha, 1988); Ś. Ānandamūrti, *Ānanda Mārga: Elementary Philosophy* (Kolkata: Ananda Marga Publications, 1991).
9. For a detailed analysis of Sarkar's Indian sources and how he varies and combines them, see C. Kang, *The Tantra of Prabhāt Ranjañ Sarkar: Critical Comparative and Dialogical Perspectives* (P. R. Sarkar Institute, 2017) especially ch. 7: The Indian Philosophical Legacy, and ch. 9 P. R. Sarkar: A Tantric Guru.

10 G. J. Larsen, *Classical Sāṃkhya: An Interpretation of Its History and Meaning* (Delhi: Motilal Banarsidass, 2010) and M. Burley, *Classical Samkhya and Yoga–An Indian Metaphysics of Experience* (London: Routledge, 2006).

11 K. Mishra, *Kashmir Saivism: The Central Philosophy of Tantrism* (Portland: Oregon Press, 1993).

12 Contrast terms, *puruṣa* roughly pure consciousness, or spirit, *prakṛti* immanent cosmic energy, potential matter.

13 M. Bussey, 'Neohumanism: Critical Spirituality, Tantra and Education' in S. Inayatullah, M. Bussey and I. Milojevic eds., *Neohumanist Educational Futures: Liberating the Pedagogical Intellect* (Taipei: Tamkang University Press, 2006), 80–95.

14 P. R. Sarkar, *Microvita in a Nutshell* (Kolkata: Ananda Marga Publications, 1991); Raymond Bates, *Microvitum: A Handbook* (P. R. Sarkar Institute, 2019) available online: https://anandamargabooks.com/books/microvitum-in-a-nutshell/ and M. Bussey, 'Microvita and Transformative Information' in *The Open Information Science Journal* 3 (2011): 28–39.

15 Kang, *The Tantra*, 393.

16 See Raymond Bates, *The Cognitive Creative Universe: A Study of Microvita Cosmogony* (Hayward, CA: Self-published, 2020); *Microvitology: Microvita Universal Subassembly Structures* (Mound Valley, KS: Self-published, 2016) and *Microcosmology: A New Paradigm of Relativity*, First electronic edn. (Mound Valley, KS: Self-published, 2017). Cf. Acarya Sutiirthananda Avadhuta ed. *The Microvita Revolution: Towards the New Science of Matter, Life and Mind* (Kolkata: Ananda Marga, 1990). For a brief but sophisticated introduction which construes microvita as a wave physics of life that is able to explain the nature of gravity, integrate the forces of nature which remain divided in modern physics, give a better account of the quantum vacuum and construe the observer as an effect of cosmic processes, see Pankaj Bābā's *New Science of the Future* (Kolkata: Ananda Marga, 2007) especially p. 20.

17 R. Bates, *The Internal Being: Reincarnational and Intuitive Psychology* (Hayward, CA: Self-published, 2016) and Kang *The Tantra*, ch. 4: 'Mind and Biopsychology' and P. R. Sarkar, *Discourses on Tantra* (Kolkata: Ananda Marga Publications, 1994), vol. 1.

18 Śrī Śrī Ānandamūrti, *Yoga Psychology* (Kolkata: Ānanda Mārga Publications, 1990). Cf. Anandamurti, *Ánanda Márga Elementary Philosophy* (Jamalpur: Ananda Marga, 1955); A. Ānandamitra, *The Spiritual Philosophy of Śrī Śrī Ānandamūrti: Commentary on Ánanda Sútram*, 2nd edn. (Kolkata: Ānanda Mārga Pracāraka Samgha, 1998), and Ś. Ś. Ānandamūrti, *The Thoughts of P. R. Sarkar*, ed. A. Ānandamitra (Kolkata: Ānanda Mārga Pracāraka Samgha, 1985).

19 See Ś. Ś. Ānandamūrti, *Human Society Part 1* (Kolkata: Ananda Marga Publications, 1959) and Ś. Ś. Ānandamūrti, *Human Society Part 2* (Ananda Nagar: Proutist Universal, 1967).

20 For a modernist interpretation which takes key Hindu referents as metaphorical, see Sohail Inayatullah, 'Sarkar's Theory of Social Change' available online: https://www.metafuture.org/sarkars-theory-of-social-change/
21 Sohail Inayatullah, *Understanding Sarkar: The Indian Episteme, Macrohistory and Transformative Knowledge* (Leiden: Brill, 2002) and *Situating Sarkar: Tantra, Macrohistory and Alternative Futures* (Queensland: Gurukula Press, 1999).
22 Sohail Inayatullah, 'Sarkar's Spiritual-dialectics: An Unconventional View of the Future' in *Futures* 20, no. 1 (1988): 54–65.
23 Johan Galtung and Sohail Inayatullah, eds., *Macrohistory and Macrohistorians Perspectives on Individual, Social and Civilizational Change* (Wesport, CT: Praeger, 1997).
24 P. R. Sarkar, *The Liberation of Intellect: Neohumanism* (Kolkata: Ananda Marga Publications, 1982) and P. R. Sarker, *Neohumanism in a Nutshell* (Kolkata: Ānanda Mārga Pracāraka Samgha, 1987).
25 Indian accounts tend to be based on a very broad conception of Sarkar's spiritual philosophy. See A. Ānandamitra, *The Spiritual Philosophy of Śrī Śrī Ānandamūrti: A Commentary on Ánanda Sútram*, 1st edn. (Denver: Ānanda Mārga Publications, 1981).
26 P. R. Sarkar, *The Thoughts of P. R. Sarkar*, ed. Acharya, Avadhutika Anandamitra (Kolkata: Ānanda Mārga Pracāraka Samgha, 1985).
27 For an introduction, see Ś. Ś. Ānandamūrti, *A Guide to Human Conduct* (Manila: Ānanda Mārga Publications, 1981). For more Indian elaborations, see Ānandamurti's Sanskrit text *Ānánda Sūtram* (Kolkata: Ananda Marga Publications, 1961); Shrii Shrii Ānandmurti, *Ananda Marga Caryacarya, Part 1*, 6th edn. (Kolkata: Ananda Marga Publications, 1995), *Ananda Marga Caryacarya, Part 2*, 4th edn. (Kolkata: Ananda Marga Publications, 1987). Sarkar's ethics appears to be a revisionist version of yoga ethics of *niyama* and *yama*, emphasing balanced rather than direct prescriptions. He specifically advocated a bill of rights for animal and plants as well as humans.
28 Ānandamūrti, *Discourses on Tantra*, ed. Vijayānanda and Acyutānanda (Kolkata: Ānanda Mārga Publications, 1994) 2 vols and Tarak ed. *Ananda Marga, Social and Spiritual Practices* (Kolkata: Ananda Marga Publications, 1990). For the wider background, see S. D. Gupta, D. J. Hoens and T. Goudriaan eds., *Hindu Tantrism* (Leiden: E. J. Brill, 1979).
29 The movement offers yoga based on forty-two *asana* positions, kiirtan retreats, as well as training in *mudras* and Indian dance. Ayurvedic medicine and Vedic nutrition are also recommended. See P. R. Sarkar, *Yoga: The Way of Tantra* (Manila: Ananda Marga Publications, 1991) and Ś. Ś. Ānandamūrti, *Yoga Sadhana: The Spiritual Practice of Yoga* (Kolkata: Ananda Marga Publications, 2010).
30 Kang, *The Tantra*, 394.

31 See Jennifer Jayanti Fitzgerald and Marcus Bussey eds., *Fire in Our Eyes, Flowers in Our Hearts: Tantric Women Tell Their Stories* (Maleny, QLD: Gurukula Press, 2007).
32 Ānandamūrti, *Yoga Sadhana*: and H. Shaman and S. Inayatullah, 'Karma Samnyasa: Sarkar's Reconceptualisation of Indian Asceticism' in *Journal of Asian and African Studies* 34, no. 1, (1999): 139–51. The details are complex. These practices range from meditation techniques to hygiene, diet and yoga. Apart from a lacto-vegetarian diet and fasting, *yoga* asanas, mudras, bandhas, pranayama and self-massage are prescribed, including two types of *asanas* allegedly unique to Ananda Marga.
33 C. Kang, *The Tantra*, 331, 333. Ananda Marga recommends that its members practice collective meditation at least once a week. These meetings called *Dharma Chakras* are preceded by the singing of 'Songs of the New Dawn' composed by Sarkar, followed by a spiritual dance (*Lalita Marmika*), along with the chanting of a universal mantra (*kiirtan*). Before meditation the Samgacchadvam *mantra* is chanted. At the end of meditation the Nityam Shuddham and the Guru Puja *mantras* are recited. Two other sacred dances, kaoshikii, the dance for mental expansion, and tandava, a vigorous dance to enhance the body, are also employed.
34 Marcus Bussey and Camila Mozzini-Alister, *Phenomenologies of Grace: The Body, Embodiment, and Transformative Futures* (London: Palgrave-Macmillan, 2020).
35 J. Karlyle and M. Towsey, *Understanding Prout: Essays on Sustainability and Transformation* (Maleny: Proutist Universal, 2010) vol. 1 and also Sohail Inyatullah, *Prout in Power: Policy Solutions That Reframe Our Futures* (Delhi: Proutist Bloc, 2012).
36 Karlyle and Towsey, *Understanding Prout*.
37 See, for example, the writings and audio books of Apek Mulay, including Apek Mulay, *Mass Capitalism: A Blueprint for Economic Revival* (Bothell, WA: Book Publishers Network, 2014) and *Economic Renaissance in the Sage of Artificial Intelligence* (Hampton, NJ: Business Expert Press, 2018).
38 For technical details, see P. R. Sarkar, *Prout in a Nutshell* (Kolkata: Ananda Marga Publications, 1987) 4 vols and *Discourses on Prout* (Kolkata: Ananda Marga Publications, 1993) and Ś. Ś., Ānandamūrti, *Ānanda Mārga Ideology and Way of Life in a Nutshell*, parts 1–11, 1st edn., trans. Vijayānanda and Vishvarūpānanda (Kolkata: Ānanda Mārga Pracāraka Samgha, 1988). For secondary literature, see R. Batra, *Prout: The Alternative to Capitalism and Marxism* (Lanham, MD: University Press of America, 1980), J. Kumar ed. *New Aspects of Prout* (Kolkata: Proutist Universal Publications, 1987) and S. Inayatullah, 'Planetary Social and Spiritual Transformation' in A. B. Shostak ed. *Viable Utopian Ideas: Shaping a Better World* (New York: M. E. Sharpe, 2003), 208–16, ch. 40; Roar Bjonnes, *Principles for a Balanced Economy: An Introduction to the Progressive Utilization Theory* (PROUT Research Institute, 2012).

39 P. R. Sarkar, *Yogic Treatments and Natural Remedies* (Kolkata: Ananda Marga Publications, 2004). Also see, P. R. Sarkar, *Natural Medicine* (Kolkata: Ananda Marga Publications, 2011).

40 P. R. Sarkar, *The New Renaissance* (Kolkata: Ananda Marga Publications, 1968). See also Ananda Marga's cultural magazine *New Renaissance,* devoted to developments in the arts. See. www.ru.org.

41 These activities are documented in Ananda Marga's educational magazine *Garukula*. See also P. R. Sarkar, *Discourses on Neohumanist Education* (Kolkata: Ananda Marga Publications, 1998) and M. Bussey, 'Embodied Education: Reflections on Sustainable Education' in *The International Journal of Environmental, Cultural, Economic and Social Sustainability* 4, no. 3 (2008): 139–48.

42 See S. Inyatullah and J. Gidley, *The University in Transformation* (Westport, CT: Bergin and Garvey, 2000).

43 P. R. Sarkar, *Namah Sivaya Santaya* (Kolkata: Ananda Marga Publications, 1982).

44 For insight into the ecstatic context associated with Ananda Marga, see Graham Double, *Walking with the Master* (Sydney: Making Waves Media, 2013).

45 See M. Bussey, 'Critical Spirituality: Neohumanism as Method' in *Journal of Future Studies* 5, no. 2 (2010): 21–35.

Chapter 5

1 Tamasin Ramsay, Chapter 8 - 'Spirit Possession and Purity in Orissa'- of *Custodians of Purity: An Ethnography of the Brahma Kumaris*, PhD Diss. (Melbourne: Monash University, 2009), 257–99. I am indebted in this chapter to the learnt publications and critical comments of this author.

2 For literature, see Liz Hodgkinson, *Peace and Purity: The Story of the Brahma Kumaris: A Spiritual Revolution* (London: Ryder, 2002); John Walliss, *The Brahma Kumaris as a 'Reflexive Tradition': Responding to Late Modernity* (Aldershot: Ashgate, 2002) chapter 3; Ken O'Donnell, *New Beginnings: Raja Yoga Meditation Course* (Mt Abu: Brahma Kumaris World University, 1995); Frank Whaling, *Understanding the Brahma Kumaris* (Dunedin: Dunedin Press, 2012); L. Babb, 'The Brahma Kumaris: History as Movie' in L. Babb ed., *Redemptive Encounters: Three-Modern Styles in the Hindu Tradition* (Berkeley: University of California Press, 1986), 110–55; D. V. Barrett, *The New Believers: A Survey of Sects, Cults and Alternative Religions* (London: Cassell, 2001); T. Ramsay, W. A. Smith and L. H. Manderson, 'Brahma Kumaris: Purity and the Globalization of Faith' in L. Manderson, W. Smith and M. Tomlinson eds., *Flows of Faith: Religious Reach and Community in Asia and the Pacific* (Dordrecht: Springer, 2012), 51–70, ch. 4. For basic information, see the Brahma Kumaris entry in Wikipedia and the Brahma Kumaris website.

3   T. Ramsay, 'Making a Model of Madhuban: The Brahma Kumaris' Journey to and Presence in Europe' in Knut A. Jacobsen and Ferdinando Sardella eds., *Handbook of Hinduism in Europe*, 2 vols. (Leiden: Brill, 2020), 528–54.
4   Babb, *Redemptive Encounters*.
5   Modernist presentations can be found in their countless self-help books and in their magazine, *World Renewal,* which gives a more positive interpretation of their teaching about immanent world destruction.
6   See Jagdish Chander, *The One Week Course.* Available at http://brahmakumarisresearch.org/resources.
7   Jagdish Chander, *Adi Dev: The First Man* (Mt Abu: Brahma Kumaris, 1983), 122, 128 and *Eternal Drama of Souls, Matter and God* (Mt Abu: Brahma Kumaris, 1985).
8   Chander, *Adi Dev.* Eventually a distinction was made between the founder as Brahma Baba and the supreme Soul Shiv Baba.
9   See the handbook *Visions of the Future* (Mt Abu: Brahma Kumaris, 1996).
10 For the full cosmogony in all its complexity, see Jagdish Chander, *The Eternal World Drama* (Mt Abu: Brahma Kumaris, 1985) and N. Nair, *The Mysteries of the Universe* (Mt Abu: Brahma Kumaris, 2008).
11 Nair, *The Mysteries,* 52.
12 Nikki De Carteret, Christopher Drake, Gayatri Naraine, Jagdish Chander Hassija, *Visions of a Better World* (Mt Abu: Brahma Kumaris World Spiritual University, 1993).
13 See Chander, *Adi Dev,* and De Carteret et al. *Visions of a Better World.*
14 Ibid., and De Carteret et al. *Visions of a Better World,* 68.
15 Chander, *The Eternal World Drama,* 323.
16 Ibid., 605.
17 Brahma Kumaris, *Visions,* 18. See also Tamasin Ramsay, Lenore Manderson, and Wendy Smith, 'Changing a Mountain into a Mustard Seed: Spiritual Practices and Responses to Disaster among New York Brahma Kumaris' in *Journal of Contemporary Religion* 25, no. 1 (2010): 89–105.
18 J. Chander, *Science and Spirituality* (Mt Abu: Brahma Kumaris, 1988).
19 Nair, *The Mysteries,* ch. 2.
20 Ibid., 96.
21 Wendy Smith and Tamasin Ramsay, 'Spreading Soul Consciousness: Managing and Extending the Global Reach of the Brahma Kumaris' in W. Smith, H. Nakamaki, L. Matsunaga, and T. Ramsay eds., *Globalizing Asian Religions: Management and Marketing* (Amsterdam: Amsterdam University Press, 2019), 205–34.
22 Nair, *The Mysteries,* 87.
23 Ibid.
24 For discussion, see Emily McKendry-Smith, '"Baba Has Come to Civilize Us": Developmental Idealism and Framing the Strict Demands of the Brahma Kumaris' in *Journal for the Scientific Study of Religion* 55, no. 4 (2016): 698–716.

25 Jagdish Chander, *Values for a Better World* (Mt Abu: Brahma Kumaris, 1995).
26 See Janus Bojesen Jensen, 'An Investigation of Sustainable Yogic Agriculture as a Mind-Matter Farming Approach' in Julia Wright ed. and Nicholas Parrott, contributed, *Subtle Agroecologies: Farming with the Hidden Half of Nature* (Boca Raton: CRC Press, 2021) 247–56, ch. 22.
27 For a study of Brahma Kumari reversing sexual polarity by casting females as spiritually superior to men, see J. D. Howell, 'Gender Role Experimentation in New Religious Movements: Clarification of the Brahma Kumaris Case' in *Journal for the Scientific Study of Religion* 37, no. 3 (1998): 453–61.
28 V. S. Lalrinawma, *The Liberation of Women in and through the Movement of the Prajapita Brahma Kumaris* (Delhi: Cambridge Press, 2003).
29 For the Brahma Kumaris approach to reincarnation, see Chander, *Eternal Drama*, 24–101.
30 Brahma Kumaris, *Visions*, 45.
31 Walliss, *The Brahma Kumaris as a 'Reflexive Tradition' Responding to Late Modernity*.
32 Chander, *The Eternal World Drama*, 297, 78–9.
33 See R. Musselwhite, *Possessing Knowledge: Organizational Boundaries among the Brahma Kumaris*, PhD thesis (Chapel Hill, NC: University of North Carolina, 2009).
34 I owe this important qualification to the social anthropologist Professor Julia Howell, an internationally acknowledged scholar of the movement.

Chapter 6

1 For the wider theosophical background, see Joscelyn Godwin, *The Theosophical Enlightenment*, 2nd edn. (Albany, NY: State University of New York Press, 1994); Bruce F. Campbell, *Ancient Wisdom Revived: A History of the Theosophical Movement* (Berkeley: University of California Press, 1980); Paul K. Johnson, *The Masters Revealed: Madame Blavatsky and Myth of the Great White Lodge* (Albany, NY: State University of New York Press, 1994) and M. Abravanel, 'The Summit Lighthouse: Its Worldview and Theosophical Heritage' in Olav Hammer and Mikael Rothstein eds., *Handbook of the Theosophical Current* (Leiden: Brill, 2013), 173–91.
2 See, however, J. R. Lewis and J. G. Melton eds., *Church Universal and Triumphant in Scholarly Perspective* (Stanford: Centre for Academic Publication, 1994) and Bradley C. Whitsel, *The Church Universal and Triumphant: Elizabeth Clare Prophet's Apocalyptic Movement* (Syracuse: Syracuse University Press, 2003) and Jocelyn H. DeHaas, 'The Church Universal and Triumphant: Controversy, Change and

Continuance' in James R. Lewis and Jesper Aa Petersen eds., *Controversial New Religions*, 2nd edn. (Oxford: Oxford University Press, 2014), 270–85 ch. 15. For criticism of the AWARE study of the church, see Robert W. Balch and Stephan Langdon, 'How the Problem of Malfeasance Gets Overlooked in Studies of New Religions: An Examination of the AWARE Study of the Church Universal and Triumphant' in Anson D. Shupe ed., *Wolves within the Fold: Religious Leadership and Abuses of Power* (New Brunswick, NJ: Rutgers University Press, 1998), 191–211. All these studies are primarily sociological. For an insider's perspective, see Erin Prophet, *Prophet's Daughter: My Life with Elizabeth Clare Prophet Inside the Church Universal and Triumphant* (Guilford, CT: Lyons Press, 2008).

3   For performance as a term in hermeneutics, see R. Schechner, *Performance Studies: An Introduction* (London: Routledge, 2011).

4   Many of these accusations are linked to the period when the Church through its seer Elizabeth Prophet warned of imminent nuclear catastrophe, built underground shelters, acquired weapons and encouraged members to sell their possessions and prepare for apocalypse. When these prophecies failed, about one third of the members left the Church, but the impression that it was a dangerous sect continued in the media. Happily, prophecies of world destruction have now ceased.

5   For the background, see J. Gordon Melton, 'The Church Universal and Triumphant: Its Heritage and Thought World' in J. R. Lewis and J. G. Melton eds., *Church Universal and Triumphant in Scholarly Perspective* (Stanford: Centre for Academic Publication, 1994), 1–20. Baird Spalding who wrote six volumes about Far Eastern Ascended Masters, and William D. Pelley are also sometimes suggested as possible sources.

6   For the details of the I Am movement, see Saint Germain Foundation, *The History of the 'I AM' Activity and Saint Germain Foundation: In The Ascended Masters Words and the Recollections of Those Who Were There* (Schaumburg, IL: Saint Germain Press, 2003).

7   M. L. Prophet and E. C. Prophet, *Foundations of the Path* (Corwin Springs, MT: Summit University Press, 1999), 10.

8   Erin Prophet, 'Church Universal and Triumphant and the Summit Lighthouse' in *Critical Dictionary of Apocalyptic and Millenarian Movements*, eds., James Crossley and Alastair Lockhart 11 February 2021. Available online www.cdamm.org/articles/CUT-TSL.

9   For Prophet's own account of her life, see E. C. Prophet, *In My Own Words* (Gardiner, MT: Summit Publications, 2009) and E. C. Prophet, *Preparation for My Mission*, ed. Erin Prophet and Tatiana Prophet (Bloomington: iUniverse, 2009). I do not discuss controversies about her conduct and personal life.

10 The Summit Lighthouse catalogue list more than one hundred and fifty books, some co-authored with Mark Prophet. See Appendix 1.

11 Erin Prophet, 'Church Universal and Triumphant'.
12 For context and background, see J. Mills, *100 Years of Theosophy: A History of the Theosophical Society in America* (Wheaton, IL: Theosophical Publishing House, 1987).
13 There may be a parallel here with AMORC, an American popularization of European Rosicrucian ideas and practices using Disneyland sites autodidact mail outs, although the degree to which spiritual transformation is achieved in the lives of members is harder to assess.
14 E. C. Prophet, *Fallen Angels and the Origins of Evil: Why Church Fathers Suppressed the Book of Enoch and Its Startling Revelations* (Corwin Springs, MT: Summit University Press, 2000).
15 'We accept the authentic sacred scriptures of the world and their spiritual interpretation by the Messengers Mark L. Prophet and Elizabeth Clare Prophet. We also accept the progressive revelation of God as dictated by the hierarchy of the Great White Brotherhood to the anointed Messengers. We accept this revelation as the Word of God, as the Everlasting Gospel (Rev. 14:6), as the prophecy of the two witnesses (Rev.11) and as the sacred scripture for the 2,150-year dispensation of Aquarius.' (Church Universal and Triumphant, *Tenets*, IV).
16 See, for example, Elizabeth Clare Prophet, *The Astrology of the Four Horsemen: How You Can Heal Yourself and Planet Earth* (Livingston, MT: Summit University Press, 1991) and Elizabeth Clare Prophet, Patricia R. Spadaro and Murray L. Steinman, *Saint Germain's Prophecy for the New Millennium: Includes Dramatic Prophecies From Nostradamus, Edgar Cayce, and Mother Mary* (Corwin Springs, MT: Summit University Press, 1999).
17 See M. L. Prophet and E. C. Prophet, *The Lost Teachings of Jesus*. 4 vols (Livingston, MT: Summit University Press, 1986) and E. C. Prophet, *The Lost Years of Jesus* (Livingston, MT: Summit University, 1984).
18 M. L. Prophet and E. C. Prophet, 'How to Decree Effectively' by 'The Messengers' in their *The Science of the Spoken Word* (Corwin Springs, MT: Summit University Press, 1991) ch. 6, 49–54.
19 See E. C. Prophet, *Is Mother Nature Mad? How to Work with Nature Spirits to Mitigate Natural Disasters* (Gardiner, MT: Summit University Press, 2008).
20 E. C. Prophet and Mark L. Prophet, *St Germain on Alchemy: Formulas for Self-Transformation* (Malibu: Summit University Press, 1985); E. C. Prophet, *Saint Germain: The Master Alchemist*, compiled by editors of The Summit Lighthouse Library (Gardiner, MT: Summit Lighthouse Library, 2004) and E. C. Prophet, *Violet Flame: Alchemy for Personal Change* (Gardiner, MT: Summit University Press, 2016).
21 See G. R. King, (Pseudonym of G.W. Ballard) through Saint Germain, *The 'I AM' Discourses*, ed. G.W. Ballard (Chicago: St Germain Press, 1935).

22 Prophet taught that the concept of 'commanding' God was based on Isaiah 45:11. For more about decrees, see Prophet and Prophet, *The Science of the Spoken Word* and E. C. Prophet, *The Creative Power of Sound: Affirmations to Create, Heal and Transform* (Corwin Springs, MT: Summit University Press, 1998).
23 Mark L. Prophet and Elizabeth Clare Prophet, *The Path of Christ or Antichrist* (Gardiner, MT: Summit University Press, 2007), 15.
24 Elizabeth Prophet claimed that the use of decrees followed the example of the use of mantra by followers of Hinduism and Buddhism in the East and the use of the rosary and the Jesus prayer in Christian traditions. Members of the anti-cult movement and some ex-members, however, have claimed that decrees have a 'hypnotic' or 'mind-control' effect.
25 See Prophet and Prophet, 'How to Decree Effectively'.
26 Elizabeth Clare Prophet, *Forbidden Mysteries of Enoch: The Untold Story of Men and Angels* (Los Angeles: Summit University Press, 1983).
27 M. Prophet and E. Prophet, *Prayers Meditations and Dynamic Decrees for Personal and World Transformation* (Gardiner, MT: The Summit Lighthouse Press, 1962), see section 7.03A 'Invocation of the Mother of the Flame', 81–2.
28 Erin Prophet, 'Church Universal and Triumphant'.
29 The Keepers of the Flame Fraternity was formed within the organization in 1961. Members paid nominal monthly dues (two dollars per month initially) and in return received monthly lessons as well as personal assistance from the Ascended Masters for their spiritual path.
30 M. L. Prophet and E. C. Prophet with Annice Booth compiler and editor, *The Masters and Their Retreats* (Corwin Springs, MT: Summit University Press, 2003), 176–7.
31 For interpretations of religious doctrines and activities as providing compensations, see R. Stark and W. S. Bainbridge, *A Theory of Religion* (New York: Peter Lang, 1987).
32 See M. L. and E. C. Prophet, *Mary's Message for a New Day* (Corwin Springs, MT: Summit University Press, 2004).
33 E. C. Prophet and Annice Booth, *Mary Magdalene and the Divine Feminine: Jesus' Lost Teachings on Woman* (Gardiner, MT: Summit University Press, 2005).
34 E. C. Prophet, *Afra, Brother of Light: Spiritual Teachings from an Ascended Master* (Corwin Springs, MT: Summit University Press, 2003).
35 E. C. Prophet and A. Booth compiler and editor, *Predict Your Future: Understand the Cycles of the Cosmic Clock* (Corwin Springs, MT: Summit University Press, 2004).
36 For material culture as a crucial dimension of religion, see the journal *Material Religion* and Manuel A. Vásquez, *More than Belief: A Materialist Theory of Religion* (New York and Oxford: Oxford University Press, 2011).

37 M. L. Prophet and E. C. Prophet, 'Saint Germain on Freedom: A Prophecy of America's Destiny' in *Pearls of Wisdom* 20, nos. 46, 47: 215–30.

38 Elizabeth Prophet spoke of an 'International Capitalist/Communist Conspiracy' by which leaders of the West collaborated with Communist leaders to eliminate national sovereignty and individual freedoms and bring about a one-world government. They saw this conspiracy as being directed primarily by disembodied fallen angels, who would work through leaders and organizations of East or West who could be used to further this agenda. These individuals might have varying degrees of awareness of the ultimate goal. See E. C. Prophet, *Saint Germain on Prophecy: Coming World Changes* (Livingston, MT: Summit University Press, 1986) and E. C. Prophet, *The Astrology of the Four Horsemen: How You Can Heal Yourself and Planet Earth* (Livingston, MT: Summit University Press, 1991).

39 Erin Prophet, 'Church Universal and Triumphant'.

40 While Summit University confers no degrees and has no accredited academic staff, focusing instead on in-depth training in the organization's teachings, plans have been announced to eventually offer a full accredited liberal arts curriculum.

41 Prophet and Prophet, *The Masters*, 14.

42 For the wider background, see W. J. Hanegraaff, *New Age Religion and Western Culture: Esotericism in the Mirror of Secular Thought* (Leiden: Brill, 1996).

43 Cf. Olav Hammer, 'Jewish Mysticism Meets the Age of Aquarius: Elizabeth Clare Prophet on the Kabbalah' in Julie Chajes and Boaz Huss eds., *Theosophical Appropriations: Esotericism, Kabbalah, and the Transformation of Traditions* (Beer Sheva: Ben-Gurion University of the Negev Press, 2016), 223–42.

44 Christopher Partridge, 'Occulture Is Ordinary' in Egil Asprem and Kennet Granholm eds., *Contemporary Esotericism* (Sheffield: Equinox, 2013), 113–133 and Christopher Partridge, *The Re-Enchantment of the WestAlternative Spiritualities, Sacralization, Popular Culture and Occulture*, vol. 1 (London: T & T Clark International, 2004).

45 For rejected knowledges, see W. J. Hanegraaff, *Esotericism and the Academy: Rejected Knowledge in Western Culture* (Cambridge: Cambridge University Press, 2012).

46 Cf. DeHaas, 'The Church Universal and Triumphant', 270–86.

Chapter 7

1 See H. Bloom, *The American Religion: The Emergence of the Post-Christian Nation* (New York: Simon & Schuster, 1992) and R. Remini, *Joseph Smith* (New York: Penguin, 2002). Cf. D. Vogel, *Joseph Smith: The Making of a Prophet*

(Salt Lake City, UT: Signature Books, 2004) and F. M. Brodie, *No Man Knows My History: The Life of Joseph Smith*, 2nd edn. (New York: Vintage, 1995). For a republican interpretation, see K. Winn, *Exiles in a Land of Liberty* (Chapel Hill, NC: UNC Press, 1989). See also D. Vogel, *Religious Seekers and the Advent of Mormonism* (Salt Lake: Signature Press, 1988). Cf. R. Stark, *The Rise of Mormonism*, ed. Reid L. Neilson (New York: Columbia University Press, 2005); L. J. Arrington and D. Bitton, *The Mormon Experience: A History of the Latter-day Saints*, 2nd edn. (Urbana, IL: University of Illinois Press, 1992); M. P. Leone, *The Roots of Modern Mormonism* (Cambridge, MA: Harvard University Press, 1979) and M. Bowman, *The Mormon People: The Making of an American Faith* (New York: Random House, 2012).

2 R. L. Bushman, *Joseph Smith: Rough Stone Rolling* (New York: Alfred Knopf, 2005) and *Believing History: Latter-day Saint Essays* (New York: Columbia University Press, 2004).

3 See T. L. Givens, *By the Hand of Mormon: The American Scripture That Launched a New World Religion* (Oxford: Oxford University Press, 2002).

4 T. Givens, *The Latter-day Saint Experience in America* (Westport, CN: Greenwood, 2004), xv. Cf. J. Shipps, *Mormonism: The Story of a New Religious Tradition* (Illinois: University of Illinois Press, 1987).

5 D. J. Davies, *The Mormon Culture of Salvation* (London: Ashgate, 2000) and *An Introduction to Mormonism* (Cambridge: Cambridge University Press, 2003) and *Joseph Smith, Jesus, and Satanic Opposition: Atonement, Evil and the Mormon Vision* (London: Ashgate, 2010).

6 Miranda Wilcox and John D. Young, eds., *Standing Apart: Mormon Historical Consciousness and the Concept of Apostasy* (Oxford: Oxford University Press, 2014).

7 R. L. Bushman, *Believing History: Latter-day Saint Essays* (New York: Columbia University Press, 2007), 165.

8 For information about the Church in general see, D. H. Ludlow ed., *Encyclopedia of Mormonism* (New York: Macmillan, 1992).

9 For nineteenth century materials, see R. Turley Jr, ed., *Selected Collections from the Archives of the Church of Jesus Christ of Latter-day Saints*, 2 vols (Provo, UT: Brigham Young University Press, 2002) and D. Vogel, ed., *Early Mormon Documents*. 5 vols (Salt Lake City, UT: Signature Books, 1996–2003).

10 Remini, *Joseph Smith*, 36–7.

11 Howard Bloom famously claimed that Joseph Smith was a gnostic, but this is too strong. See Bloom, *The American Religion*.

12 The Smith family were treasure hunters and Joseph hired himself out searching for buried treasure. In 1826 he was arrested as a glass looker under New York state law. He also wore an astrological medal all his life. Cf. D. M. Quinn, *Early Mormonism and the Magic World View* (Salt Lake City, UT: Signature Books, 1987).

13 The details of the story are well known.

14 W. Hudson, 'The Prophethood of Joseph Smith' in R. Neilson and T. Givens eds., *Joseph Smith Jr: Reappraisals after Two Centuries* (Oxford: Oxford University Press, 2008), 201–7 ch. 13.

15 Emma, Joseph's wife, declared that the plates lay in a box under her bed for months but also admitted that she did not see them. Subsequently Emma and her family rejected the theology and the economics of the twelve and stayed in Nauvoo. A reorganized Church was set up in 1860 with Joseph Smith III as president. However, the Church has now been renamed The Community of Christ. See L. K. Newell and V. T. Avery, *Mormon Enigma: Emma Hale Smith, Prophet's Wife, 'Elect Lady', Polygamy's Foe*, 1804–1879 (New York: Doubleday and Company, 1984). Latter-day Saints tend to believe that there is some strength in the reports of witnesses. They insist that eight witnesses 'hefted and handled' the plates, although their detailed testimonies, when we have them, are ambiguous. Some of the witnesses saw spiritually rather than physically, three of the main witnesses to the plates (Oliver Cowdery, Martin Harris and David Whitmer) subsequently left the Church, and two of them subsequently gave equal credence to revelations by a female prophet who engaged in ecstatic orgies. That is, they were not exactly sceptical inquirers.

16 After Joseph's death Strang also claimed to have received three metal plates which he 'translated' and published as The Law of the Lord, but his content was not revolutionary and his movement subsequently declined.

17 See G. Underwood, *The Millenarian World of Early Mormonism* (Urbana: University of Illinois Press, 1993).

18 Joseph often relied on direct inspiration for these translations since he had no real mastery of any foreign language. His translations from ancient Egyptian were problematic. See R. L. Millet and R. J. Matthews, eds., *Plain and Precious Truths Restored: The Doctrinal and Historical Significance of the Joseph Smith Translation* (Salt Lake City, UT: Deseret, 1995); M. S. Nyman and R. L. Millet, eds., *The Joseph Smith Translation: The Restoration of Plain and Precious Things* (Provo, UT: Religious Studies Center, Brigham Young University, 1985) and Robert J. Matthews, *'A Plainer Translation': Joseph Smith's Translation of the Bible, a History and Commentary* (Provo, UT: Brigham Young University Press, 1975). Cf. Julie M. Smith, 'Five Impulses of the Joseph Smith Translation of Mark and Their Implications for LDS Hermeneutics' in *Studies in the Bible and Antiquity* 7, article 2 (2015): 1–21.

19 Joseph's creativity here remains controversial, and it is clear that he did not literally translate the Egyptian papyri which came into his hands and that he misidentified an Egyptian sex god with God the Father (the text Joseph identified as the *Book of Abraham* in fact consisted of Egyptian funeral rites dating from some 2,200 years later). Latter-day Saint scholars contest this.

See John Gee and Kerry Muhlestein, 'An Egyptian Context for the Sacrifice of Abraham' in *Journal of Book of Mormon and Other Restoration Scripture* 20, no. 2 (2011): 70–7.

20 Enoch has a special place in Latter-day Saint discourses, partly because Joseph worked to give him greater prominence and partly because he provides a precedent for the mixture of seership and leadership found in Smith. See J. R. Johansen, *Enoch's Zion, Joseph's Zion and the Future Zion* (Bountiful, UT: Horizon Publishers, 2003).

21 T. Givens, *The Book of Mormon: A Very Short Introduction* (Oxford: Oxford University Press, 2009) and G. Hardy, *Understanding the Book of Mormon: A Reader's Guide* (Oxford: Oxford University Press, 2010). Latter-day Saint interpretations of the book are changing and James E. Faulconer suggests that the work can be understood as scripture divinely ordering conduct even if it is not representational.

22 Some Latter-day Saints defend the historicity of the text, claiming that the names in the book are found in Arabia, that the book gives the lost history of ancient America, that its reformed Egyptian is close to ancient Meroitic, that the text is based on Middle Eastern chiasms, that it is full of Hebraisms, that the prophet Lehi accurately describes Jerusalem as it was prior to the Babylonian captivity – and so on. See the apologetical volumes from FARMS and the writings of Hugh Nibley arguing that the *Ur*-Church restored by Joseph can be found in the ancient Middle East. See, the multivolume Collected Works of Hugh Nibley published by Deseret Books. Latter-day Saints seem to be making more use of serious academic outlets as the decades pass, including Brigham Young University Studies and the Neal A. Maxwell Institute for Religious Scholarship which publishes *Mormon Studies Review, Journal Book of Mormon Studies* and *Studies in the Bible and History*.

23 See, for example, J. M. Spencer, *1st Nephi: A Brief Theological Introduction* (Provo, UT: The Neal A. Maxwell Institute for Religious Scholarship, 2020) and T. Givens, *2nd Nephi: A Brief Theological Introduction* (Provo, UT: The Neal A. Maxwell Institute for Religious Scholarship, 2020).

24 Givens, *The Book of Mormon*, 125. Consistent with this, the Church reserves the right to edit and refine its scriptures. Thus, the present text of the *Book of Mormon* differs from that originally published in both minor and substantial respects.

25 A. K. Thompson, 'The Doctrine of Resurrection in the Book of Mormon' in *Interpreter: A Journal of Mormon Scripture* 16 (2015): 101–29.

26 Jan Shipps characterized Mormonism as a movement with a new cosmology. See Shipps, *Mormonism*, and Jan Shipps, *Sojourner in the Promised Land: Forty Years among the Mormons* (Urbana and Chicago: University of Illinois Press, 2000). Cf.

T. Givens, *Wrestling the Angel: The Foundations of Mormon Thought: Cosmos, God, Humanity* (Oxford: Oxford University Press, 2014).

27 See H. Nibley, 'Temple and Cosmos: Beyond This Ignorant Present' in *The Collected Works of Hugh Nibley*. Vol. 12, ed. Don E. Norton (Salt Lake City, UT: Deseret Book Company, 1992), 42–90.

28 Assertive materialism of this kind was found in Orson Pratt's essay 'Absurdities of Immaterialism' (1849).

29 *Doctrines and Covenants*, 131:78.

30 Some Latter-day Saint intellectuals have defended these ideas as exemplifying extreme realism and metaphysical pluralism. On this view, the Saints have a unique conception of reality. More recent Latter-day Saint writers, however, have tended to regard these ideas as speculative views specific to Joseph and some other Latter-day Saint thinkers, not revelation.

31 See here the Society for Mormon Philosophy and see J. M. McLachlan and L. Ericson, eds., *Discourses in Mormon Theology: Philosophical and Theological Possibilities* (Salt Lake City, UT: Greg Kofford Books, 2007) and *Element: A Journal of Mormon Philosophy and Theology*. Currently there is a turn to continental philosophy in the work of James Faulconer, Adam Miller and Joseph Spenser. These Mormon philosophers accept what they hold to be the postmodern critique of truth and reject what they take to be the metaphysical basis of traditional Christianity. Miller rejects representational concepts of truth. See A. S. Miller, *Future Mormon: Essays in Mormon Theology* (Salt Lake City, UT: Greg Kofford Books, 2016).

32 For Latter-day Saint anthropology see T. G. Madsen, *Eternal Man* (Salt Lake City, UT: Deseret Book Company, 1966).

33 L. Checketts, 'Thomas Aquinas Meets Joseph Smith: Toward a Mormon Ethics of Natural Law', in *Dialogue: A Journal of Mormon Thought* 51, no. 1 (2018): 79–100.

34 I discuss these doctrinal innovations in an Appendix.

35 It is now clear that magical practices including seer stones continued in the Church until the end of the nineteenth century. See J. Stapley, *The Power of Godliness: Mormon Liturgy and Cosmology* (New York: Oxford University Press, 2018).

36 Joseph introduced plural 'celestial marriage' among his close followers in Nauvoo together with secret doctrines. His ritual sacred marriage allowed men and women to become priests and priestesses, kings and queens and ultimately gods and goddesses. A few women seem to have taken second spouses as well. The crucial point was the change in celestial status thus assured.

37 E. T. Benson, *The Teachings of Ezra Taft Benson* (Salt Lake City, UT: Bookcraft, 1988), 7.

38 G. D. Smith, *Nauvoo Polygamy: '... but we called it celestial marriage'* (Salt Lake City, UT: Signature Books, 2008). Cf. L. Foster, *Religion and Sexuality: The Shakers, the Mormons, and the Oneida Community* (Urbana: University of Illinois Press, 1984), ch. 3.
39 There is some evidence that overcoming the death was a major concern in early Mormonism. See Samuel Morris Brown, *In Heaven as It Is on Earth: Joseph Smith and the Early Mormon Concept of Death* (Oxford: Oxford University Press, 2012).
40 D. J. Buerger, *The Mysteries of Godliness: A History of Mormon Temple Worship* (Salt Lake City, UT: Signature Books, 2002).
41 D. J. Buerger, 'The Development of the Mormon Temple Endowment Ceremony', in *Dialogue: A Journal of Mormon Thought* 20, no. 4 (1987): 67.
42 See Joseph Smith, *Journals, Volume 3: May 1843–June 1844*, edited by A. Hedge, A. Smith and B. Rogers. The Joseph Smith Papers ed. A. Hedge, A. Smith and B. Rogers (Salt Lake City, UT: Church Historian's Press, 2015).
43 E. B. Firmage and R. C. Mangrum, *Zion in the Courts: A Legal History of the Church of Jesus Christ of Latter-day Saints 1830–1900* (Urbana: University of Illinois Press, 1988).
44 See R. L. Bushman, *Joseph Smith and the Beginnings of Mormonism* (Urbana: University of Illinois Press, 1988); Johansen, *Enoch's Zion*; and B. E. Park, *Kingdom of Nauvoo: The Rise and Fall of a Religious Empire on the American Frontier* (New York City: Liveright Publishing, 2020).
45 Here fruitful comparisons can be made between Mormons and Sikhs. Sikhs are also characterized by extraversion. They too are a new people, with a separate identity and distinctive identifiers (clothing, beards, turbans, temples, food kitchens, engaged in worldly affairs especially economic activities. They practise equality and democratic self-government, have only lay clergy, and reject distinctions based on caste, race or creed. Their religion is based on direct communication with God and they often exhibit higher moral standards than their neighbours. On the other hand, they have a positive view of violence and give the sword pride of place in their ceremonies. See W. H. McLeod, *The Sikhs: History, Religion, and Society* (New York: Columbia University Press, 1989).
46 R. D. Potter, 'Liberation Theology in the Book of Mormon,' in *Discourses in Mormon Theology*, ed. J. M. McLachlan and L. I. Ericson (Salt Lake: Greg Kofford Books, 2007), ch. 8.
47 N. A. Carmack, 'Images of Christ in Latter-day Saint Visual Culture, 1900–1999' in *BYU Studies* 39, no. 3 (2000): 18–76.
48 T. L. Givens, *People of Paradox: A History of Mormon Culture* (Oxford: Oxford University Press, 2007) and *The Latter-day Saint Experience in America*.
49 T. Carter, *Building Zion: The Material World of Mormon Settlement* (Minneapolis, MN: University of Minnesota Press, 2015).

50 The Saints also have *The Pearl of Great Price*, a compilation of revisions to the King James translation of the Bible and the *13 Articles of Faith*. It is generally agreed that the Church had edited the *Doctrine and Covenants* and Joseph's multi-volume *History of the Church* to the point of reversing meanings, and added both concepts and entire paragraphs to individual revelations. There are related problems with Church versions of many texts currently attributed to Joseph. From a Latter-day Saint point of view this is justified because what matters is what the text means as scripture for the Church now. Moreover, there is some historical basis for this approach in Joseph's own habit of changing his revelations from time to time, including the text of the *Book of Mormon*. See Bushman, *Joseph Smith: Rough Stone Rolling*. It is also important to note that important texts once attributed to Joseph are now largely attributed to others, including the *Lectures on Faith*, which seems to be mainly the work of Sidney Rigdon.

51 Joseph himself ordained some blacks to the priesthood. On Race generally see A. L. Mauss, *All Abraham's Children: Changing Mormon Conceptions of Race and Lineage* (Urbana: University of Illinois Press, 2003).

52 On race generally see M. P. Mueller, *Race and the Making of the Mormon People* (Chapel Hill: The University of North Carolina Press, 2017).

53 There is now literature on homosexual Saints and on the contributions of Black women. See L. R. Strickling, *On Fire in Baltimore: Black Mormon Women and Conversion in a Raging City* (Salt Lake City, UT: Greg Kofford Books, 2018) and C. L. Bushman, *Mormon Sisters: Women in Early Utah* (Logan, UT: Utah State University Press, 1997). Homosexuals are no longer considered apostates and children of same-sex marriages may be baptized. More generally, see J. Riess, *The Next Mormons: How Millennials Are Changing the L D S Church* (New York: Oxford University Press, 2019).

54 See T. G. Petrey, 'Toward a Post-Heterosexual Mormon Theology' in *Dialogue: A Journal of Mormon Thought* 44, no. 4 (2011): 107–43.

55 See A. Mauss, *The Angel and the Beehive: The Mormon Struggle with Assimilation* (Urbana: University of Illinois Press, 1994). Some Latter-day Saints interpret these tensions as evidence of a distinctive culture which allows the Church to change rapidly and to make its way successfully through divergent cultures all over the world.

56 Latter-day Saint scholars have been more successful in showing that semblances of some of their doctrines can be found in apocryphal texts cited by Jesus or St Paul, than their predecessors' efforts to ground the *Book of Mormon* in Latin American archaeology would lead one to expect. For example, the teaching that souls pre-exist and the teaching that creation is not *ex nihilo* can be found in the Wisdom of Solomon. Cf. T. Givens, *When Souls Had Wings: Pre-Mortal Existence in Western Thought* (Oxford: Oxford University Press, 2010).

57 See the brilliant study by Givens, *By the Hand of Mormon*.

Appendix

1. Mormons were denounced as heretics from early on. See T. Givens, *The Viper on the Hearth: Mormons, Myths, and the Construction of Heresy* (New York: Oxford University Press, 2013).
2. Blake T. Ostler, *Exploring Mormon Thought: The Attributes of God*, vol. 1 (Salt Lake City, UT: Greg Kofford Books, 2001), 11.
3. A. Keith Thompson, *Trinity and Monotheism: A Historical and Theological Review of the Origins and Substance of the Doctrine* (Redland Bay, QLD: Modotti Press, 2019).
4. Moses 3:4–5.
5. Some Latter-day Saints distinguish the Holy Ghost, a distinct person, from the Holy Spirit as the all-pervading agent of God's actions. For a sophisticated treatment of Mormon conceptions of embodiment, see J. E. Faulconer, 'The Transcendence of the Flesh, Divine and Human,' in P. Y. Hoskisson and D. C. Peterson, eds., *'To Seek the Law of the Lord': Essays in Honor of John W. Welch* (Orem, UT: The Interpreter Foundation, 2017), 113–34. Cf. D. J. Davies, 'The Holy Spirit in Mormonism' in *International Journal of Mormon Studies* 2 (2009): 23–41.
6. Here the famous King Follett sermon remains a crucial if controversial text. See D. Q. Cannon, 'The King Follett Discourse: Joseph Smith's Greatest Sermon in Historical Perspective' in *BYU Studies* 18, no. 2 (1978): 179–92.
7. Ostler, *Exploring Mormon Thought* in three volumes, especially *Exploring Mormon Thought: The Attributes of God*, 78.
8. According to some Bible scholars 'gods' in this sense were not supreme but dependent on Yahweh, although it is not clear that Joseph understood 'gods' in this sense. Indeed, Joseph himself taught that there were other divine persons before the Father became mortal.
9. During the Nauvoo period Joseph began to reject the notion of Trinity and to teach the plurality of gods. Different Mormons deal with this differently. At times there have been manifest tensions between rationalistic Church intellectuals and more conservative Church authorities. Thus, Sterling Mc Murrin (1914–96) argued for the moral neutrality of the universe in which a finite God strove to extend his dominion, a conception which he claimed allowed Latter-day Saints, unlike other Christians, to solve the problem of evil. Parley Pratt (1807–57) and Orson Pratt (1811–81) interpreted Joseph's teaching on eternal intelligences to mean that reality consisted of infinite eternal particles, each of which possessed independent creativity and mind, thus providing the Church with a variation on Leibniz's monadology. Subsequently the theologian scientist John Widtsoe (1872–1952) produced a perfectionist theology, while Brigham H. Roberts (1857–1933) adopted panentheism in his attempt to reconcile plural theology with absolutism. See B. T. Ostler, 'The Restoration and Systematic Theologies,' in *Exploring Mormon*

Thought: The Attributes of God, ch. 3, and his subsequent volumes, *Exploring Mormon Thought: The Problems of Theism and the Love of God*, vol. 2 (Salt Lake City, UT: Greg Kofford Books, 2006) and *Exploring Mormon Thought: Of God and Gods*, Vol. 3 (Salt Lake City, UT: Greg Kofford Books, 2008).

10 Brigham Young claimed that God the Father had lived on earth as a mortal and later evolved into God. He also taught that God became Adam and brought one of his plural wives with him as Eve. Later after his ascension he returned to earth to physically as father Jesus. See D. J. Buerger, 'The Adam-God Doctrine' in *Dialogue: A Journal of Mormon Thought* 15, no. 1 (1982): 14–58. This doctrine is now disapproved. It is only one of several elaborations of Joseph's polytheism. Another was Eliza B. Snow's identification of Eve as a goddess.

11 Latter-day Saint scholars sometimes find Trinitarianism in the Book of Mormon and/or read monotheism as an error missing from ancient Israel with its anthropomorphic deity and council of gods and also from New Testament Christianity, despite later developments. See Thompson, *Trinity* and *Monotheism: A Historical and Theological Review of the Origins and Substance of the Doctrine*.

12 T. Givens and F. Givens, *The God Who Weeps: How Mormonism Makes Sense of Life* (Salt Lake City: Ensign Peak, 2012).

13 The Latter-day Saint philosopher, James Faulconer doubts that it will ever be possible to integrate the conflicting Latter-day Saint philosophies and theologies into a coherent system. Following French philosophical discussions, Faulconer claims that Latter-day Saints reject the ontotheological tradition entirely and are a-theological and also a-theists in so far as they reject the *theos*, even though they do not have a single coherent world view to propose. See J. E. Faulconer, *Faith, Philosophy, Scripture* (Provo, UT: Neal A. Maxwell Institute, 2010).

14 Brigham H. Roberts, for example, held that there was one eternal God immanent in the universe who radiated into many individual gods.

15 L. H. Gentry, 'What of the Lectures on Faith?' in *BYU Studies* 19, no. 1 (1978): 5–19. Other Latter-day Saint apologists, however, argue that the *Book of Mormon* contains a new theology which is definitely not that of traditional Christianity. See Givens, *By the Hand of Mormon: The American Scripture That Launched a New World Religion*.

16 See, for example, Joseph M. Spencer, *For Zion: A Mormon Theology of Hope*, (Salt Lake City, UT: Greg Kofford Books, 2014); Miller, *Future Mormon: Essays in Mormon Theology*.

17 Blake Ostler has produced a massive re-evaluation of Latter-day Saint theology and philosophy at the price of radically reinterpreting or dismissing as non-canonical much of the teaching of Joseph, Brigham Young and other past Church Presidents. Ostler largely rejects classical theism. He denies that God exists in eternity with the timeless attributes attributed to the *theos* in Greek philosophy. Ostler also struggles to allow God relative omniscience (God has present omniscience but

cannot know the future contingent acts of free agents). He reads the teaching about God's embodiment as negative: as a denial of the traditional doctrine of God and its associated metaphysics. It implies, he suggests, that the difference between God and humanity may not be as great as has been assumed. In addition, Ostler adopts a kenotic Christology and a form of social Trinitarianism. Accordingly, he revises the classic the polytheist interpretation of Joseph's theology and argues that even the King Follett sermon can be read as social Trinitarian. Ostler also offers a compassion theory of atonement for which God becomes what we are to show us that he loves us so much that he is willing to be in relationship with us, even though it causes him extensive and intensive suffering. He also provides a Latter-day Saint ethics for which moral laws, grounded in the eternal nature of uncreated realities, define the conditions that are necessary for the growth and progress of the individual and the community. Ostler appeals to the fallacy of composition in order to insist that there is no need for the Godhead as a whole to have the same properties in each of its parts. See Ostler, *Exploring Mormon Thought: The Attributes of God*.

18 There is some evidence that the early Latter-day Saints were closer to a form of Protestant orthodoxy than later developments would suggest. Specifically, before 1835 they seem to have been close to the Disciples of Christ and to Methodists, a view supported in part by the emergence of the Reformed Church which refused to accept Joseph's later non-Protestant doctrines. For a spirited but controversial defence of Latter-day Saint materialism, see Stephen Webb, *Jesus Christ, Eternal God: Heavenly Flesh and the Metaphysics of Matter* (New York: Oxford University Press, 2011), ch. 9.

19 Classical Mormonism identifies Jesus with Adam, who was Michael as well as Jehovah. Current teaching has both Adam and Christ as part of the Council of the Gods who bring about mankind's experience of probation on earth.

20 For the neo-orthodox version see R. L. Millet, *A Different Jesus? The Christ of the Latter-day Saints* (Grand Rapids, MI: Eerdmans, 2000). For an attempt to provide a Latter-day Saint Christology informed by analytical philosophical theology, see Ostler, *Exploring Mormon Thought: The Attributes of God*, ch. 14. Steven E. Robinson argues in How Wide the Divide?, see C. L. Blomberg and S. E. Robinson, *How Wide the Divide? A Mormon and an Evangelical in Conversation* (Downers Grove, IL: InterVarsity Press, 1997) that Latter-day Saints can come close to reform Christianity and accept that the Scriptures are literally true. For him God is omniscient, omnipotent and unchangeable. See also John G. Turner, *The Mormon Jesus: A Biography*, (Cambridge, MA and London: Belknap Press of Harvard University Press, 2016).

21 'The Olive Leaf' revelation of 1832.

22 *Doctrine and Covenants* 130:22. Cf. Davies, *The Mormon Culture of Salvation*.

23 Latter-day Saint enthusiasm for science has often been positivistic in spirit, but Brigham Young University in Utah is held to be one of the best universities for science in the United States.
24 Latter-day Saints assimilate their revelation to the Patristic doctrine of *theosis*, but the comparison is somewhat forced. See N. Russell, *The Doctrine of Deification in the Greek Patristic Tradition* (Oxford: Oxford University Press, 2004).
25 Ostler, *Exploring Mormon Thought: The Attributes of God*, 456.
26 *Doctrine and Covenants* 76, 88:17–28. Latter-day Saint scholars insist that this does not mean that human beings ever become equal to the Father (nineteenth-century statements are more ambiguous). For Latter-day Saint conceptions of progression, see Kirk. D. Hagen, 'Eternal Progression in a Multiverse: An Explorative Mormon Moment' in *Dialogue: A Journal of Mormon Thought* 39, no. 2 (2006): 1–45.
27 Givens, *The Book of Mormon: A Very Short Introduction*, ch. 2.
28 *The Word of Wisdom*.
29 Ibid., 70.
30 Latter-day Saint scholars tend to update Latter-day Saint theology and philosophy as intellectual trends change, while associations such as Element, The Society for Latter-day Saint Philosophy and Theology attempt to show that Church teaching anticipates doctrines currently fashionable in academia from process theology to deconstruction.
31 Moses 6:64 in the *Pearl of Great Price*.
32 For Latter-day Saints the form of the Church derives from revelational events. Joseph restored the true Church in 1830. John the Baptist appeared to Joseph and Sydney Rigdon and renewed the Aaronic priesthood in 1829. Peter, James and John restored the priesthood of Melchizedek shortly afterwards after a gap of 1,800 hundred years. Joseph Moses appeared to Joseph and Cowdery in the Kirkland temple in 1833 and Peter, James and John gave the Keys of the Kingdom in 1836.
33 Mormon apologists search for evidence that Christians originally believed in premortal existence. See Givens, *When the Soul Had Wings: Pre-Mortal Existence in Western Thought*.
34 Consistent with this cosmological literalism, Joseph expected new astronomical knowledge to come by revelation in the future.
35 The term 'paranormal' captures the fact that Latter-day Saints characteristically posit preternatural phenomena which they claim are to be understood in naturalistic terms. There are now several intellectually oriented Mormon journals which explore new perspectives and relate Church teaching to current theological and philosophical trends. See *Dialogue: A Journal of Mormon Thought*, *Sunstone*, *BYU Studies*, *FARMS Review of Books*, *The Journal of Mormon History* and *Element: The Journal of the Society for Mormon Philosophy and Theology*.

Bibliography

'Abdu'l-Bahá. *Tablets of Abdu'l-Bahá Abbas*. Vol. 1. Chicago, IL: Bahá'í Publishing Trust, 1919.
'Abdu'l-Bahá. *Paris Talks*. 4th edn. London: Bahá'í Publishing Trust, 1969.
'Abdu'l-Bahá. *The Secret of Divine Civilization*. Wilmette, IL: Bahá'í Publishing Trust, 1975.
'Abdu'l-Bahá. *The Promulgation of Universal Peace*. Wilmette, IL: Bahá'í Publishing Trust, 1982.
'Abdu'l-Bahá. *Some Answered Questions*. Wilmette, IL: Bahá'í Publishing Trust, 1985.
'Abdu'l-Bahá. 'Tablet of the Universe', *Makátib-i 'Abdu'l-Bahá* 1 (1997): 13–32.
Able, John. *'Apocalypse Secrets' Bahai Interpretation of the Book of Revelation*. John Able Books, 2011.
Abravanel, M. 'The Summit Lighthouse: Its Worldview and Theosophical Heritage'. In *Handbook of the Theosophical Current*, edited by Olav Hammer and Mikael Rothstein, 173–91. Leiden: Brill, 2013.
Agamben, G. *The Highest Poverty: Monastic Rules and Form-of-Life*. Translated by Adam Kotsko. Stanford: Stanford University Press, 2013.
Ānandamitra, A. *The Spiritual Philosophy of Śrī Śrī Ānandamūrti: A Commentary on Ánanda Sútram*. 1st edn. Denver: Ānanda Mārga Publications, 1981.
Ānandamitra, A. *The Spiritual Philosophy of Śrī Śrī Ānandamūrti: A Commentary on Ánanda Sútram*. 2nd edn. Kolkata: Ānanda Mārga Pracāraka Samgha, 1998.
Anandamurti, Ś. *Ánanda Márga Elementary Philosophy*. Jamalpur: Ananda Marga, 1955.
Ānandamūrti, Ś. *Human Society Part 1*. Kolkata: Ananda Marga Publications, 1959.
Ānandamūrti, Ś. *Ānānda Sūtram*. Kolkata: Ananda Marga Publications, 1961.
Ānandamūrti, Ś. *Human Society Part 2*. Ananda Nagar: Proutist Universal, 1967.
Ānandamūrti, Ś. *A Guide to Human Conduct*. Manila: Ānanda Mārga Publications, 1981.
Ānandamūrti, Ś. *The Thoughts of P. R. Sarkar*, edited by A. Ānandamitra. Kolkata: Ānanda Mārga Pracāraka Samgha, 1985.
Ānandamūrti, Ś. *Ananda Marga Caryacarya, Part 2*. 4th edn. Kolkata: Ananda Marga Publications, 1987.
Ānandamūrti, Ś. *Ānanda Mārga Philosophy in a Nutshell*. Parts 1–4. Translated by A.V. Avadhuta and A.V. Avadhuta. Kolkata: Ānanda Mārga Pracāraka Samgha, 1988.
Ānandamūrti, Ś. *Ānanda Mārga Ideology and Way of Life*. Parts 1–11. 1st edn. Translated by A.V. Avadhuta and A.V. Avadhuta. Kolkata: Ānanda Mārga Pracāraka Samgha, 1988.
Ānandamūrti, Ś. *Yoga Psychology*. Kolkata: Ānanda Mārga Publications, 1990.

Ānandamūrti, Ś. *Ānanda Mārga: Elementary Philosophy*. Kolkata: Ananda Marga Publications, 1991.

Ānandamūrti, Ś. *Discourses on Tantra*. 2 vols., ed. Vijayānanda and Acyutānanda. Kolkata: Ānanda Mārga Publications, 1994.

Anandmurti, Ś. *Ananda Marga Caryacarya, Part 1*. 6th edn. Kolkata: Ananda Marga Publications, 1995.

Ānandamūrti, Ś. *Yoga Sadhana: The Spiritual Practice of Yoga*. Kolkata: Ananda Marga Publications, 2010.

Ashcraft, W. Michael. *A Historical Introduction to the Study of New Religious Movements*. London: Routledge, 2018.

Asprem, E. *The Problem of Disenchantment: Scientific Naturalism and Esoteric Discourse. 1900–1939*. Leiden: Brill, 2014.

Asprem, E. with Kennet Granholm, eds. *Contemporary Esotericism*. Sheffield: Equinox, 2012.

Asprem, Egil and Markus Altena Davidsen, eds. *Aries: Journal for the Study of Western Esotericism*, Special Issue on Esotericism and the Cognitive Science of Religion 3, no. 1 (2017).

Arrington, L. J. and D. Bitton. *The Mormon Experience: A History of the Latter-day Saints*. 2nd edn. Urbana, IL: University of Illinois Press, 1992.

Atran, Scott. *In Gods We Trust: The Evolutionary Landscape of Religion*. New York: Oxford University Press, 2002.

Avadhuta, Acarya Sutiirthananda, ed. *The Microvita Revolution: Towards the New Science of Matter, Life and Mind*. Kolkata: Ananda Marga, 1990.

Babb, L. 'The Brahma Kumaris: History as Movie'. In *Redemptive Encounters: Three-Modern Styles in the Hindu Tradition*, edited by L. Babb, 110–55. Berkeley: University of California Press, 1986.

Badiee, J. *An Earthly Paradise: Bahá'í Houses of Worship around the World*. Oxford: George Ronald, 1992.

Badi'i, H. *The True Foundation of all Economics (A Compilation)*. 2nd rev. ed. Canada: Webcom, 1996.

Bahá'í Publishing Trust ed. *Bahá'í Marriage and Family Life: Selections from the Writings of the Bahá'í Faith*. Wilmette, IL: Bahá'í Publishing Trust, 1997.

Bahá'í Publishing Trust ed. *Bahá'u'lláh, the Bab and 'Abdu'l-Bahá: Bahá'í Prayers*. Wilmette, IL: Bahai Publishing Trust, 2020.

Bahá'u'lláh. *Gleanings from the Writings of Bahá'u'lláh*. Translated by Shoghi Effendi. Wilmette, IL: Bahá'í Publishing Trust, 1952.

Bahá'u'lláh. *Epistle to the Son of the Wolf*. Translated by S. Effendi. Wilmette, IL: Bahá'í Publishing Trust, 1953.

Bahá'u'lláh. *The Proclamation of Bahá'u'lláh to the Kings and Leaders of the World*. Haifa: World Centre Publications, 1967.

Bahá'u'lláh. *The Kitáb-i-Íqán: The Book of Certitude*. Translated by Shoghi Effendi. Wilmette, IL: Bahá'í-Publishing Trust, 1974.

Bahá'u'lláh. *The Hidden Words of Bahá'u'lláh*. Translated by S. Effendi. Wilmette, IL: Bahá'í Publishing Trust, 1975.

Bahá'u'lláh. *The Seven Valleys and the Four Valleys*. Translated by M. Gail with A. K. Khan. 3rd edn. Wilmette, IL: Bahá'í Publishing Trust, 1978.

Bahá'u'lláh. 'A Tablet of Mirzá Husayn 'Alí Bahá'u'lláh of the Early Iraq Period: The Tablet of All Food', Translated by Stephen N. Lambden. *Bahá'í Studies Bulletin* 3, no. 1 (June 1984): 4–67.

Bahá'u'lláh. *The Kitáb-i- Aqdas: The Most Holy Book*. Haifa: Bahá'í World Centre, 1992.

Bahá'u'lláh. 'The Riḍvánu'l-'Adl, the Tablet of the Paradise of Justice?', *Bahá'í Studies Review* 20 (2014/2018): 97–134.

Bahá'u'lláh. *The Call of the Divine Beloved: Selected Mystical Works of Bahá'u'lláh*. Haifa: Bahá'í World Centre, 2019.

Balch, Robert W. and Stephan Langdon. 'How the Problem of Malfeasance Gets Overlooked in Studies of New Religions: An Examination of the AWARE Study of the Church Universal and Triumphant'. In *Wolves within the Fold: Religious Leadership and Abuses of Power*, edited by Anson D. Shupe, 191–211. New Brunswick, NJ: Rutgers University Press, 1998.

Balyuzi, H. M. *Edward Granville Browne and the Bahá'í Faith*. Oxford: George Ronald, 1970.

Balyuzi, H. M. *'Abdu'l-Bahá: The Centre of the Covenant of Bahá'u'lláh*. Oxford: George Ronald, 1971.

Balyuzi, H. M. *Bahá'u'lláh: The King of Glory*. Oxford: George Ronald, 1980.

Barker, E. ed. *New Religious Movements*. Lewiston, NY: Edwin Mellen Press, 1982.

Barker, E. ed. *Of Gods and Men: New Religious Movements in the West Macon*. Macon, GA: Mercer University Press, 1983.

Barker, E. *The Making of a Moonie: Choice or Brainwashing?*. Oxford and New York, NY: B. Blackwell, 1984.

Barrett, D. V. *The New Believers: A Survey of Sects, Cults and Alternative Religions*. London: Cassell, 2001.

Barrett, Justin L. 'Counterfactuality and Counterintuitive Concepts', *Behaviour and Brain Sciences* 27, no. 6 (2005): 731–2.

Bates, R. *The Internal Being: Reincarnational and Intuitive Psychology*. Hayward, CA: Self-published, 2016a.

Bates, R. *Microvitology: Microvita Universal Subassembly Structures*. Mound Valley, KS: Self-published, 2016b.

Bates, R. *Microcosmology: A New Paradigm of Relativity*. First electronic edn. Mound Valley, KS: Self-published, 2017.

Bates, R. *Microvita A Handbook*. P. R. Sarkar Institute, 2019. Available online: https://prsinstitute.org/downloads/related/natural-sciences/microvita/MicrovitaHandbook.pdf

Bates, R. *The Cognitive Creative Universe: A Study of Microvita Cosmogony*. Hayward, CA: Self-published, 2020.

Batra, R. *Prout: The Alternative to Capitalism and Marxism*. Lanham, MD: University Press of America, 1980.

Bednarowski, M. F. *New Religions and the Theological Imagination in America*. Bloomington: Indiana University Press, 1989.

Bell, Alice and Marie-Laure Ryan, eds. *Possible Worlds Theory and Contemporary Narratology*. Lincoln, NE and London: University of Nebraska, 2019.

Benson, E. T. *The Teachings of Ezra Taft Benson*. Salt Lake City, UT: Bookcraft, 1988.

Bergsmo, M. ed. *Studying The Writings of Shoghi Effendi*. Oxford: George Ronald, 1991.

Bethel, D. M. *Makiguchi the Value Creator: Revolutionary Japanese Educator and Founder of Soka Gakkai*. New York and Tokyo: John Weatherill Inc., 1973.

Bethel, D. M. ed. *Education for Creative Living. Ideas and Proposals of Tsunesaburo Makiguchi*. Translated by A. Birnbaum and D. M. Bethel. Ames: Iowa State University, 1989.

Bjonnes, Roar. *Principles for a Balanced Economy: An Introduction to the Progressive Utilization Theory*. PROUT Research Institute, 2012.

Bloch, Ernst. *Christian Thomasius: Ein deutscher Gelehrter ohne Misere*. East Berlin: Aufbau Verlag, 1953.

Bloch, Ernst. *Avicenna and the Aristotelian Left*. Translated by Loren Goldman and Peter Thompson. New York: Columbia University Press, 2018.

Bloch, Ernst. *Thomas Münzer als Theologe der Revolution*. Munich: Kurt Wolf, 1921, *Christian Thomasius*.

Blomberg, C. L. and S. E. Robinson. *How Wide the Divide? A Mormon and an Evangelical in Conversation*. Downers Grove, IL: InterVarsity Press, 1997.

Bloom, H. *The American Religion: The Emergence of the Post-Christian Nation*. New York: Simon & Schuster, 1992.

Bogdanov, A. *Essays in Tektology: The General Science of Organization*. Translated by George Gorelik. Seaside, CA: Intersystems Publications, 1980.

Boulding, E. and D. Ikeda. *Into Full Flower Making Peace Cultures Happen*. Cambridge, MA: Dialogue Path Press, 2010.

Bowman, M. *The Mormon People: The Making of an American Faith*. New York: Random House, 2012.

Brahma, K. *Visions of the Future*. Mt Abu: Brahma Kumaris, 1996.

Brannen, N. S. *Soka Gakkai: Japan's Militant Buddhists*. Richmond, VA: John Knox Press, 1968.

Brodie, F. M. *No Man Knows My History: The Life of Joseph Smith*. 2nd edn. New York: Vintage, 1995.

Browman, M. *The Mormon People: The Making of an American Faith*. New York: Random House, 2012.

Brown, Keven. 'A Bahá'í Perspective on the Origin of Matter', *Journal of Bahá'í Studies* 2-3 (1990): 15-44.

Brown, Samuel Morris. *In Heaven as It Is on Earth: Joseph Smith and the Early Mormon Concept of Death*. Oxford: Oxford University Press, 2012.

Browne, E. G. 'Introduction'. In *Abbas Effendi: His Life and Teaching*, 2nd rev. edn. edited by Myron Phelps. New York: Putnam's Sons, 1912, xi–xxx.

Browne, E. G. *Materials for the Study of the Bábí Religion*. Cambridge: The University Press, 1918.

Buck, C. *Paradise and Paradigm: Key Symbols in Persian Christianity and the Bahá'í Faith*. Albany, NY: State University of New York Press, 1999.

Buck, C. and A. Ma'sumian. 'Baha'u'llah's Paradise of Justice: Commentary and Translation', *Baha'i Studies Review* 20 (2014): 97–134.

Buerger, D. J. 'The Adam-God Doctrine', *Dialogue: A Journal of Mormon Thought* 15, no. 1 (1982): 14–58.

Buerger, D. J. 'The Development of the Mormon Temple Endowment Ceremony', *Dialogue: A Journal of Mormon Thought* 20, no. 4 (1987): 67.

Buerger, D. J. *The Mysteries of Godliness: A History of Mormon Temple Worship*. Salt Lake City, UT: Signature Books, 2002.

Burley, M. *Classical Samkhya and Yoga–An Indian Metaphysics of Experience*. London: Routledge, 2006.

Busacchi, V. *Philosophy and Human Revolution: Essays in Celebration of Daisaku Ikeda's 90th Birthday*. Newcastle: Cambridge Scholars Publishing, 2018.

Bushman, C. L. *Mormon Sisters: Women in Early Utah*. Logan, UT: Utah State University Press, 1997.

Bushman, R. *Joseph Smith and the Beginnings of Mormonism*. Urbana, IL: University of Illinois Press, 1988.

Bushman, R. *Believing History: Latter-day Saint Essays*. New York: Columbia University Press, 2004.

Bushman, R. *Joseph Smith: Rough Stone Rolling*. New York: Alfred Knopf, 2005.

Bussey, M. 'Neohumanism: Critical Spirituality, Tantra and Education'. In *Neohumanist Educational Futures: Liberating the Pedagogical Intellect*, edited by S. Inayatullah, M. Bussey and I. Milojevic, 80–95. Taipei: Tamkang University Press, 2006.

Bussey, M. 'Embodied Education: Reflections on Sustainable Education', *The International Journal of Environmental, Cultural, Economic and Social Sustainability* 43, no. 3 (2008): 139–48.

Bussey, M. 'Critical Spirituality: Neohumanism as Method', *Journal of Future Studies* 5, no. 2 (2010): 21–35.

Bussey, M. 'Microvita and Transformative Information', *The Open Information Science Journal* 3 (2011): 28–39.

Bussey, M. and C. Mozzini-Alister. *Phenomenologies of Grace the Body, Embodiment, and Transformative Futures*. London: Palgrave-Macmillan, 2020.

Campbell, Bruce F. *A History of the Theosophical Movement*. Berkeley: University of California Press, 1980.

Cannon, D. Q. 'The King Follett Discourse: Joseph Smith's Greatest Sermon in Historical Perspective', *BYU Studies* 18, no. 2 (1978): 179–92.

Carmack, N. A. 'Images of Christ in Latter-day Saint Visual Culture, 1900–1999', *BYU Studies* 39, no. 3 (2000): 18–76.
Carter, T. *Building Zion: The Material World of Mormon Settlement*. Minneapolis, MN: University of Minnesota Press, 2015.
Causton, R. *Nichiren Shoshu Buddhism: An Introduction*. London: Rider, 1988.
Chamberlain, E. F. (compiled). *'Abdu'l-Bahá on Divine Philosophy*. Boston, MA: Tudor Press, 1918.
Chander, J. *The One Week Course*. Available online at: http://brahmakumarisresearch.org/resources
Chander, J. *Adi Dev: The First Man*. Mt Abu: Brahma Kumaris, 1983.
Chander, J. *Eternal Drama of Souls, Matter and God*. Mt Abu: Brahma Kumaris, 1985.
Chander, J. *The Eternal World Drama*. Mt Abu: Brahmin Kumaris, 1985.
Chander, J. *Science and Spirituality*. Mt Abu: Brahma Kumaris, 1988.
Chander, J. *Values for a Better World*. Mt Abu: Brahma Kumaris, 1995.
Checketts, L. 'Thomas Aquinas Meets Joseph Smith: Toward a Mormon Ethics of Natural Law', *Dialogue: A Journal of Mormon Thought* 51, no. 1 (2018): 79–100.
Clarke, P. B. *New Religions in Global Perspective: Religious Change in the Modern World*. London: Routledge, 2005.
Crovett, H. 'Ananda Marga and the Use of Force', *Nova Religio: The Journal of Alternative and Emergent Religion* 12, no. 1 (2008): 25–56.
Cusack, C. M. *Invented Religions: Imagination, Fiction and Faith*. Farnham: Ashgate, 2010.
Cusack, C. M. and P. Kosnáč, eds. *Fiction, Invention and Hyper-reality from Popular Culture to Religion*. London: Routledge, 2017.
Chryssides, G. D. and M. Z. Wilkins, eds. *A Reader in New Religious Movements*. London: Continuum, 2006.
Chryssides, G. D. and B. E. Zeller eds. *The Bloomsbury Companion to New Religious Movements*. London and New York: Bloomsbury, 2014.
Cole, J. R. 'The Concept of Manifestation in the Bahá'í Writings', *Bahá'í Studies* 9 (1982). Available online: https://bahai-library.com/cole_concept_manifestation
Cotter, C. R. and David G. Robertson eds. *After World Religions: Reconstructing Religious Studies*. New York: Routledge, 2016.
Crovett, H. 'Ananda Marga and the Use of Force', *Nova Religio: The Journal of Alternative and Emergent Religion* 12, no. 1 (2008): 25–56.
Cusack, C. M. *Invented Religions Imagination, Fiction and Faith*. Farnham: Ashgate, 2010.
Cusack, C. M. and P. Kosnáč, eds. *Fiction, Invention and Hyper-reality from Popular Culture to Religion*. London: Routledge, 2017.
Cusack, C. M. and A. Norman, eds. *Handbook of New Religions and Cultural Production*. Leiden: Brill, 2012.
Dahl, A. L. *Mark Tobey, Art and Belief*. Oxford: George Ronald, 1984.

Dahl, A. L. *The Eco Principle Evolution: And Economy in Symbiosis*. Oxford: George Ronald, 1996.

Dahl, G. William Hatcher and John Huddleston. *Economics for a World Commonwealth: Essays on Economic Theory from a Bahá'í Perspective*. Wilmette, IL: Bahá'í Publishing Trust, 1975.

Daishonin, N. *The Writings of Nichiren Daishonin*. Vol. 1. Tokyo: Soka Gakkai, 1999.

Dasgupta, S. *Awakening: The Story of the Bengal Renaissance*. London: Random House, 2011.

Daske, D. and W. Ashcraft, eds. *New Religious Movements: A Documentary Reader*. New York: New York University Press, 2005.

Dator, J. A. *Soka Gakka, Builders of the Third Civilisation: American and Japanese Members*. Seattle: Washington University Press, 1969.

Davies, D. J. *The Mormon Culture of Salvation*. London: Ashgate, 2000.

Davies, D. J. *An Introduction to Mormonism*. Cambridge: Cambridge University Press, 2003.

Davies, D. J. 'The Holy Spirit in Mormonism', *International Journal of Mormon Studies* 2 (2009): 23–41.

Davies, D. J. *Joseph Smith, Jesus, and Satanic Opposition: Atonement, Evil and the Mormon Vision*. London: Ashgate, 2010.

Davies, J. *The Mormon Culture of Salvation: Force, Grace and Glory*. London: Routledge, 2018.

De Carteret, N. C. Drake, N. Gayatri and J. C. Hassija. *Visions of a Better World*. Mt Abu: Brahma Kumaris World Spiritual University, 1993.

DeHaas, J. H. 'The Church Universal and Triumphant and Controversy, Change and Continuance'. In *Controversial New Religions*, edited by James R. Lewis and Jesper Aa. Petersen, ch. 15., 270–85. 2nd edn. Oxford: Oxford University Press, 2014.

Dehn, U. 'Soka Gakkai'. In *Establishing the Revolutionary: An Introduction to New Religions in Japan*, edited by Birgit Staemmler and Ulrich Dehn, 201–20. Vienna, Zurich: Lit Verlag, 2011.

Dépelteau, F. and T. S. Landini eds. *Norbert Elias and Social Theory*. London: Palgrave Macmillan, 2013.

Diessner, R. *Psyche and Eros: Bahái Studies in a Spiritual Psychology*. Oxford: George Ronald, 2007.

Dolce, L. 'Criticism and Appropriation: Nichiren's Attitude towards Esoteric Buddhism', *Japanese Journal of Religious Studies* 26, no. 3–4 (Fall 1999): 349–82.

Doležel, L. *Heterocosmica: Fiction and Possible Worlds*. Baltimore: Johns Hopkins University Press, 1998.

Doležel, L. 'Possible Worlds of Fiction and History', *New Literary History* 29, no. 4, Critics without Schools? (Autumn 1998): 785–809.

Double, G. *Walking with the Master*. Sydney: Making Waves Media, 2013.

Dubuisson, D. *The Western Construction of Religion: Myths, Knowledge, and Ideology*. Translated by William Sayers. Baltimore: The Johns Hopkins University Press, 2003.

Effendi, S. *The Unfoldment of World Civilisation*. New York: Bahá'í Publishing Committee, 1936.

Effendi, S. *Gleanings from the Writings of Bahá'u'lláh*. London: Bahá'í Publishing Trust, 1949.

Effendi, S. *Bahá'í Administration: Selected Messages 1922–1932*. Wilmette, IL: Bahá'í Publishing Committee, 1953a.

Effendi, S. *Guidance for Today and Tomorrow*. London: Bahá'í Publishing Trust, 1953b.

Effendi, S. *The Advent of Divine Justice*. 3rd edn. Wilmette, IL: Bahá'í Publishing Trust, 1971.

Effendi, S. *Directives from the Guardian*. Compiled by Gertrude Garrida. New Delhi: Bahá'í Publishing Trust, 1973.

Effendi, S. *God Passes By*. rev. edn. Wilmette, IL: Bahá'í Publishing Trust, 1974.

Effendi, S. *Citadel of Faith: Messages to America 1947–1957*. Wilmette, IL: Bahá'í Publishing Trust, 1980a.

Effendi, S. *The Faith of Bahá'u'lláh: A World Religion*. Wilmette, IL: Bahá'í Publishing Trust, 1980b.

Effendi, S. *The Promised Day Is Come*. 3rd edn. Wilmette, IL: Bahá'í Publishing Trust, 1980c.

Effendi, S. *The World Order of Bahá'u'lláh'*. Wilmette, IL: Bahá'í Publishing Trust, 1991.

Faber, R. 'Bahá'u'lláh and the Luminous Mind: Bahá'í Gloss on a Buddhist Puzzle', *Lights of Irfan* 18 (2017): 53–106.

Faber, R. *The Garden of Reality: Transreligious Relativity in a World of Becoming*. Lanham: Lexington Books, 2018.

Faber, R. *The Ocean of God: On the Transreligious Future of Religions*. London: Anthem Press, 2019.

Faulconer, J. E. *Faith, Philosophy, Scripture*. Provo, UT: Neal A. Maxwell Institute, 2010.

Faulconer, J. E. 'The Transcendence of the Flesh, Divine and Human'. In *'To Seek the Law of the Lord': Essays in Honor of John W. Welch*, edited by P. Y. Hoskisson and D. C. Peterson, 113–34. Orem, UT: The Interpreter Foundation, 2017.

Firmage, E. B. and R. C. Mangrum. *Zion in the Courts: A Legal History of the Church of Jesus Christ of Latter-day Saints 1830–1900*. Urbana, IL: University of Illinois Press, 1988.

Fitzgerald, J. J. and M. Bussey eds. *Fire in Our Eyes, Flowers in Our Hearts: Tantric Women Tell Their Stories*. Maleny, QLD: Gurukula Press, 2007.

Fitzgerald, T. *Discourse on Civility and Barbarity: A Critical History of Religion and Related Categories*. New York and Oxford: Oxford University Press, 2007.

Foster, L. *Religion and Sexuality: The Shakers, the Mormons, and the Oneida Community*. Urbana, IL: University of Illinois Press, 1984.

Frisby, D. P. *Simmel and since Essays on Georg Simmel's Social Theory*. London and New York: Routledge, 1992.

Frisby, D. P. and M. Featherstone eds. *Simmel on Culture*. London: Sage, 1998.

Fořt, B. 'Possible Worlds of Fiction and History', *New Literary History* 29, no. 4 (Autumn 1998): 785–809.

Fořt, Bohumil. *An Introduction to Fictional World Theory*. Frankfurt am Main; New York: Peter Lang, 2016.

Fozdar, F. 'The Baha'i Faith: A Case Study in Globalization, Modernity and the Routinization of Charisma', *The Journal for the Academic Study of Religion* 28, no. 3 (2015): 274–92.

Galtung, J. and S. Inayatullah, eds. *Macrohistory and Macrohistorians Perspectives on Individual, Social and Civilizational Change*. Wesport, CT: Praeger, 1997.

Gare, A. 'Aleksandr Bogdanov's History, Sociology and Philosophy of Science', *Studies in the History and Philosophy of Science* 31, no. 2 (2000): 231–48.

Garrison, J. 'Nichiren Buddhism and Deweyan Pragmatism: An Eastern-Western Integration of Thought', *Educational Studies Ames* 55, no. 1 (2019): 12–27.

Gee, J. and K. Muhlestein. 'An Egyptian Context for the Sacrifice of Abraham', *Journal of Book of Mormon and Other Restoration Scripture* 20, no. 2 (2011): 70–7.

Gentry, L. H. 'What of the Lectures on Faith?', *BYU Studies* 19, no. 1 (1978): 5–19.

Givens, T. L. *By the Hand of Mormon: The American Scripture That Launched a New World Religion*. Oxford: Oxford University Press, 2002.

Givens, T. L. *The Latter-day Saint Experience in America*. Westport, CN: Greenwood, 2004.

Givens, T. L. *People of Paradox: A History of Mormon Culture*. Oxford: Oxford University Press, 2007.

Givens, T. L. *The Book of Mormon: A Very Short Introduction*. Oxford: Oxford University Press, 2009.

Givens, T. L. *When Souls Had Wings: Pre-Mortal Existence in Western Thought*. Oxford: Oxford University Press, 2010.

Givens, T. L. *The Viper on the Hearth: Mormons, Myths, and the Construction of Heresy*. New York: Oxford University Press, 2013.

Givens, T. L. *Wrestling the Angel: The Foundations of Mormon Thought: Cosmos, God, Humanity*. Oxford: Oxford University Press, 2014.

Givens, T. L. *2nd Nephi: A Brief Theological Introduction*. Provo, UT: The Neal A. Maxwell Institute for Religious Scholarship, 2020.

Givens, T. L. and F. Givens. *The God Who Weeps: How Mormonism Makes Sense of Life*. Salt Lake City, UT: Deseret Book Company, 2012.

Godart, G. C. 'Nichirenism, Utopianism and Modernity Rethinking Ishiwara Kanji's East Asia League Movement', *Japanese Journal of Religious Studies* 42, no. 2 (2015): 235–74.

Godwin, J. *The Theosophical Enlightenment*. 2nd edn. Albany, NY: State University of New York Press, 1994.

Gorbachev, M. and I. Daisaku. *Moral Lessons of the Twentieth Century: Gorbachev and Ikeda on Buddhism and Communism*. Translated by R. L. Gage. London: I.B. Tauris, 2005.

Goudsblom, J. *Sociology in the Balance: A Critical Essay*. Oxford: Blackwell, 1977.

Goulah, J. 'Daisaku Ikeda's Environmental Ethics of Humanitarian Competition: A Review of His United Nations Peace and Educational Proposals', *Peace Studies Journal* 3, no. 1 (2010): 1–23.

Goulah, J. 'Daisaku Ikeda and the Soka Movement for Global Citizenship', *Asia Pacific Journal of Education* 40, no. 1 (2020): 35–48.

Gupta, S., J. Hoens and T. Goudriaan eds. *Hindu Tantrism*. Leiden: E. J. Brill, 1979.

Hagen, K. D. 'Eternal Progression in a Multiverse: An Explorative Mormon Moment', *Dialogue: A Journal of Mormon Thought* 30, no. 2 (2006): 1–45.

Hall, J. A. and R. Schroeder eds. *The Anatomy of Power: The Social Theory of Michael Mann*. Cambridge: Cambridge University Press, 2006.

Hammer, O. and M. Rothstein eds. *The Cambridge Companion to New Religious Movements*. Cambridge: Cambridge University Press, 2012.

Hammer, O. 'Jewish Mysticism Meets the Age of Aquarius: Elizabeth Clare Prophet on the Kabbalah'. In *Theosophical Appropriations: Esotericism, Kabbalah, and the Transformation of Traditions*, edited by Julie Chajes and Boaz Huss, 223–42. Beer Sheva: Ben-Gurion University of the Negev Press, 2016.

Hammond, P. E. and D. W. Machacek. *Soka Gakkai in America: Accommodation and Conversion*. Oxford and New York: Oxford University Press, 1999.

Hanegraaff, W. J. *New Age Religion and Western Culture: Esotericism in the Mirror of Secular Thought*. Leiden: Brill, 1996.

Hanegraaff, W. *Esotericism and the Academy: Rejected Knowledge in Western Culture*. Cambridge: Cambridge University Press, 2012.

Hanley, P., ed. *The Spirit of Agriculture*. Oxford: George Ronald, 2005.

Hardy, G. *Understanding the Book of Mormon: A Reader's Guide*. Oxford: Oxford University Press, 2010.

Harper, B. D. *Lights of Fortitude: Gleanings in the Lives of the Hands of the Cause of God*. Oxford: George Ronald, 1972.

Hatcher, J. S. *The Purpose of Physical Reality: The Kingdom of Names*. Wilmette, IL: Bahá'í Publishing Trust, 1987.

Hatcher, J. S. *The Arc of Ascent: The Purpose of Reality II*. Oxford: George Ronald, 1994.

Hatcher, J. S. *The Divine Art of Revelation*. Wilmette, IL: Bahá'í Publishing Trust, 1998.

Hatcher, J. S. and W. S. Hatcher. *The Law of Love Enshrined: Selected Essays*. Oxford: George Ronald, 1996.

Hatcher, W. S. 'Economics and Moral Values', *World Order* 9, no. 2 (1974/5): 14–27.

Hatcher, W. *Logic and Logos Essays on Science, Religion and Philosophy*. Oxford: George Ronald, 1990.

Hatley, S. and S. Inayatullah. 'Karma Samnyasa: Sarkar's Reconceptualisation of Indian Asceticism'. In *Ascetic Culture: Renunciation and Worldly Engagement*, edited by K. Ishwaran, 139–51. Leiden: Brill, 1999.

Hegel, G. F. 'The Positivity of the Christian Religion'. In *Early Theological Writings*. Translated by T. M. Knox and Introduction and fragments translated by Richard Kroner, 67–181. Chicago, IL: Chicago University Press, 1948.

Henderson, H. and D. Ikeda. *Planetary Citizenship: Your Values, Beliefs, and Actions Can Shape a Sustainable World*. Santa Monica: Middleway Press, 2004.

Hexham, I. and K. Poewe. *New Religions as Global Cultures: Making the Human Sacred*. Boulder, CO: Westview Press, 1997.

Hodgkinson, L. *Peace and Purity: The Story of the Brahma Kumaris: A Spiritual Revolution*. London: Ryder, 2002.

Howell, J. D. 'Gender Role Experimentation in New Religious Movements: Clarification of the Brahma Kumaris Case', *Journal for the Scientific Study of Religion* 37, no. 3 (1998): 453–61.

Huddleston, J. 'The Economy of a World Commonwealth', *World Order* 9, no. 4 (1975): 37–43.

Huddleston, J. *The Search for A Just Society*. Oxford: George Ronald, 1991.

Huddleston, J. 'Principles of Economic Justice'. In *Toward the Most Great Justice: Elements of Justice in the New World Order*, edited by C. Lerche, 137–52. London: Bahá'í Publishing Trust, 1996.

Hudson, W. *The Marxist Philosophy of Ernst Bloch*. London and New York: Macmillan, 1982.

Hudson, W. *The Reform of Utopia*. London: Ashgate, 2003.

Hudson, W. 'Bloch and a Philosophy of the Proterior'. In *Ernst Bloch and the Privatisation of Hope*, edited by P. Thompson and S. Zizek ch.1, 21–36. Durham: Duke University Press, 2013.

Hudson, W. 'The Prophethood of Joseph Smith'. In *Joseph Smith Jr: Reappraisals After Two Centuries*, edited by T. Givens and R. Nelson, ch. 13. Oxford: Oxford University Press, 2008, 201–207.

Hudson, W. *The English Deists: Studies in Early Enlightenment*. London: Pickering and Chatto, 2009.

Hudson, W. *Enlightenment and Modernity: The English Deists and Reform*. London: Pickering and Chatto, 2009.

Hudson, W. 'Daisaku Ikeda and Innovative Education'. In *Daisaku Ikeda and Dialogue for Peace*, edited by O. Urbain, ch. 6. London: I.B. Tauris, 2013, 99–112.

Hudson, W. *Australian Religious Thought*. Clayton: Monash University Publishing, 2016.

Huff, T. *The Rise of Early Modern Science Islam, China, and the West*. 3rd edn. Cambridge: Cambridge University Press, 2017.

Ikeda, D. *Soka Education: A Buddhist Vision for Teachers, Students and Parents*. Santa Monica: Middleway Press, 2001.

Ikeda, D. *Unlocking the Mysteries of Birth and Death: ... and Everything in between*. Santa Monica: Middleway Press, 2003.

Ikeda, D., M. Kiguchi and E. Shimura. *Buddhism and the Cosmos*. London: Macdonald, 1985.

Inayatullah, S. 'Sarkar's Theory of Social Change' available online: https://www.metafuture.org/sarkars-theory-of-social-change/

Inayatullah, S. 'Sarkar's Spiritual-dialectics: An Unconventional View of the Future', *Futures* 20, no. 1 (1988): 54–65.

Inayatullah, S. *Situating Sarkar: Tantra, Macrohistory and Alternative Futures*. Queensland: Gurukula Press, 1999.

Inyatullah, S. and J. Gidley. *The University in Transformation*. Westport, CT: Bergin and Garvey, 2000.

Inayatullah, S. *Understanding Sarkar: The Indian Episteme, Macrohistory and Transformative Knowledge*. Leiden: Brill, 2002.

Inayatullah, S. 'Planetary Social and Spiritual Transformation'. In *Viable Utopian Ideas: Shaping a Better World*, edited by A. B. Shostak. New York: M. E. Sharpe, 2003.

Inayatullah, S. *Prout in Power: Policy Solutions That Reframe Our Futures*. New Delhi: Proutist Bloc, 2017.

Jaeggi, R. *Critique of Forms of Life*. Translated by Ciaran Cronin. Cambridge, MA: Harvard University Press, 2018.

Jensen, J. B. 'An Investigation of Sustainable Yogic Agriculture as a Mind-Matter Farming Approach'. In *Subtle Agroecologies Farming with the Hidden Half of Nature*, edited by Julia Wright and contributed by Nicholas Parrott, ch. 22, 247–56. Boca Raton: CRC Press, 2021.

Johansen, J. R. *Enoch's Zion, Joseph's Zion and the Future Zion*. Bountiful, UT: Horizon Publishers, 2003.

Johnson, P. K. *The Masters Revealed: Madame Blavatsky and Myth of the Great White Lodge*. Albany, NY: State University of New York Press, 1994.

Johnson, L. *Reginald Turvey Life and Art*. Oxford: George Ronald, 1986.

Kang, C. *The Tantra of Prabhāt Rañjan Sarkar: Critical Comparative and Dialogical Perspectives*. P. R. Sarkar Institute, 2017.

Kant, I. *Reason within the Limits of Reason Alone*. Translated by T. M. Greene and H. H. Hudson. New York: Harper and Row, 1960.

Kanter, R. M. *Commitment and Community: Communes and Utopias in Sociological Perspective*. Cambridge, MA: Harvard University Press, 1972.

Karlberg, M. *Beyond the Culture of Contest: From Adversarialism to Mutualism in an Age of Interdependence*. Oxford: George Ronald, 2004.

Karlberg, M. 'Western Liberal Democracy as a New World Order'. In *The Bahá'í World, 2005–2006: An International Record*, edited by Robert Weinberg, 133–56. Haifa: World Centre Publications, 2007. Available online: https://www.bahai.org/documents/essays/karlberg-dr-michael/western-liberal-democracy-new-world-order

Karlberg, M. 'The Press as a Consultative Forum: A Contribution to Normative Press Theory', *Bahá'í Studies Review* 16 (2010): 29–42.

Karlyle, J. and M. Towsey. *Understanding Prout: Essays on Sustainability and Transformation*. Vol. 1. Maleny: Proutist Universal, 2010.

Kazemi, F. 'Mysteries of Alast: The Realm of Subtle Entities ('Alam-I dharr) and the Primordial Covenant in the Babi-Bahá'í Writings', *Bahá'í Studies Review* 15, no. 1 (2009): 39–66.

King, G. R. (Pseudonym of G. W. Ballard) through *Saint Germain, The 'I AM' Discourses*. Chicago: St Germain Press, 1935.

Kumar, J. ed. *New Aspects of Prout*. Kolkata: Proutist Universal Publications, 1987.

Kumaris, B. *Visions of the Future*. Mt Abu: Brahma Kumaris, 1996.

Lalrinawma, V. S. *The Liberation of Women in and through the Movement of the Prajapita Brahma Kumaris*. Delhi: Cambridge Press, 2003.

Lample, P. *Creating a New Mind: Reflections on the Individual, the Institutions and the Community*. West Palm Beach, FL: Palabra Publications, 1999.

Lample, P. *Revelation and Social Reality: Learning to Translate What Is Written into Reality*. West Palm Beach, FL: Palabra Publications, 2009.

Larsen, G. J. *Classical Sāṃkhya: An Interpretation of Its History and Meaning*. Delhi: Motilal Banarsidass, 2010.

Laruelle, F. *Christo-Fiction: The Ruins of Athens and Jerusalem*. Translated by Robin Mackay. New York: Columbia University Press, 2015.

Latour, B. *On the Modern Cult of the Factish Gods*. Durham: Duke University Press, 2010.

Lawson, T. *Gnostic Apocalypse and Islam: Qur'an, Exegesis, Messianism and the Literary Origins of the Babi Religion*. London: Routledge, 2011.

Leach, B. with R. Weinberg ed. *Spinning the Clay into Stars: Bernard Leach and the Bahá'í Faith*. London: George Ronald, 1999.

Leone, M. P. *The Roots of Modern Mormonism*. Cambridge, MA: Harvard University Press, 1979.

Lewis, J. R. *Violence and New Religious Movements*. New York: Oxford University Press, 2011.

Lewis, J. R. ed. *The Oxford Handbook of New Religious Movements*. Oxford: Oxford University Press, 2016.

Lewis, J. R. and J. G. Melton eds. *Church Universal and Triumphant in Scholarly Perspective*. Stanford: Centre for Academic Publication, 1994.

Lewis, J. R. and J. Aa. Petersen eds. *Controversial New Religions*. 2nd edn. Oxford: Oxford University Press, 2014.

Ludlow, D. H. ed. *Encyclopedia of Mormonism*. New York: Macmillan, 1992.

MacEoin, D. *The Sources for Early Bábí Doctrine and History: A Survey*. Leiden: Brill, 1992.

MacEoin, D. *The Messiah of Shiraz: Studies in Early and Middle Babism*. Leiden: Brill, 2008.

MacEoin, D. 'From Babism to Bahai'ism'. In *Sects, Cults and New Religions: Critical Concepts in Sociology*, edited by C. M. Cusack and D. Kirby, vol. 1, ch. 7, 139–74. Oxon: Routledge, 2014.

Machacek, D. and B. Wilson eds. *The Sōka Gakkai Movement in the World*. Oxford: Oxford University Press, 2000.

Madsen, T. G. *Eternal Man*. Salt Lake City, UT: Deseret Book Company, 1966.

Makiguchi, T. 'The Geography of Human Life'. [in Japanese]. In *Complete Works of Tsunesaburo Makiguchi*, Tokyo: Daisan Bunmeisha Vol. 1, 23, 1903.

Makiguchi, T. 'The System of Value-Creating Pedagogy'. In *Complete Works of Tsunesaburo Makiguchi*, [in Japanese]. Tokyo: Daisan Bunmeisha, Vol. 5, 6–7, 1930.

Makiguchi, T. *Education for Creative Living. Ideas and Proposals of Tsunesaburo Makiguchi*. Translated by A. Birnbaum and D.M. Bethel, edited by D.M. Bethel. Ames: Iowa State University, 1989.

Makiguchi, T. *Zenshu*, (Tokyo: Daisan Bunmei-sha) 1983, vol. 6, 285, quoted in D. Ikeda, *Soka Education: A Buddhist Vision for Teachers, Students and Parents*. Santa Monica: Middleway Press, 2001.

Mann, M. *The Sources of Social Power: Volume 1, a History of Power from the Beginning to AD 1760*. Cambridge: Cambridge University Press, 1986.

Mann, M. *The Sources of Social Power: Volume 2, the Rise of Classes and Nation States 1760–1914*. Cambridge: Cambridge University Press, 1993.

Mann, M. *The Sources of Social Power: Volume 3, Global Empires and Revolution, 1890–1945*. Cambridge: Cambridge University Press, 2012a.

Mann, M. *The Sources of Social Power: Volume 4, Globalizations, 1945–2011*. Cambridge: Cambridge University Press, 2012b.

Matthews, R. J. '*A Plainer Translation': Joseph Smith's Translation of the Bible, a History and Commentary*. Provo, UT: Brigham Young University Press, 1975.

Mauss, A. *The Angel and the Beehive: The Mormon Struggle with Assimilation*. Urbana: University of Illinois Press, 1994.

Mauss, A. *All Abraham's Children: Changing Mormon Conceptions of Race and Lineage*. Urbana: University of Illinois Press, 2003.

McCutcheon, R. T. *Manufacturing Religion: The Discourse on Sui Generis Religion and the Politics of Nostalgia*. New York and Oxford: Oxford University Press, 1997.

McGilligan, J. P. *The Barli Development Institute for Rural Women: An Alternative Model of Women's Empowerment*. Oxford: George Ronald, 2012.

McGlinn, S. *Church and State: A Postmodern Political Theology*. self-published, 2005.

McKendry-Smith, E. "Baba Has Come to Civilize Us': Developmental Idealism and Framing the Strict Demands of the Brahma Kumaris', *Journal for the Scientific Study of Religion* 55, no. 4 (December 2016): 698–716.

McLachlan, J. M. and L. Ericson, eds. *Discourses in Mormon Theology: Philosophical and Theological Possibilities*. Draper, UT: Greg Kofford Books, 2007.

McLaughlin, L. *Soka Gakkai's Human Revolution: The Rise of a Mimetic Nation in Modern Japan*. Honolulu: University of Hawai'i Press, 2019.

McLean, J. 'Prolegomena to a Bahá'í Theology', *Journal of Bahá'í Studies* 5, no. 1, (March–June 1992): 25–67.

McLean, J. ed. *Revisioning the Sacred New Perspectives on a Bahá'í Theology*. (Studies in the Bábí and Bahá'í Religions, Vol. 8). Los Angeles: Kalimat Press, 1997.

McLeod, W. H. *The Sikhs: History, Religion, and Society*. New York: Columbia University Press, 1989.

Melton, J. Gordon. 'The Church Universal and Triumphant: Its Heritage and Thought World'. In *Church Universal and Triumphant in Scholarly Perspective*, edited by J. R. Lewis and J. G. Melton. 1–20. Stanford: Centre for Academic Publication, 1994.

Métraux, D. A. *The Sōka Gakkai Revolution*. Washington and Lanham, MD: University of America Press, 1994.

Mihrshahi, R. 'Ether, Quantum Physics and the Bahá'í Writings', *Australian Bahá'í Studies Journal*, 4 (2002/2003): 3–20.

Miller A. S. *Future Mormon: Essays in Mormon Theology*. Salt Lake City, UT: Greg Kofford Books, 2016.

Millet, R. L. *A Different Jesus? The Christ of the Latter-day Saints*. Grand Rapids, MI: Eerdmans, 2005.

Millet, R. L. and R. J. Matthews, eds. *Plain and Precious Truths Restored: The Doctrinal and Historical Significance of the Joseph Smith Translation*. Salt Lake City, UT: Deseret Book Company, 1995.

Mills, J. *100 Years of Theosophy: A History of the Theosophical Society in America*. Wheaton, IL: Theosophical Publishing House, 1987.

Mishra, K. *Kashmir Saivism: The Central Philosophy of Tantrism*. Portland: Oregon Press, 1993.

Momen, M. 'Relativism: A Basis for Bahá'í Metaphysics' Studies in Honor of the Late Hasan M. Balyuzi. In *Studies in the Babi and Bahá'í Religions*, Vol. 5, edited by M. Momen, 185–217. Los Angeles: Kalimát Press, 1988.

Momen, M. *Hinduism and the Bahá'í Faith*. Oxford: George Ronald, 1990.

Momen, M. *Buddhism and the Bahá'í Faith*. Oxford: George Ronald, 1994.

Momen, M. *The Phenomenon of Religion*. Oxford: Oneworld, 1999.

Momen, M. *Islam and the Bahá'í Faith: An Introduction to the Bahá'í Faith for Muslims*. Oxford: George Ronald, 2000.

Momen, M. ed. *The Bahá'í Faith and the World Religions*. Oxford: George Ronald, 2005.

Momen, M. *Bahá'u'lláh: A Short Biography*. Oxford: Oneworld, 2007.

Momen, M. 'Power and the Baha'i Community', *Lights of Irfan*, 19 (2018): 209–32. Available online: http://irfancolloquia.org/54/momenpower

Momen, W. and M. Momen. *Understanding the Bahai Faith*. Edinburgh: Dunedin Academic Press, 2006.

Morgan, D. *The Embodied eye: Religious Visual Culture and the Social Life of Feeling*. Berkeley: University of California Press, 2012.

Mueller, M. P. *Race and the Making of the Mormon*. Chapel Hill: The University of North Carolina Press, 2017.

Mulay, A. *Mass Capitalism: A Blueprint for Economic Revival*. Bothell, WA: Book Publishers Network, 2014.

Mulay, A. *Economic Renaissance in the Sage of Artificial Intelligence*. Hampton, NJ: Business Expert Press, 2018.

Murata, K. *Japan's New Buddhism: An Objective Account of Soka Gakkai*. New York: Weatherhill, 1969.

Musselwhite, R. *Possessing Knowledge: Organizational Boundaries among the Brahma Kumaris*. PhD thesis, Chapel Hill, NC: University of North Carolina, 2009.

Nabil-i-A'zam. *The Dawn-Breakers: Nabíl's Narrative of the Early Days of the Bahá'í Revolution*. Translated by Shoghi Effendi. Wilmette, IL: Bahá'í Publishing Trust, 1932.

Nair, N. The *Mysteries of the Universe*. Mt Abu: Brahma Kumaris, 2008.

Newell, L. K. and V. T. Avery. *Mormon Enigma: Emma Hale Smith. Prophet's Wife, 'Elect Lady', Polygamy's Foe. 1804–1879*. New York: Doubleday and Company, 1984.

Nibley, H. *Enoch the Prophet*. Salt Lake City, UT: Deseret Book Company, 1986a.

Nibley, H. *Old Testament and Related Studies*. Salt Lake City, UT: Deseret Book Company, 1986b.

Nibley, H. *Mormonism and Early Christianity*. Salt Lake City, UT: Deseret Book Company, 1987a.

Nibley, H. *The World and the Prophets*. Salt Lake City, UT: Deseret Book Company, 1987b.

Nibley, H. *An Approach to the Book of Mormon*. Salt Lake City, UT: Deseret Book Company, 1988a.

Nibley, H. *Lehi in the Desert*. Salt Lake City, UT: Deseret Book Company, 1988b.

Nibley, H. *Since Cumorah*. Salt Lake City, UT: Deseret Book Company, 1988c.

Nibley, H. *Approaching Zion*. Salt Lake City, UT: Deseret Book Company, 1989a.

Nibley, H. *The Prophetic Book of Mormon*. Salt Lake City, UT: Deseret Book Company, 1989b.

Nibley, H. *The Ancient State*. Salt Lake City, UT: Deseret Book Company, 1991a.

Nibley, H. *Tinkling Cymbals and Sounding Brass*. Salt Lake City, UT: Deseret Book Company, 1991b.

Nibley, H. *Temple and Cosmos*. Salt Lake City, UT: Deseret Book Company, 1992a.

Nibley, H. 'Temple and Cosmos: Beyond This Ignorant Present'. In *The Collected Works of Hugh Nibley*, Vol. 12, edited by Don E. Norton, 42–90. Salt Lake City, UT: Deseret Book Company, 1992b.

Nibley, H. *Brother Brigham Challenges the Saints*. Salt Lake City, UT: Deseret Book Company, 1994.

Nibley, H. *Abraham in Egypt*. Salt Lake City, UT: Deseret Book Company, 2000.

Nibley, H. *Apostles and Bishops in Early Christianity*. Salt Lake City, UT: Deseret, 2004.

Nibley, H. *The Message of the Joseph Smith Papyri: An Egyptian Endowment*. Salt Lake City, UT: Deseret Book Company, 2005.

Nibley, H. *Eloquent Witness: Nibley on Himself, Others, and the Temple*. Salt Lake City, UT: Deseret Book Company, 2008.

Nibley, H. *An Approach to the Book of Abraham*. Salt Lake City, UT: Deseret Book Company, 2010.

Nyman M. S. and Robert L. Millet, eds. *The Joseph Smith Translation: The Restoration of Plain and Precious Things*. Provo, UT: Religious Studies Center, Brigham Young University, 1985.

O'Connell, J. T. 'Bengali Religions'. In *The Encyclopedia of Religion*. Vol. 2, edited by Mircea Eliade, 100–9. New York: Macmillan Publishing, 1987.

O'Donnell, K. *New Beginnings: Raja Yoga Meditation Course*. Mt Abu: Brahma Kumaris World University, 1995.

Oliver, P. *New Religious Movements: A Guide for the Perplexed*. London and New York: Continuum, 2012.

Ostler, B. T. *Exploring Mormon Thought: The Attributes of God*. Vol. 1. Salt Lake City, UT: Greg Kofford Books, 2001.

Ostler, B. T. *Exploring Mormon Thought: The Problems of Theism and the Love of God*. Vol. 2. Salt Lake City, UH: Greg Kofford Books, 2006.

Ostler, B. T. *Exploring Mormon Thought: Of God and Gods*. Vol. 3. Salt Lake City, UH: Greg Kofford Books, 2008.

Pankaj, T. *Bāba's New Science of the Future*. Kolkata: Ananda Marga Publications, 2007.

Park, B. E. *Kingdom of Nauvoo: The Rise and Fall of a Religious Empire on the American Frontier*. New York City: Liveright Publishing, 2020.

Partridge, C. ed. *New Religions: A Guide to New Religious Movements, Sects and Alternative Spiritualities*. New York: Oxford University Press, 2004.

Partridge, C. *The Re-Enchantment of the West: Alternative Spiritualities, Sacralization, Popular Culture and Occulture*. Vol 1. London: T & T Clark International, 2004.

Partridge, C. 'Occulture Is Ordinary'. In *Contemporary Esotericism*, edited by E. Asprem and K. Granholm, 113–33. Sheffield: Equinox, 2013.

Petrey, G. 'Toward a Post-Heterosexual Mormon Theology', *Dialogue: A Journal of Mormon Thought* 44, no. 4 (2011): 107–43.

Possamai, A. *Sociology of Religion for Generations X and Y*. London: Equinox, 2009.

Possamai, A. ed. *Handbook of Hyper-Real Religions*. Leiden: Brill, 2012.

Potter, R. D. 'Liberation Theology in the Book of Mormon.' In *Discourses in Mormon Theology: Philosophical and Theological Possibilities*, edited by J. M. McLachlan and L. I. Ericson, ch. 8. Salt Lake City: Greg Kofford Books: 2007.

Prakash, B. 'The Hindu Philosophy of History', *Journal of the History of Ideas* 16, no. 4 (1955): 494–505.

Prestwich, M. ed. *International Calvinism 1541–1715*. Oxford: Clarendon Press, 1986.

Pritchard, E. P. *Theories of Primitive Religion*. Oxford: Oxford University Press, 1965.

Prophet, E. C. *Forbidden Mysteries of Enoch: The Untold Story of Men and Angels*. Los Angeles: Summit University Press, 1983.

Prophet, E. C. *The Lost Years of Jesus*. Corwin Springs, MT: Summit University, 1984.

Prophet, E. C. *Saint Germain on Prophecy: Coming World Changes*. Livingston, MT: Summit University Press, 1986.

Prophet, E. C. *The Astrology of the Four Horsemen: How You Can Heal Yourself and Planet Earth*. Livingston, MT: Summit University Press, 1991.

Prophet, E. C. *The Creative Power of Sound: Affirmations to Create, Heal and Transform*. Corwin Springs, MT: Summit University Press, 1998.

Prophet, E. C. *Fallen Angels and the Origins of Evil: Why Church Fathers Suppressed the Book of Enoch and Its Startling Revelations*. Corwin Springs, MT: Summit University Press, 2000.

Prophet, E. C. *Afra, Brother of Light: Spiritual Teachings from an Ascended Master*. Corwin Springs, MT: Summit University Press, 2003.

Prophet, E. C. *Saint Germain: The Master Alchemist*. Compiled by editors of The Summit Lighthouse Library. Gardiner, MT: Summit Lighthouse Library, 2004.

Prophet, E. C. *Is Mother Nature Mad? How To Work with Nature Spirits to Mitigate Natural Disasters*. Gardiner, MT: Summit University Press, 2008.

Prophet, E.C. *In My Own Words*. Gardiner, MT: Summit Publications, 2009.

Prophet, E. C. *Violet Flame: Alchemy for Personal Change*. Gardiner, MT: Summit University Press, 2016.

Prophet, E. C. and A. Booth compiler and editor. *Predict Your Future: Understand the Cycles of The Cosmic Clock*. Corwin Springs, MT: Summit University Press, 2004.

Prophet, E. C. and A. Booth. *Mary Magdalene and the Divine Feminine: Jesus' Lost Teachings on Woman*. Gardiner, MT: Summit University Press, 2005.

Prophet, E. C. *Preparation for My Mission*. Edited by Erin Prophet and Tatiana Prophet. Bloomington: iUniverse, 2009.

Prophet, E. C. and M. L. Prophet. *St Germain on Alchemy: Formulas for Self-Transformation*. Malibu: Summit University Press, 1985.

Prophet, E. C., P. R. Spadaro and M. L. Steinman. *Saint Germain's Prophecy for the New Millennium: Includes Dramatic Prophecies from Nostradamus, Edgar Cayce, and Mother Mary*. Corwin Springs, MT: Summit University Press, 1999.

Prophet, M. L. and E. C. Prophet. 'Invocation of the Mother of the Flame'. 7.03A. In *Prayers Meditations and Dynamic Decrees for Personal and World Transformation*, 81–2. Gardiner, MT: The Summit Lighthouse Press, 1962.

Prophet, M. L. and E. C. Prophet. 'Saint Germain on Freedom: A Prophecy of America's Destiny'. In *Pearls of Wisdom*, Vol. 20, nos. 46, 47, 215–30. Livingston, MT: Summit University Press, 1977.

Prophet, M. L. and E. C. Prophet. *The Lost Teachings of Jesus*. 4 vols. Livingston, MT: Summit University Press, 1986.

Prophet, M. L. and E. C. Prophet. 'How to Decree Effectively' by 'The Messengers'. In *The Science of the Spoken Word*. ch. 6, 49–54. Corwin Springs, MT: Summit University Press, 1991.

Prophet, M. L. and E. C. Prophet. *Foundations of the Path*. Corwin Springs, MT: Summit University Press, 1999.

Prophet, M. L. and E. C. Prophet with Annice Booth compiler and editor. *The Masters and Their Retreats*. Corwin Springs, MT: Summit University Press, 2003.

Prophet, M. L. and E. C. Prophet. *Mary's Message for a New Day*. Corwin Springs, MT: Summit University Press, 2004.

Prophet, M. L. and E. C. Prophet. *The Path of Christ or Antichrist*. Gardiner, MT: Summit University Press, 2007.

Prophet, E. *Prophet's Daughter: My Life with Elizabeth Clare Prophet Inside the Church Universal and Triumphant*. Guilford, CT: Lyons Press, 2008.

Prophet, E. 'Church Universal and Triumphant and the Summit Lighthouse'. In *Critical Dictionary of Apocalyptic and Millenarian Movements*, edited by James Crossley and Alastair Lockhart, 11 February 2021. Available online: www.cdamm.org/articles/CUT-TSL.

Queen, C. S. and S. B. King, eds. *Engaged Buddhism: Buddhist Liberation Movements in Asia*. Albany: State University of New York Press, 1996.

Quinn, D. M. *Early Mormonism and the Magic World View*. Salt Lake City, UT: Signature Books, 1987.

Ramsay, T. 'Spirit Possession and Purity in Orissa'. *Custodians of Purity An Ethnography of the Brahma Kumaris*, PhD Thesis, Melbourne: Monash University, 2009.

Ramsay, T. 'Making a Model of Madhuban: The Brahma Kumaris' Journey to and Presence in Europe'. In *Handbook of Hinduism in Europe*, 2 vols., edited by Knut A. Jacobsen and Ferdinando Sardella, 528–54. Leiden: Brill, 2020.

Ramsay, T., L. Manderson, and W. Smith. 'Changing a Mountain into a Mustard Seed: Spiritual Practices and Responses to Disaster among New York Brahma Kumaris', *Journal of Contemporary Religion* 25, no. 1 (2010): 89–105.

Ramsay, T., W. A. Smith, and L. H. Manderson. 'Brahma Kumaris: Purity and the Globalization of Faith'. In *Flows of Faith: Religious Reach and Community in Asia and the Pacific*, edited by L. Manderson, W. Smith and M. Tomlinson, ch. 4, 51–70. Dordrecht: Springer, 2012.

Remini, R. *Joseph Smith*. New York: Penguin, 2002.

Riess, J. *The Next Mormons: How Millennials Are Changing the LDS Church*. New York: Oxford University Press, 2019.

Russell, N. *The Doctrine of Deification in the Greek Patristic Tradition*. Oxford: Oxford University Press, 2004.

Saiedi, N. *Logos and Civilization: Spirit, History and Order in the Writings of Bahá'u'lláh*. Bethesda, MD: University Press of Maryland, 2000.

Saint Germain Foundation. *The History of the 'I AM' Activity and Saint Germain Foundation: In The Ascended Masters Words and the Recollections of Those Who Were There*. Schaumburg, IL: Saint Germain Press, 2003.

Sarakāra, S. *Prabháta Samgiita: A Literary and Philosophical Appreciation*. Ananda Nagar: Ananda Marga Publications, 2010.

Sargent, L. T. *Utopianism: A Very Short Introduction*. Oxford: Oxford University Press, 2010.

Sarkar, P. R. *The New Renaissance*. Kolkata: Ananda Marga Publications, 1968.
Sarkar, P. R. *The Liberation of Intellect: Neohumanism*. Kolkata: Ananda Marga Pracaraka Samgha, 1982.
Sarkar, P. R. *Namah Sivaya Santaya*. Kolkata: Anand Marga Publications, 1982.
Sarkar, P. R. *The Thoughts of P. R. Sarkar*. Edited by Avadhutika Anandamitra Acharya. Kolkata: Ānanda Mārga Pracāraka Samgha, 1985.
Sarkar, P. R. *Neohumanism in a Nutshell*. Part1. Kolkata: Ānanda Mārga Pracāraka Samgha, 1987.
Sarkar, P. R. *Prout in a Nutshell*, 4 vols. Kolkata: Ānanda Mārga Pracāraka, 1987.
Sarkar, P. R. *Discourses on the Mahábhárata*. Kolkata: Ánanda Márga Pracáraka Samgha, 1991.
Sarkar, P. R. *Microvita in a Nutshell*. Kolkata: Ānanda Mārga Pracāraka, 1991.
Sarkar, P. R. *Yoga: The Way of Tantra*. Manila: Ānanda Mārga Pracāraka, 1991.
Sarkar, P. R. *Discourses on Prout*. Kolkata: Ānanda Mārga Pracāraka, 1993.
Sarkar, P. R. *Discourses on Tantra*. Vol. 1. Kolkata: Ānanda Mārga Pracāraka, 1993.
Sarkar, P. R. *Discourses on Neohumanist Education*. Kolkata: Ānanda Mārga Pracāraka, 1998.
Sarkar, P. R. *Varńa Vijinána - The Science of Letters*. Ananda Nagar: Ānanda Mārga Pracāraka, 2000.
Sarkar, P. R. *The Electronic Edition of the Works of P. R. Sarkar*. Version 6.0. Compiled by G. Dhara and Acyutānanda Kolkata: Ānanda Mārga Publications, 2001.
Sarkar, P. R. *Yogic Treatments and Natural Remedies*. Kolkata: Ānanda Mārga Pracāraka, 2004.
Sarkar, P. R. *Natural Medicine*. Kolkata: Ānanda Mārga Pracāraka, 2011.
Savi, J. *The Eternal Quest for God: An Introduction to the Divine Philosophy of 'Abdu'l-Bahá*. Oxford: George Ronald, 1989.
Savi, J. *Towards the Summit of Reality: An Introduction to the Study of Bahá'u'lláh's Seven Valleys and Four Valleys*. Oxford: George Ronald, 2008.
Schaefer, U. *Heilsgeschichte und Paradigmenwechsel: Zwei Beiträge zur Bahá'í Theologie*. Prague: Zero Palm Press, 1992.
Schaefer, U. 'The New Morality: An Outline', *Bahá'í Studies Review* 5, no. 1 (1995): 65–81.
Schaefer, U. *Beyond the Clash of Religions: The Emergence of a New Paradigm*. 2nd edn. Stockholm, Sweden: Zero Palm Press, 1998.
Schaefer, U. 'Infallible Institutions?'. In *Reason and Revelation: New Directions in Bahá'í Thought*, edited by S. Fazel and J. Danesh, 3–37. Los Angeles: Kalimat Press, 2002.
Schaefer, U. *Introduction to Bahá'í Ethics*. Oxford: George Ronald, 2005.
Schaefer, U. *Bahá'í Ethics in Light of Scripture: An Introduction Doctrinal Fundamentals*. Vol 1. Oxford: George Ronald, 2007.
Schaefer, U. *Bahá'í Ethics in Light of Scripture: Virtues and Divine Commandments*. Vol 2. Oxford: George Ronald, 2009.
Schechner, R. *Performance Studies: An Introduction*. London: Routledge, 2011.

Scott, D. and C. Hirschkind, eds. *Powers of the Secular Modern: Talal Asad and His Interlocutors*. Stanford: Stanford University Press, 2006.

Seager, R. H. *Encountering the Dharma Daisaku Ikeda, Soka Gakkai, and the Globalization of Buddhist Humanism*. Berkeley: University of California Press, 2006.

Sergeev, M. ed. *Studies in Bahá'í Philosophy: Selected Articles*. Leiden: Brill, 2015.

Sergeev, M. *Theory of Religious Cycles: Tradition, Modernity and the Bahái Faith*. Leiden: Brill, 2015.

Shaman, H. and S. Inayatullah. 'Karma Samnyasa: Sarkar's Reconceptualisation of Indian Asceticism', *Journal of Asian and African Studies* 34, no. 1 (1999): 139–51.

Shipps, J. *Mormonism: The Story of a New Religious Tradition*. Illinois: University of Illinois Press, 1987.

Shipps, J. *Sojourner in the Promised Land: Forty Years among the Mormons*. Urbana and Chicago: University of Illinois Press, 2000.

Sil, N. P. 'Anatomy of Ānanda Mārga: Hindu Anabaptists', *Asian Culture Quarterly* 16, no. 2 (1988): 1–18.

Sil, N. P. 'The Troubled World of the Ananda Marga: An Examination', *Quarterly Review of Historical Studies* 27, no. 4 (1988): 3–19.

Sil, N. P. 'The Odyssey of the Ananda Marga: A Comparative Study', *Journal of Asian and African Studies* 48, no. 2 (2013): 229–41.

Smith, G. D. *Nauvoo Polygamy: '... But We Called It Celestial Marriage'*. Salt Lake City, UT: Signature Books, 2008.

Smith, J. *Joseph Smith Papers – Journals, Volume 3: May 1843–June 1844*. Salt Lake City, UT: Church of Jesus Christ and the Latter Day Saints, 2015.

Smith, J. M. 'Five Impulses of the Joseph Smith Translation of Mark and Their Implications for LDS Hermeneutics', *Studies in the Bible and Antiquity* 7, article 2 (2015): 1–21.

Smith, W. and T. Ramsay. 'Spreading Soul Consciousness: Managing and Extending the Global Reach of the Brahma Kumaris'. In *Globalizing Asian Religions: Management and Marketing*, edited by W. Smith, H. Nakamaki, L. Matsunaga, and T. Ramsay, 205–34. Amsterdam: Amsterdam University Press, 2019.

Snow, D. and N. Machalek. 'The Sociology of Conversion', *Annual Review of Sociology* 10 (1984): 167–90.

Spencer, J. M. *For Zion: A Mormon Theology of Hope*. Salt Lake City, UT: Greg Kofford Books, 2014.

Spencer, J. M. *1st Nephi: A Brief Theological Introduction*. Provo, UT: The Neal A. Maxwell Institute for Religious Scholarship, 2020.

Stapley, J. *The Power of Godliness: Mormon Liturgy and Cosmology*. New York: Oxford University Press, 2018.

Stark, R. and W. S. Bainbridge. *A Theory of Religion*. New York: Peter Lang, 1987.

Stark, R. with R. L. Neilson ed. *The Rise of Mormonism*. Edited by Reid Y. Neilson. New York: Columbia University Press, 2005.

Stetzer, F. *Religion on the Healing Edge What Bahá'ís Believe*. Wilmette, IL: Bahá'í Publishing Trust, 2007.

Stone, J. I. 'Nichiren's activist heirs: Sōka Gakkai, Risshō Kōseikai, Nipponzan Myōhōji'. In *Action Dharma: New Studies in Engaged Buddhism*, edited by C. Queen Damien Keown, C. Prebish and D. Keown, 63–94. London: Routledge Curzon, 2003.

Strickling, l. R. *On Fire in Baltimore: Black Mormon Women and Conversion in a Raging City*. Salt Lake City, UT Utah: Greg Kofford Books, 2018.

Sutcliffe, S. and C. M. Cusack eds. *The Problem of Invented Religions*. London: Routledge, 2016.

Taherzadeh, A. *The Revelation of Bahá'u'lláh*. 4 vols. Oxford: George Ronald, 1974–1987.

Tarak, ed. *Ananda Marga, Social and Spiritual Practices*. Kolkata: Ānanda Mārga Pracāraka, 1990.

Tehranian, M. and D. Ikeda. *Reflections on the Global Civilisation: A Dialogue*. London: I. B. Tauris, 2016.

Thompson, A. K. 'The Doctrine of Resurrection in the Book of Mormon'. *Interpreter: A Journal of Latter-day Saint Faith and Scholarship* 16 (2015): 101–29.

Thompson, A. K. *Trinity and Monotheism: A Historical and Theological Review of the Origins and Substance of the Doctrine*. Redland Bay, QLD: Modotti Press, 2019.

Turley, R. ed. *Selected Collections from the Archives of the Church of Jesus Christ of Latter-day Saints*. 2 vols. Provo, UT: Brigham Young University Press, 2002.

Turner, B. *The Religious and the Political: A Comparative Sociology of Religion*. Cambridge: Cambridge University Press, 2013.

Turner, J. G. *The Mormon Jesus: A Biography*. Cambridge, MA and London: Belknap Press of Harvard University Press, 2016.

Underwood, G. *The Millenarian World of Early Mormonism*. Urbana: University of Illinois Press, 1993.

Urbain, O. *Daisaku Ikeda's Philosophy of Peace*. London: I. B. Tauris, 2010.

Vásquez, M. A. *More than Belief: A Materialist Theory of Religion*. New York: Oxford: Oxford University Press, 2011.

Vick, H. H. *Social and Economic Development: A Bahá'í Approach*. Oxford: George Ronald, 1989.

Vogel, D. *Religious Seekers and the Advent of Mormonism*. Salt Lake City, UT: Signature Press, 1988.

Vogel, D. ed. *Early Mormon Documents*. 5 vols. Salt Lake City, UT: Signature Books, 1996–2003.

Vogel, D. *Joseph Smith: The Making of a Prophet*. Salt Lake City, UT: Signature Books, 2004.

Walbridge, J. *Sacred Arts, Sacred Space, Sacred Time*. Oxford: George Ronald, 1996.

Walliss, J. *When Prophecy Fails: The Brahma Kumaris and the Pursuit of the Millenniums*. Sheffield: British Association for the Advancement of Science, September, 1999.

Walliss, J. *The Brahma Kumaris as a 'Reflexive Tradition' Responding to Late Modernity*. Aldershot: Ashgate, 2002.

Warburg, M. *Citizens of the World: A History and Sociology of the Bahá'í s from a Globalisation Perspective*. Leiden: Brill Academic, 2006.

Wark, M. *Molecular Red: Theory for the Anthropocene*. London: Verso, 2015.

Williamson, T. *The Philosophy of Philosophy*. Oxford: Blackwell, 2007.

Wilson, B. and K. A. Dobbelaere. *A Time to Chant: The Sōka Gakkai Buddhists in Britain*. New York: Oxford University Press, 1994.

Winn, K. *Exiles in a Land of Liberty*. Chapel Hill, NC: UNC Press, 1989.

Webb, S. *Jesus Christ, Eternal God: Heavenly Flesh and the Metaphysics of Matter*. New York: Oxford University Press, 2011.

Whaling, F. *Understanding the Brahma Kumaris*. Dunedin: Dunedin Press, 2012.

White, J. *The Sokagakkai and Mass Society*. Stanford: Stanford University Press, 1970.

Whitsel, B. C. *The Church Universal and Triumphant: Elizabeth Clare Prophet's Apocalyptic Movement*. Syracuse: Syracuse University Press, 2003.

Wilcox, M. and J. D. Young, eds. *Standing Apart: Mormon Historical Consciousness and the Concept of Apostasy*. Oxford: Oxford University Press, 2014.

Index

'Abdu'l-Bahá 23
Adventist 18–19, 22, 24
Agamben, G. 8
AMORC 91, 156 n.13
Ananda Marga 19, 52–5, 65–6, 115
   biopsychology 57
   cognitive materials 55–9
   cooperative economic system 118–19
   education system 63
   Neohumanism 58
   pan-species universalist ethics 116
   philosophy of mind 57
   postreligious features 64
   revealed conception of history 57
   spiritual practices 59–60
   universalist ethics 58
apotheosis 125, 128
Articles of Faith 128–9

Báb 22–3, 27, 140 n.12
Bahá'ís 15, 18, 21–4, 36–7, 118–23, 144 n.60
   activism 32
   cognitive materials 24–7
   faith 34
   humanity, unification of 31–2
   interpretative pluralism 34, 121
   organizational revelations 35–6
   political arrangements 29
   positivity 28–30
   reframe religion 33–4, 118
   spiritual practices 27
Bahá'u'lláh 23–4, 26–9, 33, 35–6, 140 n.12
Benson, E. T. 102, 125
Bloch, E. 2, 32, 136 n.20
Bogdanov, A. 138 n.37
Book of Enoch 83–4, 100
Book of Mormon, The 98, 100, 102, 107, 109, 125–6, 128, 161 n.24
Book of Moses, The 100–1
Brahma Kumaris 19, 67–70, 78–9, 115–16, 120–3
   cognitive materials 70–3

cosmosophy 72–3
organizational forms 77–8
postreligious features 76–7
social and cultural activism 74–6
spiritual practices 73–4
Buddhism 38–47, 49, 51, 145 n.6
Bushman, R. 95–6

charismatic spiritual movement 50, 81, 83, 95–6, 98–9, 104, 113
Chih-i 45
Christianity 5, 36, 77, 80, 82, 84, 87, 94–6, 99–101, 103, 105–6, 129–31
Church Universal and Triumphant, The 19, 80–94, 104, 119, 121, 123
cognitive materials 8, 10–15, 18–20, 24–7, 41–4, 50–1, 55–9, 70–3, 77, 84–6, 93, 100–3, 115–16, 124, 136 n.20
cognitive science 6, 92, 136 n.13
concrete utopianism 2–3, 30, 37–8, 113–14, 118
cosmic historicism 52, 67, 70, 72, 116
cosmic humanism 39, 42–4, 50–1, 116, 121
cosmosophy 15–16, 19, 24–6, 43–4, 56, 70–3, 84–5, 97, 101, 103, 115
counterfactual doctrines 6, 8, 10, 13–14, 16, 22, 37
covenant 23, 25, 27, 30, 32–5, 99, 104, 106–7, 122
creativity 3–4, 6, 9–11, 16, 19–20, 22, 32, 38–9, 48, 50–1, 55–6, 60, 63, 66, 78, 81–2, 92, 95–7, 110–11, 113, 120, 123, 160 n.19
cultural productivity 2, 7, 9, 22, 113, 120, 131
cultural reform 16, 46–8, 60–4, 89–92, 107–8, 120

Davies, D. 95
Dharma Chakras 60, 151 n.33
disaggregative approach 10–12, 111, 123
Doctrine and Covenants 100, 109, 126
dualist 8, 20, 37, 56, 111, 130

economic reform 16, 46–8, 60–4, 89–92, 107–8
educational reform 16, 46–8, 60–4, 89–92, 107–8, 119
Effendi, S. 23, 33, 36, 139 n.9, 140 n.12
esho funi 42
esoteric aspects 15–16, 19, 22, 26–7, 34, 41, 59–60, 64–5, 70, 74–5, 80, 82, 84–5, 91–3, 104, 117, 121
exoteric practices 15, 104, 117

Faber, R. 24, 32
faith 33–5, 49, 98, 129
fantastic 13, 85, 93
Faulconer, J. E. 161 n.21, 166 n.13
fictionality 13–14
futurist 17, 19–20, 39, 58, 62, 65–7, 116

Galtung, J. 58
Givens, T. 100–1, 128
global civilization 22, 36–7, 47, 89, 118, 122–3
  positivity to 28–30
  socio-cultural activism for 30–2
God 23–6, 28, 68–74, 77, 82, 84–8, 98–9, 101, 103–7, 124–31, 140 n.16, 156 n.15, 165 n.8, 166 nn.9–10, 166–167 n.17
Gohonzon 45–6, 49, 145 n.6

Hamann, J. G. 6
Hegel, G. F. 5, 14, 71, 113
hermeneutics 24–5, 70
Hinduism 52–3, 71–2, 75–6, 78, 90
historical sociology 17, 57–8, 99
Holy Spirit 84, 86, 125, 127
Huff, T. 17

Ikeda, D. 40–2, 46–7, 49–50, 118, 145 nn.6, 8, 10, 146 n.13
intentional meaning 105, 121
interpretative pluralism 34, 121
Islam 23, 35–6, 108, 120

James, W. 44

Kalpa Tree 71
Kant, I. 5, 102
Kitáb-i-Aqdas (Bahá'u'lláh) 29
Komeito 47, 118

Lamanite Handbook 109
Latour, B. 10
Latter-day Saints 19–20, 95–110, 115–31, 161 n.22, 162 n.30, 164 nn.55, 56, 168 nn.23, 24, 26, 30, 32, 35
Lekhraj, D. 68, 70, 72, 76
Lessing, G. E. 23

McGlinn, S. 142 n.38
Makiguchi, T. 39, 41, 43–4, 47–8, 122, 147 nn.27, 30
Manifestations 23–5, 28, 32, 34–6
Mann, M. 17
medical reform 63, 74–5, 88, 117, 120
Messianism 21
microvita 56–7, 122
model ideas 13–14, 24, 44, 55, 71, 103, 115, 131
moderate naturalism 11
modernist 24–5, 34–5, 38–41, 43–4, 58, 61, 64–5, 67–8, 75, 77–9, 83, 123
Momen, M. 34
Mormonism 95, 98, 100, 102, 104–9, 125–8, 161 n.26, 167 n.19, 168 n.33
Murlis 70, 72
mystic law 43

Nelson, R. M. 130
Neohumanism 58, 63, 122
New Religious Movements 7, 67, 80
Nichiren Buddhism 19, 38–43, 45–7, 49, 145 n.6, 146 n.12
Nietzsche, F. 43–4, 103
nominalism 12
non-standard conception of faith 103, 129

occulture 19, 80, 91–2
organizational forms 17–18, 28, 35–6, 50, 64–5, 77–8, 93, 108–10, 122–3
Ostler, B. 166–167 n.17

paranormal 168 n.35
Pearl of Great Price, The 100
Pelagian 84
performative 80, 85–6, 90, 121
  counterfactuality 80, 90
philosophical anthropology 73, 116
political reform 16, 46–8, 60–4, 89–92, 107–8

positivity 4–6, 8, 10, 14, 18–22, 24, 28–30, 36–7, 39, 47, 71, 80–1, 83, 94, 96–9, 107, 109, 111–13, 115, 130
possible worlds theory 14
postmodernism 29, 142 n.38
postreligion 92–3
postreligious features 32–5, 49, 64
postsecular 21
practical ethics 24, 26
preternatural 83, 109, 131
Pritchard, E. 14–15
projective imagination 13, 22, 85, 93
Prophet, E. C. 81–3, 86, 88–90, 93, 157 n.24, 158 n.38
Prophet, M. L. 81–2, 89
prosocial 21, 24, 28–9, 36, 62, 114, 118–19, 122
Prout (Progressive Utilization Theory) 60–2, 118

radical pluralism 24
reincarnation 71–2
religion 1–2, 5, 10
    generic 6–8, 10–12, 20, 22, 96, 111
    postreligion 16–17, 49, 92–3, 120
    reframe 33–4, 118
    strong 104
Religion within the Limits of Reason Alone (Kant) 5
religious reform 120
revealed cosmosophy 19, 24–5, 43, 56, 71–2, 84, 101, 115
Roy, R. M. 58

Sarkar, P. R. 53–65, 122
secularism 8–9, 21, 75–6, 97, 103, 121–2
Shaykh Ahmad Ahsá'í of Bahrain 22–3
Sikhs 163 n.45
Simmel, G. 17
Smith, J. 98
social holism 10
social reform 16, 46–8, 60–4, 89–92, 107–8, 119

Soka Gakkai 18–19, 38–41, 50–1, 65, 116, 118–23, 146 nn.11, 13
    Buddhism, version of 49
    cognitive materials 41–4
    and cosmic humanism 39, 42–4, 50–1, 116, 121
    Lotus Sutra 41–2, 44–5
    organizational form 50
    sociocultural vision 47
    spiritual practices 45–6
    value creation 43–4, 47, 51, 116, 122
spiritual movements 2–9, 11, 13–14, 16–22, 24–5, 28, 33, 37, 50, 52, 60, 64–8, 74, 82, 95–6, 108, 111, 115–16, 121, 123
spiritual practices 8, 11, 15–16, 27, 29, 38, 45–6, 59–60, 65–6, 73–6, 86–9, 104–7, 117, 120
spiritual republicanism 39, 50, 112, 121
Stirner, M. 43–4
Strang, J. 99
Summit University 84, 90, 92–3, 121

Tantra 59–60, 64, 74
Taylor, J. 131
teleological 30
thaumaturgic features 98, 101, 104
theosophical 19, 83, 86, 89–91, 130
theosophy 15, 70, 81
thought experiment 10–11, 13–14
Toda, J. 41, 145 nn.6, 10
tri-modalism 127
Turner, B. 137 n.22

Universal House of Justice 23, 28–9, 35, 140 n.12, 142 n.35
Urbain, O. 145 n.8
utopian intentionality 10, 27, 30, 112, 114, 117, 121, 131

veridiction 10

www.ingramcontent.com/pod-product-compliance
Lightning Source LLC
Chambersburg PA
CBHW061831300426
44115CB00013B/2336